Thackeray the Writer

From *Pendennis* to *Denis Duval*

Edgar F. Harden

First published in Great Britain 2000 by
MACMILLAN PRESS LTD
Houndmills, Basingstoke, Hampshire RG21 6XS and London
Companies and representatives throughout the world

A catalogue record for this book is available from the British Library.

ISBN 0-333-79048-0

First published in the United States of America 2000 by
ST. MARTIN'S PRESS, INC.,
Scholarly and Reference Division,
175 Fifth Avenue, New York, N.Y. 10010

ISBN 0-312-22929-1

The Library of Congress catalogued the first volume as follows:
Harden, Edgar F.
Thackeray the writer : from journalism to Vanity Fair / Edgar F. Harden.
  p. cm.
Includes bibliographical references and index.
ISBN 0-312-21226-7 (cloth)
1. Thackeray, William Makepeace, 1811-1863—Criticism and interpretation. 2. Thackeray, William Makepeace, 1811-1863--Aesthetics. 3. Thackeray, William Makepeace, 1811-1863—Technique. 4. Journalism—England—History—19th century. 5. Authorship--History—19th century. I. Title.
PR5638.H34 1998
823'.8—dc21   97-43870
                                                                         CIP

© Edgar F. Harden 2000

All rights reserved. No reproduction, copy or transmission of this publication may be made without written permission.

No paragraph of this publication may be reproduced, copied or transmitted save with written permission or in accordance with the provisions of the Copyright, Designs and Patents Act 1988, or under the terms of any licence permitting limited copying issued by the Copyright Licensing Agency, 90 Tottenham Court Road, London W1P 0LP.

Any person who does any unauthorised act in relation to this publication may be liable to criminal prosecution and civil claims for damages.

The author has asserted his right to be identified as the author of this work in accordance with the Copyright, Designs and Patents Act 1988.

This book is printed on paper suitable for recycling and made from fully managed and sustained forest sources.

10 9 8 7 6 5 4 3 2 1
09 08 07 06 05 04 03 02 01 00

Printed and bound in Great Britain by
Antony Rowe Ltd, Chippenham, Wiltshire

For my son, Edgar

Contents

Preface ix

List of Abbreviations xi

Chapter One: *The History of Pendennis* 1

Chapter Two: *The English Humourists of the Eighteenth Century* and *The History of Henry Esmond, Esq.* 29

Chapter Three: *The Newcomes* 70

Chapter Four: *The Four Georges* and *The Virginians* 94

Chapter Five: *Lovel the Widower* 143

Chapter Six: *The Adventures of Philip* 160

Chapter Seven: *Roundabout Papers* 181

Appendix: *Denis Duval* 215

Notes 220

Index 226

Preface

This volume completes my study of Thackeray's literary development, which began with *Thackeray the Writer: From Journalism to "Vanity Fair"* (1998). Like that work, it is intended for general readers as well as for an academic audience. Hence I concentrate on Thackeray's texts rather than devote any extensive attention to what critics, including myself, have written about them. As in the first volume, I do not document all statements about Thackeray, assuming as I do general agreement about the major facts of his life and about his basic outlook—agreement based upon the evidence of his correspondence and upon the findings of biographical studies.

For assistance in preparing this volume I am very much indebted, as usual, to the computing expertise of Anita Mahoney of the Dean of Arts office, Simon Fraser University.

List of Abbreviations

Annotations   *Annotations for the Selected Works of William Makepeace Thackeray: The Complete Novels, the Major Non-Fictional Prose, and Selected Shorter Pieces.* Ed. Edgar F. Harden. 2 vols. New York and London: Garland, 1990.

Letters   *The Letters and Private Papers of William Makepeace Thackeray.* Ed. Gordon N. Ray. 4 vols. Cambridge, Mass.: Harvard University Press, 1945-46.

Letters [H]   *The Letters and Private Papers of William Makepeace Thackeray. A Supplement.* Ed. Edgar F. Harden. 2 vols. New York and London: Garland, 1994.

Works   *The Oxford Thackeray.* 17 vols. London, New York, and Toronto: Oxford University Press, 1908.

CHAPTER ONE:

THE HISTORY OF PENDENNIS

During his career as a writer before the appearance of *Vanity Fair,* Thackeray had published 568 pieces as a contributor to newspapers and periodicals—works that included parodies, burlesques, extravaganzas, political reports, art criticism, book reviews, tales, comic verses, and installments of a full-length novel.[1] In addition he had published 7 works as separate imprints, most of them containing new material ranging from pictorial caricature and news reporting to travel books reflecting his experiences in Ireland and on a journey to the Near East. During the serial appearance of *Vanity Fair* on 19 occasions between January 1847 and July 1848, Thackeray also wrote and published 88 pieces for magazines and periodicals, besides drawing and publishing 106 comic illustrations. What was he to do after the appearance of the masterpiece that had established him as one of England's two leading novelists? Clearly, more of the same: continuing the incredibly energetic, bubbling flow of usually comic, occasionally more somber journalism, and of course beginning another ambitious serial novel.

In *Vanity Fair* Thackeray had for the first time in his imaginative life articulated a comprehensive system of forces defining a moral universe. Inevitably, therefore, all of his subsequent works unfolded within the force-field of this powerful articulation. Henceforth the words "Vanity Fair" openly defined the assumptions of the author in his fictions and non-fictions, and also identified the fundamental signpost that his readers needed in order for them to see and to understand the comical and absurd world that he and they shared—both the fictional world and the reality that it reflected.

He had also given quintessential definition to the Thackerayan narrator—an omnipresent, protean figure who mirrors the archetypal configurations of human society, and who reflects Thackeray's belief that one cannot see and understand the ambiguities of human existence from a single, stable point of view. Every utterance is the utterance of a moment, trapped in the flux of time and therefore limited. Consequently, his narrator manifests an intense historical awareness that constantly reveals itself in the precise, concrete details of an evoked visible world, as well as in his persistent consciousness of the flow of time, which ages both things and human experience, diminishing both and calling the value of both into question. Thackeray's satire, therefore, operates in creative interaction with this historical awareness. It is a satire that can be limited and local, but that also ranges beyond time and place, radically challenging a reader's most fundamental assumptions about human life. The brilliant wit and comedy of a Thackerayan narrative like *Vanity Fair* constantly entertain us, but the frequent shifting of narrative perspective also reminds us of the profound indeterminacy at the heart of it.

His next narrative, a serial, like all but one of its successors, *The History of Pendennis. His Fortunes and Misfortunes, His Friends and His Greatest Enemy* (November 1848-December 1850) is also a novel without a hero, and a novel firmly set in the Fair. *Pendennis,* however, is a case-study, so to speak, and like ensuing Thackerayan narratives reveals the same general types and the same recurring patterns of human conduct and lives rendered in *Vanity Fair,* but it also illustrates a certain humanindividuality. Whereas the emblematic illustration on the monthly wrappers of the serial parts of *Vanity Fair* had emphasized the role of the clown-narrator addressing his audience of fellow fools, the

CHAPTER ONE

corresponding illustration on the wrappers of *Pendennis* pictured the title-figure making a choice between two female figures, one representing worldly temptation and the other the fulfillments of domesticity—an archetypal choice rendered in individual terms.

Pendennis is Thackeray's pre-eminent version of the great nineteenth-century theme of the young man from the provinces, impoverished, simple, and under-educated, but intelligent and full of high hopes, who comes to a disillusioning but also maturing understanding of himself and of his place in the world. In tracing Pen's progress, Thackeray typically drew upon his own experiences: boyhood memories of Larkbeare in Devon, youthful absurdity and victimization at Cambridge, naïve beginnings in bohemian Grub Street, and presumably silly posturings on the fringes of fashionable life in London.

As these statements suggest, however, the novel gives great emphasis not only to Pen but also to the various contexts of his existence. All of the characters are prominent inhabitants of the Fair, possess the inevitable limitations of their virtues, have to give up enticing possibilities, and—although they may seek to have their conduct governed by desirable values—can find only limited happiness. In typical Thackerayan fashion, Pen is quite flawed, a crucial aspect of Thackeray's presentation of him being the ironic relationship between Pen's hopes and enthusiasms and the narrator's more mature perspectives. At the same time, however, as Thackeray reveals that Laura's love is a partial renewal of Helen Pendennis's love for her son ("and arms as tender as Helen's once more enfold him"[2]), the novelist implies his awareness that he is dramatizing his own frustrated need for domestic affection.

Clearly the most prominent literality and metaphor defining the context of Pen's life is theatricality, which the novel renders with notable elaborateness and rich comedy. In *Pendennis*, theatricality epitomizes human isolation as well as intended deception—of oneself as well as of others—and can be seen as an analogue of *Vanity Fair's* charade and puppet metaphors. In Thackeray all the world tends to be a stage and all men and women merely players, yet one can at times perceive one's "true" being and communicate it directly. Although other individuals tend to see one's behavior as performance, and although one's "true" being tends to dissipate and delude itself as well as others in a surrender to role-playing, it can also express itself even amid the theatrics.

Surrounding the histrionic title-figure we see various characters who illuminate for us and sometimes for him the extensiveness and complexity of theatrical behavior. In showing us a series of responses to such behavior, extending from a considerable number of actual playhouse visits to a variety of social gatherings and private conversations, the narrator focuses our attention especially upon the degree of a character's ability to distinguish between the human actor and the role. We see Pen's growth, for example, not only by the gradual change in his attitude towards the Fotheringay but also by the decline of his interest in Mrs. Leary and by the fact that in the latter instance he does not, as he had with the Fotheringay, confuse the performer with the role—unlike the still naïve Mr. Huxter.

From the very beginning of Pen's early infatuation during a performance of *The Stranger*—a play about a man imprisoned by a role that isolates him from himself as well as from others—the narrator emphasizes both the extent of Pen's confusion and the degree to which it separates him from the audience of which he is a part. The narrator gives us an elaborate sense of the play's sham, from its extraordinary dialogue, costumes, properties and style of acting, to the considerably disengaged behavior of the actors, and he frequently reminds us of the reactions of spectators other than Pen. To the initiated Foker, "The Stranger" is Bingley in tights and Hessians, and the woman opposite him is "the Fotheringay" (I, iv, 35), but in Pen's eyes she is

"Mrs. Haller" (I, iv, 36), even when he sees her privately (I, v, 48). To us she begins "her business," but to the awestruck Pen "she's speaking." A further contrast is provided by her coach, Bows, who, even while about to be overcome by the pathos of a moment, is able to cry out "Bravo" in approval of his pupil's successful handling of her part. Whatever the limitations of Bows himself, this ability to respond sympathetically even while he knows he is observing a rehearsed mimetic act points to a larger ability possessed by the narrator, who can respond to what is genuine within the sham—to the "reality of love, children, and forgiveness of wrong" that is to be found "in the midst of the balderdash" (I, iv, 37).

The theatricality into which Pen's infatuation leads him becomes especially evident when he arranges to see *Hamlet* with his mother; by deciding that "the play should be the thing" (I, vi, 56) to test Helen, he implicitly acknowledges that his own life is a play, within which *Hamlet* will be staged. Like Hamlet, he is both actor and stage-manager, but because Helen has no knowledge of his intentions, she responds to the play-within-the-play as a stage-piece without a dramatic context and sees only a beautiful Ophelia (I, vi, 59). The next spectators who witness a performance of *Hamlet*—Dr. Portman and Major Pendennis—have that additional knowledge and therefore see more than a character in a play. The clergyman finds her not only "a very clever actress" but also a woman "endowed with very considerable personal attractions," while the Major ignores her abilities as a Shakespearean performer and comments on her physical attractiveness as an object of sexual desire: "Gad, . . . the young rascal has not made a bad choice." The Major's attention focuses on the larger human drama within which *Hamlet* is being played; more aware than Dr. Portman of the audience in the theatre and perfectly cognizant of an actress's ability to be alertly self-conscious, the Major sees her appeal for male admiration in the look she gives Sir Derby Oaks and he cynically thinks: "that's their way" (I, ix, 90). It is Dolphin who gives professional testimony to the Fotheringay's mastery of attitudinizing and her ability to learn the occasional "dodge" (I, xiv, 124).

Although Pen attends the Chatteris theatre night after night, he fails to see the mechanical quality of the dull girl's performance, and even when personal contact between them has ended and he has become a mere spectator, he does not become aware that he has always seen her as though across footlights. The memory of his passion and a persistent sense of his humiliation bring him to watch her in London, but by the next year "she was not the same, somehow." At last he seems to recognize "coarse and false" accents, "the same emphasis on the same words," and her "mechanical sobs and sighs" (I, xx, 190). His continuing association of her with misery, repudiation, and failure, however, makes understandable his following visit, after he has been plucked at Oxbridge.

When next he sees her—in a theatre audience, appropriately—she has changed her name and position; having become Lady Mirabel, she has permanently joined the audience and henceforth spends her energies perfecting her new, and now metaphorical role. By a striking complication, then, fantasy—the belief that an ignorant actress could be socially acceptable as a wife—having been exposed as illusion, suddenly becomes fact and yet retains its illusoriness; the fantasy becomes a reality that yet remains fantastic. London society has its private reservations (I, xxix, 282, 284), but publicly it allows the role to define the person and thereby encourages her to simulate the part she has chosen by marrying Sir Charles Mirabel, that most "theatrical man" (II, vi, 53).[3]

Her success in finding acceptance, moreover, not only implicates London society but also helps make her come to seem like a lady in her own right. The range of her accomplishments gradually increases, from patronizing new authors (II, vi, 60-1) to penning neat little notes (II, x, 100-1). Major Pendennis comes to term her "a most respectable woman, received everywhere—everywhere, mind" (II, vi, 53). She gives receptions and seems to Pen "as grave and collected as if she had been born a Duchess, and had never seen a trap-door in her life" (II, vi, 60). The main implications are clear: not only do people almost inevitably play roles, often deluding even themselves, but with money and a certain amount of study they find their great arena in society—where human beings are isolated from each other by the very roles that fit the overall performance.

The precocious Harry Foker serves as a perfect introduction to these two arenas, both in Chatteris and London. He also makes an appearance at the moment of Pen's re-emergence into London life and again that evening at the theatre (I, xxix, 281). In Chatteris he knows all the actors and in his own way unconsciously emulates them as well. Difficult to identify at first beneath his elaborate costume (I, iii, 29), Foker, like "one of our great light comedians," offers us "great pleasure and an abiding matter for thought" (I, iv, 34). Whether calling for "his mixture," ordering turtle, venison, and carefully chilled wine, dancing the hornpipe while "looking round for the sympathy of his groom, and the stable men" (I, iii, 30), or twirling "like Harlequin in the Pantomime" (I, xiii, 117), Foker is playing his role as man of the world with all the enthusiasm of youthful naïvety.

For all his simplicity, of course, he does have a certain shrewd acuteness of insight, especially into devious behavior: hence the irony of his partly duplicating Pen's early infatuation and of his failure to perceive the degree to which Miss Amory, an even more accomplished performer than the Fotheringay, is providing herself with "two strings to her bow" (I, x, 93). In terms of the general theatrical metaphor, Foker's illusion is epitomized for us when, after being smitten with Blanche, he feels he needs a new appearance, and in response to his command, "*Cherchy alors une paire de tongs,—et—curly moi un pew,*" the valet wonders "whether his master was in love or was going masquerading" (II, i, 8).[4] As the woodcut initial of the third last chapter reminds us, in seeking Blanche he plays Clown to Pen's Harlequin; yet, to his credit, Foker finally draws a just conclusion from the evidence presented to him about her.

Like Foker and especially Pen, Alcides Mirobolant shows how vanity and infatuation motivate theatrical behavior. A superlatively unconscious role-player, Mirobolant receives unusual attention from the novelist for a minor character because of his usefulness in parodying those who are self-deluded and, in the unconsciously ironic words of Morgan, those who "has as much pride and hinsolence as if they was real gentlemen" (I, xxxvii, 360). Like Pen in London, Mirobolant possesses an exalted sense of his own professional importance; in addition to his own library, pictures, and piano, he requires an array of assistants, his own maid, his own apartments, and all the deference due to a hypersensitive artist—a role that he plays even in private: "It was a grand sight to behold him in his dressing-gown composing a *menu*. He always sate down and played the piano for some time before that. If interrupted, he remonstrated pathetically with his little maid. Every great artist, he said, had need of solitude to perfectionate his works" (I, xxiii, 218). As a deluded lover, like the youthful Pen he uses loftily inflated language for the very earthbound object of his passion, and he conceives of himself in an overtly theatrical way: in replying to his confidante, who accuses him of being perfidious, he says, "with a deep bass voice, and a tragic accent worthy of the Porte St. Martin and his favourite melo-drames, 'Not perfidious, but fatal. Yes, I am a fatal man, Madame Fribsbi. To inspire hopeless passion is my destiny'" (I, xxiv, 234).

CHAPTER ONE

But it is as a mock-gentleman that he most clearly serves to parody the attitudinizing of young Pen. At the Baymouth ball, where his vanity conflicts directly with Pen's, Mirobolant's self-esteem clothes itself in a blue ribbon and a three-pointed star, but even then Arthur fails to see the implications: the idea "that such an individual should have any feeling of honour at all, did not much enter into the mind of this lofty young aristocrat, the apothecary's son" (I, xxvii, p. 262). As a Gascon, Mirobolant stands on the one side of Pen, while Costigan, Mirobolant's Irish counterpart, stands on the other; both represent parodic versions of the strut and swagger found in Pen.

Because Mirobolant has an exaggerated belief in the distinctions that set him apart, he insists that he is a *chef*, not a *cuisinier*, and that being a *Chevalier de Juillet* he has a special duty to defend his honor—like that other mock-gentleman, Costigan, by means of a duel. Here too, his attitude shows itself akin to Pen's theatrical sense of his own dignity, both in his own formal challenge to a fellow schoolboy and in his response to Mirobolant's tapping him on the shoulder. The conflict between the two expresses itself in such approved melodramatic forms as the grinding of teeth, the jabbering of oaths, the stamping of feet, the challenge to a duel, and the high incidence of French, but like most melodramatic threats in the book it is quickly deflated.

The connectedness of all this role-playing receives further extension in the depiction of another highly theatrical figure who believes himself to be a thorough man of the world: "General or Captain Costigan—for the latter was the rank which he preferred to assume" (I, v, 43). Costigan is a mock-gentleman and a mock-warrior—a veritable "Sir Lucius O'Trigger, which character he had performed with credit, both off and on the stage" (I, xii, 108). He resembles the infatuated Pen as an often unconscious role-player, but where the boy is drunk on poetry and adolescent longings, the source of Costigan's illusions is a Celtic imagination excessively stimulated by alcohol. Ending as a fixture of the singer's table at the Back Kitchen, this performer inevitably characterizes himself in theatrical terms, speaking often and sadly "of his resemblance to King Lear in the plee—of his having a thankless choild, bedad" (II, iv, 36). When "this aged buffoon" (II, xvii, 163) finds himself in pawn for drink, however—at "the Roscius's Head, Harlequin Yard, Drury Lane" (II, iv, 37), of course—he successfully appeals to that same child, but, inevitably, with an invented story. In fact, "the Captain was not only unaccustomed to tell the truth,—he was unable even to think it—and fact and fiction reeled together in his muzzy, whiskified brain" (I, v, 45). Inevitably, then, his language is highly theatrical, for he cannot distinguish himself from his role. Appropriately making his initial appearance in the company of an actor, Costigan habitually speaks with elaborate rhetoric; he exaggerates the language and "[suits] the action to the word" (I, xi, 102).

Inordinate in his sense of honor, and extravagant also in his sense of embarrassment, which he is capable of expressing "in a voice of agony, and with eyes brimful of tears" (I, xii, 108), he unwittingly serves to parody Pen's own excessive pride and shame from the very beginning of the novel to the moment when the series of jokes by Warrington and others about Pen's "noble" family and his residence at Fairoaks "Castle" culminates as the imagination of the "tipsy mountebank" (I, xiii, 115) actually bodies forth the marvellous structure and the impressive life lived there: "I've known um since choildhood, Mrs. Bolton; he's the proproietor of Fairoaks Castle, and many's the cooper of Clart I've dthrunk there with the first nobilitee of his neetive countee" (II, viii, 83). As a dueller we cannot take him even as seriously as Sir Lucius, but since Costigan has a respect for people that is based chiefly upon their wealth or future prospects, we can perceive in him a comic representation of the values of the fashionable society to which he constantly alludes and which he uses to help bolster his role. He thereby reveals his similarity to Major Pendennis.

The Major, another old warrior of limited financial means and fictional ancestry, actually associates with the kind of people Costigan pretends to have known, but such association produces a false sense of personal importance not unlike Costigan's: as the narrator ironically puts it, "The Major lived in such good company that he might be excused for feeling like an Earl" (I, vii, 70). At one point he even seems to feel like a Duke, for after greeting Wellington the Major begins "to imitate him unconsciously" (I, xxxvii, 363). In fact, we have a strong impression of his being an actor. Like his chest, "manfully wadded with cotton" (I, viii, 81), he is perfect on the outside but rickety within—both physically and metaphorically. Hence the considerable emphasis on his elaborate toilettes, which become more lengthy and complicated as he grows more feeble, and which become the basis for the narrator's elevating Major Pendennis to the mock-eminence of "hero" alongside Costigan (II, x, 100).

Like Sir Charles Mirabel, an inveterate "theatrical man" (II, vi, 53), "Colonel" Altamont, a notorious imposter, and those two aged youths, Blondel and Colchicum (II, vii, 72), Major Pendennis wears a wig—and that fact receives unusual attention in the novel, as does the elaborate and mysterious curling the wig receives. To a number of scoffers, it even defines him; he is "Wigsby" (I, xxix, 282, II, vi, 54, xxix, 294). Indeed, on one memorable occasion, later briefly re-evoked (I, xiv, 126), it is used to epitomize not only age but sham sentiment, as he tells a story of losing a young heiress: "We returned our letters, sent back our locks of hair (the Major here passed his fingers through his wig), we suffered—but we recovered" (I, vii, 71). Here, as often elsewhere, Major Pendennis is also an actor in the broadest sense: one whose wholehearted commitment to the values of Vanity Fair marks him as a participant in fundamental and extended illusion. We see this in the very ring he wears so prominently, "emblazoned with the famous arms of Pendennis" (I, i, 2). Like Bingley's it is a sham ring, and like the family motto as interpreted by the Major (II, xxxii, 318), it represents a dedication to worldly aspirations alone. Though the linking of Major Pendennis and Costigan is established from the very beginning of the novel in Pen's letter to his uncle, no one would question that the Major is a far more conscious and adept poseur than Costigan; like most role-players, indeed, like Becky Sharp, however, he himself is partly taken in by the illusion he tries to sustain. With "a mournful earnestness and veracity," he urges young Pen to begin his genealogical studies but not to concentrate upon the pedigrees, for many are "very fabulous, and there are few families that can show such a clear descent as our own" (I, ix, 85; repeated II, xix, 185). So too, the Major believes that his conduct is "perfectly virtuous" as well as perfectly "respectable" (I, ix, 86).

One of the judgments that best epitomizes him appears in the delightful phrase, "He was perfectly affable" (I, i, 2). Such a desirable quality as affability, of course, can give great pleasure and amusement, even when it is the perfection of pose. If the performance is carried on at great length, however, we come to see the human strain and debilitation involved, as the Major's condition after his performance at the Gaunt House ball demonstrates. Like Pen, Blanche, Lady Clavering, and Lord Steyne, who introduces himself to her "at the request of the obsequious Major Pendennis" (II, vii, 69), the Major participates in many a "little play" (II, vii, 70) that goes to make up the entertainment of the evening. But since extended perfection is too much to ask of a human, to be "perfectly affable" for very long is to be inhumanly artificial.

Though the Major is capable of such consistency, we also see flaws from the very start of the performance, not only in his neglect of the humble rural petitioner in favor of the entreaties of more fashionable women but also in the "rage and wonder" (I, i, 3) that show themselves on his face and make Glowry feel for his lancet. Later in the novel, therefore, when we are told "it was curious how emotion seemed to olden him" (II, xiv, 137), the narrator is saying not simply that emotion ages the Major but also that emotion reveals his age; being a break in the pose, it discloses the aging process that has been taking place underneath, much as the sudden glimpse of Becky's haggard face opposite Rawdon asleep in his chair shows us how the unremitting effort to maintain her role has debilitated her.

Finally, the passage of time[5] not only reveals weakness and leads to artifice that is both more elaborate and more apparent, but it also changes the perspective in which the artifice is viewed. The Major's practised grin comes to be termed a smirk (II, vi, 54, xviii, 180, xx, 202) and thereby, like Smirke himself, more of a subject for caricature. His club, Bays's, even comes in the eyes of young men to take on the name of Dolphin's theatre: "It's a regular museum" (I, xxxvii, 362). Likewise, as men of the Major's time begin to die and he becomes more isolated, he thereby seems more theatrical and more clearly a subject for laughter. Hence it is appropriate that he at last retires from "the Pall Mall *pavé*," where "he has walked . . . long enough" (II, xxxi, 311), as a stage actor might at last retire from the boards. He never fully understands the play, however, even when he recalls so potentially illuminating an example as Sheridan's comedy—"We have him at a dead-lock, like the fellow in the play— the Critic, hey?" (II, xxxii, 318)—for in *Pendennis* as in *The Critic*, contrivance is easily overcome by counter-contrivance, and the Major's elaborate plot, like Puff's, is negated by the recalcitrance of actors who alter their parts.

The Major never really understands the meaning of his part either, not even towards the end when he quotes Shakespeare's Wolsey and implicitly identifies himself with that role. Shakespeare's great worldling came at last to recognize that the cause of his defeat and misery lay in himself, that one cannot build on corruption; hence his injunction: "Be just and fear not." It is a mark of Pen's maturity that he understands this and renounces the corruption, but Major Pendennis does not. Hence his pitifully theatrical act of kneeling to Pen and his final comment: ""'and had I but served my God as I've served you"— . . . I mightn't have been—Goodnight, sir, you needn't trouble yourself to call again.' . . . He looked very much oldened; it seemed as if the contest and defeat had quite broken him" (II, xxxii, 320).

Major Pendennis believes that his desires for his nephew, which he thinks of as unselfish, have only exposed him to defeat and misery. Implying, then, that unselfishness opens one to unhappiness, he inverts the meaning of Wolsey's speech and maintains his own worldly consistency, just as he does when he accepts Pen's marriage to Laura because Lady Rockminster approves. Though we are told that he "became very serious in his last days," that seriousness seems to take the form solely of telling "his stories" to Laura or listening to her reading to him (II, xxxvii, 371). His stories could hardly be very edifying and one has reason for doubting whether he understands what she reads any more than he understood the folly of Wolsey or Cymbeline (II, xiv, 137-38).

The man whom Strong finally calls "Jack Alias" (II, xxxvii, 370) seems for a time to represent the triumph of theatricality. Whether his real name is "John Armstrong," like the famous outlaw, or whether that is as fictitious as "Ferdinand," "Amory," and "Altamont," it is as "Colonel Altamont, of the body-guard of his Highness the Nawaub of Lucknow" (I, xxvi, 256), that he is introduced and generally known in the novel. Appearing in a black wig (I, xxvii, 263) and in accompanying "whiskers, dyed evidently with the purple of Tyre" (I, xxvi, 256), beribboned like Mirobolant, bejewelled like the mountebank, Bloundell-Bloundell, with whom he associates on several occasions, and generally overdressed, Altamont is a blatant masquerader whose function is to emphasize the spuriousness of the relationships in the Clavering family and elsewhere, to serve as a standard for measuring other kinds of make-believe in the novel, and finally to demonstrate the basic folly of human plots and exploitative desires.

As a thoroughgoing performer, he endures repeated exposure, so deeply does he believe in his role or roles, as we can see when, in speaking of himself, he tells Strong that "a man of honour may take any name he chooses" (II, v, 46) or, at an equally comic moment, in excusing some deplorable behavior of his, he calmly says to Sir Francis Clavering: "I told you I was drunk, and that ought to be sufficient between gentleman and gentleman" (II, v, 49). Altamont not only has difficulty in distinguishing himself from his role, but he also, with the assistance of drink, confuses matters in the actual theatre as well, to the exasperation of Captain Strong: "I took him to the play the other night; and, by Jove, sir, he abused the actor who was doing the part of villain in the play, and swore at him so, that the people in the boxes wanted to turn him out. The after-piece was the 'Brigand,' where Wallack comes in wounded, you know, and dies. When he died, Altamont began to cry like a child, and said it was a d——d shame, and cried and swore so, that there was another row, and everybody laughing" (II, iv, 40).

Altamont, in short, is the epitome of disorder in the novel, for he is not only the chief threat but he is compulsive, even joyful in his unruliness, and his last cry is an exultant challenge to all comers: "Hurray, who's for it!" (II, xxxvii, 368). A true squire of Alsatia (II, iv, 33), he cannot be permanently assimilated by society, nor does he really wish to be. A brigand, an outlaw, an ex-convict, guilty of forgery and manslaughter, he is even more fundamentally what Strong terms him at the end of the novel: "a madman" (II, xxxvii, 360). Full of "wild stories and adventures" (II, vi, 56), he represents a romantically alluring irrationality to simple novel-reading females like Miss Snell and Miss Fribsby; exploiting one after the other, like "a perfect Don Juan" (II, xxxvii, 369), he offers in return "to give anybody a lock of his hair" (II, xxxvii, 370).

Only Pen deliberately renounces the attempt to trade off of what Altamont seems to represent; consequently he is free to find stability in a good marriage. Altamont, of course, renounces nothing and, being the irrational force that he is, sweeps free of all attempts to capture him. All these plots fail and it is entirely fitting that Altamont should escape the careful Morgan because of a drunken innkeeper's sudden fears, and because of a most theatrical man's unexpected impulse of dashing down the gutterpipe that separates Altamont from his pursuers, being reminded of that "aisy sthratagem by remembering his dorling Emilie, when she acted the pawrt of Cora in the Plee—and by the bridge in Pezawro, bedad" (II, xxxvii, 370). And with that phrase, we are carried back to the beginning of the novel and realize that all these plots reflect each other.

Though equally as much a masquerader as her father, Blanche Amory is of a rather different kind, despite certain similarities. For one thing, an important part of her alien tone comes from habits she has picked up in France. Called "the French girl" (I, xxvii, 258) by one character, she uses French not only to crown herself with a false name but especially to express her affectations, notably her sentimental ones. Her flippant and arch use of the Gallic tongue, however, reveals not only affectation but moral insensitivity—lightly calling Pen a *"monstre,"* for example, as a means of teasing him about supposedly having a sexual dalliance with Fanny (II, xx, 201).

Blanche's exposure to French literature, especially the romances of George Sand, causes her to play at being in love with literary heroes and to change capriciously from one to another; she indulges the same expectations and conducts herself in the same way when she transfers her attentions to actual human beings. It is little wonder, therefore, that she encourages Mirobolant (I, xxxvii, 360), flirts simultaneously with Foker and Pen, and at last, in a desperate search for legitimacy, marries an apparently bogus count with a superlatively grand name: de Montmorenci (the same family with which Becky Sharp claimed kinship) de Valentinois.

When she has no other audience she enjoys posing to herself, whether in a mirror or in her book of verse, the title of which serves the narrator as a metonym for her (II, xxvii, 275). When she is not "the Muse," "*Mes Larmes,*" or "the Lady of *Mes Larmes,*" then she is often "the Sylphide," and like Marie Taglioni in the ballet of that name (I, xxxix, 377), she simulates an ethereal being whose association with earth-bound humanity proves impossible. As a *"femme incomprise"* (I, xxiii, 216), she cultivates sentiment and so, "by practice" (I, xxiv, 227), increases both her dissatisfaction and its expression. Irony becomes one form of utterance, especially irony directed against members of the Clavering family. At other times her annoyance takes the form of open quarrels with them, even before visitors like Laura and Major Pendennis.

Though at moments she feels a certain chagrin at having let her role slip, she always has another at hand. Most capable of responding to her circumstances by speaking dramatically and making "appropriate, though rather theatrical" gestures, she characteristically thinks of herself as "a heroine" (II, xxxvii, 366). When paying a patronizing and inquisitive visit to Fanny Bolton, for example, "Blanche felt a queen stepping down from her throne to visit a subject, and enjoyed all the bland consciousness of doing a good action" (II, xxvii, 274). Inevitably, Mrs. Bolton, a former member of the theatre, sees the play-acting and, worse, the prostitution of feeling.

Blanche wants "an establishment" (II, vi, 59) and wide social acceptance, but she also wants to continue her immature indulgence in "dreaming pretty dramas" (II, xxxiv, 329). Playing at being in love with Pen and genuinely attracted by Foker's wealth, her performance for each at the piano (captured also, for emphasis, by two illustrations) helps to epitomize her artful duplicity. Though she plays various characters, she also has certain stock gestures and devices that recur in her performances: "If ever this artless young creature met a young man, . . . she confided in him, so to speak—made play with her beautiful eyes—spoke in a tone of tender interest, and simple and touching appeal, and left him, to perform the same pretty little drama in behalf of his successor." If at first there are "very few audiences before whom Miss Blanche could perform" (I, xxvi, 246), she does for a time secure more attention, but her repetitions become apparent to Pen, as had the Fotheringay's.

When Pen asks her whether she wishes him "to come wooing in a Prince Prettyman's dress from the masquerade warehouse, and . . . feed my pretty princess with *bonbons?*" her answer is, of course, "*Mais j'adore les bonbons, moi*" (II, xxvi, 266). Indeed, it is Pen's ability as a play-actor that in part makes her equivocate between him and the wealthy Foker, for with the latter she has to carry much of the burden of the relationship. Hence also we understand part of the "strange feeling of exultation" that takes "possession of Blanche's mind" (II, xxxvii, 365) when she loses Foker at last. It takes possession of her mind because, as several people in the novel point out, she has no heart; like Becky Sharp she can feel no kindness, warmth, sympathy, or love.

Without these capabilities, "life is nothing" (I, xxiv, 227) indeed, and Blanche unwittingly emphasizes the emptiness of her life for us by variously repeating, in effect, her cry: "*Il me faut des émotions*" (II, xxxv, 345). As one who from a very early age "had begun to gush" (I, xxiv, 227), she appropriately tells Pen, in her deceptive letter, "To you I bring the gushing poesy of my being" (II, xxxiv, 331); even at this point, however, he fails to realize how complete a sham she is, for "he saw more than existed in reality" (II, xxxv, 345). What really exists at the heart of this circle of sham emotions is precisely nothing; at the center of the roles, their motive and epitome, exists complete emptiness, for the self has been dissipated through a surrender to role-playing. With the Fotheringay we are amused by seeing the ironic discrepancy between her theatrical role and her dull, stolid, everyday self, but with Blanche Amory, the more we see into her the more we understand that behind the role is only a void.

The last form of theatricalism by which Pen is tested derives rather intimately from the actual theatre; it is represented by Fanny Bolton, whose mother was "in the profession once, and danced at the Wells." Fanny herself has attended a day-school run by two former actresses and she is "a theatrical pupil" of Bows's, like the Fotheringay. "She has a good voice and a pretty face and figure for the stage," and having heard "of her mother's theatrical glories, . . . longs to emulate [them]" (II, iv, 34-35). Like her mother, Fanny is a "theatrical person" (II, ix 96). Hence she responds readily to spectacle and freely participates in the illusions to which it gives rise.

Vauxhall is therefore a perfect place for her romance to begin. It offers singing, horse-riding, fireworks, dancing, and a general glitter that makes it seem to "blaze before her with a hundred million of lamps, with a splendour such as the finest fairy tale, the finest pantomime she had ever witnessed at the theatre, had never realised" (II, viii, 82). She is of course ready to make a hero of the young man who takes her through such a wealth of splendor as Vauxhall, and somewhat like Blanche and her Savoyard organ-grinder (I, xxiv, 228), she romanticizes Pen by imagining hardship as well as glory: "I'm sure he's a nobleman, and of ancient famly, and kep out of his estate." Thinking of Bulwer's *The Lady of Lyons*, she asks, "And if everybody admires Pauline . . . for being so true to a poor man—why should a gentleman be ashamed of loving a poor girl?" (II, xiii, 124). The other member of "this couple of fools" (II, xi, 108), as the narrator forthrightly terms them, her mother, encourages these fantasies with recollections of former actresses who married theatrical men of one kind or another: not only the Fotheringay, but Emily Budd, who danced Columbine in *Harlequin Hornpipe* (II, x, 98, xiii, 125).

Fanny, who, like young Pen (I, viii, 78), would "do on the stage" (II, xxxiv, 334), eventually has to accept Huxter as her harlequin, but the brief association with Pen helps the girl to supplement her powers of fantasy with cunning, notably when she coaxes information about him out of Costigan, "tripping about the room as she had seen the dancers do at the play" (II, xi, 107), flattering him, learning what she wants to know, and then abandoning him. Though she suffers "fever and agitation, and passion and despair" (II, xvii, 167), the "drama" (II, xxvi, 263) with Pen ends when she consoles herself like the heroine of Pen's poem, Ariadne. As he sees at last, the ultimate root of her theatricality lies in her "coquetry and irrepressible desire of captivating mankind" (II, xxxvi, 348).[6]

The object of much of this role-playing, cool or passionate, is of course also frequently theatrical in his behavior, but less so as he grows older. Pen's lack of a father, his spoiled domination of Helen and young Laura, his reading of Inchbald's *Theatre* (I, iii, 24), and supplementary literature, his lively imagination, adolescent longings, isolation, and inexperience all help to account for his youthful fantasies. He becomes a reciter of gloomy, romantic verses, a poet-playwright himself, and a person most ready to respond to the pathos and beauty of Ophelia and Mrs. Haller by seeing himself in the appropriate roles: "He was Hamlet jumping into Ophelia's grave: he was the Stranger taking Mrs. Haller to his arms, beautiful Mrs. Haller" (I, vii, 69). He puts on "his most princely air" (I, vi, 64) when addressing inferior mortals like Dr. Portman, while with the Major he strings up his nerves for "his tragic and heroical air," "armed *cap-à-pié* as it were, with lance couched and plumes displayed" (I, viii, 77). It is only appropriate that the conclusion of the affair should be parodied by Hobnell, who "flung himself into a theatrical attitude near a newly-made grave, and began repeating Hamlet's verses over Ophelia, with a hideous leer at Pen" (I, xv, 135).

After the end of this first major episode of his life, however, his extravagant theatricalism is essentially at an end. Though Pen momentarily looks down at Fanny, "splendidly protecting her, like Egmont at Clara in Goethe's play" (II, viii, 84-85), and sees himself as a potential Faust to her Margaret, he terms that vision "nonsense," and vows there will be none of that "business" (II, ix, 93) for him. Finally, when he asks Blanche, "will you be the . . . Lady of Lyons, and love the penniless Claude Melnotte?" (II, xxxiv, 329), he is acting a part more to amuse her than to satisfy himself.

Along with these romantic roles, Pen has, from the very beginning of the novel, tried to simulate "a man of the world." The family legends, his father's pretensions, and his own tacit pseudo-aristocratic position as "head of the Pendennises" (I, i, 5), provide initial encouragement, as does the Fotheringay affair itself, for Pen becomes "famous" (I, xix, 176) at the university by making known his former passion for her, who is now a successful London actress: "his brow would darken, his eyes roll, his chest heave with emotion as he recalled that fatal period of his life, and described the woes and agonies which he had suffered" (I, xix, 175). Strutting, swaggering, entertaining bounteously, and indulging expensive tastes for clothing, jewelry, rare editions, prints, and gambling, while neglecting his studies (somewhat like his creator), Pen boyishly overplays his role—nowhere more so than in his admiring association with Bloundell-Bloundell, who is as flamboyantly fraudulent as Macheath

(I, xx, 186), and whose stories Pen believes as implicitly as Fanny does Costigan's.

During the "Ball-Practising" (I, xxvii, 257), Pen seems at his most typical as a would-be man of the world when "performing *cavalier seul* . . . [and] drawling through that figure" (I, xxvii, 260), but, as before, his triumphs end, like Fitz-Boodle's: though he and Blanche whirl round "as light and brisk as a couple of opera-dancers," they bump into recalcitrant actuality. His "waltzing career" (I, xxvii, 261) having ended, he soon turns to law and then to a literary career (again like his creator). Here Warrington, the novel's primary counter-force to pretensions of theatricality, makes sure that Pen is taken down at the start, calling Pen's old poem about Ariadne "miserable weak rubbish" that is "mawkish and disgusting," and his Prize Poem both "pompous and feeble" (I, xxxii, 312). Pen therefore begins with humble hack-writing for bread and gradually moves up to the modest eminence of being a published novelist.

In his parallel social career, however, away from Warrington's superintendence, Pen's mimetic instincts seem more under the influence of personal vanity: "Pen was sarcastic and dandyfied when he had been in the company of great folks; he could not help imitating some of their airs and tones, and having a most lively imagination, mistook himself for a person of importance very easily." Living in prominent society, we are reminded, makes one an actor, as we see again when Pen tells Foker of the Major's efforts to secure Blanche for him, and when, by "flinging himself into an absurd theatrical attitude," he reveals not only "high spirits" (II, vii, 72) but also perhaps a mostly unconscious discomfort at what he sees and may sense of the Major's plotting.

Pen's next bit of theatricalism shows clear discomfort, however—this time at a lurking purpose in himself—as he tries to dispel "a gloomy and rather guilty silence" when he and Fanny happen to meet Bows in the porter's doorway by attempting "to describe, in a jocular manner, the transactions of the night previous, and . . . to give an imitation of Costigan vainly expostulating with the check-taker at Vauxhall. It was not a good imitation" (II, x, 97), and Bows understands why. Deciding that his "calling is not seduction" (II, xi, 110), Pen turns again to Blanche Amory and to his more public aspirations. Having played the part of the experienced old gentleman to Laura and Fanny, he now tries it on Warrington: "I am older than you, George, in spite of your grizzled whiskers, and have seen much more of the world than you have in your garret here, shut up with your books and your reveries and your ideas of one-and-twenty" (II, xxiii, 232). Though a severe judgment, it is clearly self-serving, causing Warrington to respond with a shrewd exposure of Pen's motive for proclaiming himself a worldly old Sadducee, one who takes things as they are: "This is the meaning of your scepticism, . . . my poor fellow. You're going to sell yourself" (II, xxiii, 238).

Pen in effect accepts a stock role imposed upon him; in the appropriately ironic words of Morgan, he is now "young Hopeful" (II, xxx, 303). Before the play is over, however, Pen clearly sees that he must not accept a ready-made role: "you must bear your own burthen, fashion your own faith, think your own thoughts, and pray your own prayer" (II, xxxv, 340). When he puts on his last "tragedy air" and tells Lady Rockminster that "a villain has transplanted me" (II, xxxvi, 347) in the affections of Blanche Amory, the pose reflects in part his mortified vanity, and consequently it distorts the truth about Foker in the use of the word "villain"; hence that theatrical and inappropriate term must be rejected. Even more, however, the exaggerated pose also represents a conscious self-parody that is a sign of health and insight, and that is rooted in a joyous new sense of his own identity that has arisen from Laura's agreement to marry him. His last role is decidedly self-effacing: together with Laura he serves the Huxters by arranging to soften the father, "bring in the young people, extort the paternal benediction, and finish the comedy" (II, xxxvi, 349). Finally, as the novel's last sentence tells us, he "does not claim to be a hero, but only a man and a brother" (I, xxxvii, 372).

That tempered claim is an emancipation, the ultimate mark of Pen's maturity, for it implies his awareness that when theatricalism is mere strutting and gesticulating—without humility and the recognition of kinship, which includes charity—it is an epitome of human isolation. In effect, he understands at last the meaning of that short and quietly resonant scene with Bows on Chatteris bridge, when two isolations meet in brief sympathy (I, xiv, 128). Warrington, of course, has long had a similar understanding, and therefore it is entirely fitting that at the end of the novel he not only affirms his kinship to Pen and Laura, his "brother and sister" as he calls them, but that also, by "practising in the nursery here, in order to prepare for the part of Uncle George" (II, xxxvii, 370), he acknowledges the potentially positive value of theatricality. *The History of Pendennis* reminds us that we all inevitably play roles in the over-arching comedy, but that we need to choose them with great care so as to dramatize genuine feelings of sympathy and love, and thereby to bring a temporary end to human isolation.

* * * * *

Like the narrator of *The Book of Snobs* and *Vanity Fair*,[7] his counterpart in *Pendennis* maintains a close relationship with the individual members of his audience, addressing them sometimes as males, sometimes as females, often as mature, and at least once as youthful. Continuing the practice established in those earlier works, he addresses the reader as "worthy" (I, xv, 129, xix, 170, II, xv, 144), "respected" (I, xiii, 115, II, iii, 27), "friendly" (I, xvi, 142), and even "beloved" (II, xiii, 119). We are called "brother and sister" (II, xxiii, 229) and "Brother wayfarer" (I, xviii, 165) because we are members of the human family sharing the experience of living in the Fair and attempting to make our way through it. As such we are collaborators who help bring his narrative into being and who authenticate it. Like him we know the implied answer to the question, "which of us knows his fate?" (I, iii, 32). Although our infatuations mock us all, young "Pen is a man who will console himself like the rest of us" (I, xv, 130). "We should all of us, I am sure, have liked to see the Major's grin, when the worthy old gentleman made his time-honoured joke" (I, xviii, 164). "What generous person is there that has not been so deceived" (I, xxv, 240) as Laura was in Blanche? In short, it is not simply his tale but "our tale" (II, xxxvii, 367).

At the same time, he invites us to participate more amusedly and at other times more profoundly in the comicality, absurdity, folly, and darkness of human life. Costigan's tattered hat, boots, and gloves suggest that "Poverty seems as if it were disposed, before it takes possession of a man entirely, to attack his extremities first" (I, v, 44). "When a gentleman is cudgelling his brain to find any rhyme for sorrow, besides borrow and to-morrow, his woes are nearer at an end than he thinks for" (I, xv, 131). "How lonely we are in the world; how selfish and secret, everybody! . . . you and I are but a pair of infinite isolations, with some fellow-islands a little more or less near to us" (I, xvi, 143).

If *performance* crucially defines our behavior as inhabitants of Vanity Fair—indeed, almost forty of the characters are literally actors, actresses, and dancers—so too does our reenactment of archetypal configurations articulated in literature, in history, and in mythological awareness. At times we see the mirroring by means of proverbial or proverb-like narrative statements. The experiences of Smirke literally tumbling head over heels off his horse in an impossible love-sick hope to see Helen and to move her emotions, and of Pen rushing off in a whirlwind to see with rapture the performance of a dull actress both prompt the comical observation "Thus love makes fools of all of us" (I, iv, 40). Nevertheless, even in response to fractured French, we must acknowledge that *"Etre soul au monde est bien ouneeyong"* (I, xvi, 144). Old Lord Colchicum's sexual pursuit of a young female circus rider with the help of Tom Tufthunt leads to the sardonic remark: "When Don Juan scales the wall, there's never a want of a Leporello to hold the ladder" (II, viii, 83). Contradictory views of marriage remind the narrator of "the old allegory of the gold and silver shield, about which the two knights quarrelled, each [being] right according to the point from which he looks: so about marriage; the question whether it is foolish or good, wise or otherwise, depends upon the point of view from which you regard it" (I, vii, 67). The most fundamental Thackerayan articulation of the archetypal nature of our performances is of course his frequently quoted Horatian epitome: *Mutato nomine, de te fabula narratur* (With a change of name, the tale is told of you [II, xxxiv, 335]).

Pen's father taking his pedigree out of a trunk recalls to the narrator Sterne's officer calling for his sword (I, ii, 8). Helen, silently keeping within herself what her love has divined of her son's secret thoughts and feelings, prompts narrative recollection of Mary "keep[ing] these things in her heart" (I, iii, 29). More comically, men and women are like Titania seeing "good looks in donkey's ears, wit in their numskulls, and music in their bray" (II, xxvi, 264). "Was Titania the first who fell in love with an ass, or Pygmalion the only artist who has gone crazy about a stone?" (I, v, 52). Garbetts, the actor, unexpectedly meeting a lawyer who has got out a writ against him, "with a face as blank as Macbeth's when Banquo's ghost appears upon him, gasped some inarticulate words, and fled out of the room" (I, xiii, 117).

The Major is an unsatisfactory Mentor to Pen's Telemachus (II, vi, 53). The Major and Costigan reenact the prelude to the battle of Fontenoy (chapter vignette: I, xi, 97). Warrington is a Diogenes (I, xxxiii, 327, II, viii, 80). The love-sick Foker could "no more escape the common lot than Achilles, or Ajax, or Lord Nelson, or Adam our first father" (II, i, 1). Foker is like "the heir in Horace pouring forth the gathered wine of his father's vats; . . . human nature is pretty much the same in Regent Street as in the Via Sacra" (II, xxxiii, 324). Fanny is the Ariadne of Shepherd's Inn (II, xxvi, 263). Blanche is Foker's Armida (II, xxxvii, 362). Strong is down on his luck like "Marius at Miturnæ, Charles Edward in the Highlands, Napoleon before Elba" (II, xxiii, 226). The headmaster of Greyfriars School loses his momentary magnificence like Cinderella after the ball (I, ii, 18). And Smirke, like so many Thackerayan characters, has an unwanted Horatian companion riding behind him on his pony: black Care (I, xvi, 143).

Pen often sees himself in terms of prototypes. With absurd youthful pretentiousness he introduces himself as someone with an Odysseus-like breadth of experience, *qui mores hominum multorum videt et urbes* (who has seen the many cities and customs of men [I, i, 5]). By pompously quoting Thackeray's master, Horace, who is conveying Homer's characterization of Odysseus, Pen unwittingly identifies for readers one of Thackeray's basic assumptions: our culture transmits archetypal renderings of human experience that provide the basis for an understanding of our own experience (if we are capable of it). Given his slow growth into understanding, Pen youthfully creates romantic images of himself adopted from his reading: he is a fire-worshipper, he is Conrad, he is Selim—not from real experience, but from exotic, near-Eastern fantasies by Moore and Byron (I, iii, 25).

Gradually, however, he sees himself more in terms of actual historical experience and literary articulation. He seeks counterparts for his feelings in passages from Anacreon and Lucretius, and from late seventeenth and early eighteenth century poets like "Waller, Dryden, Prior" and similar poets of pre-Romantic elegance and sophistication. He sees his mother in terms of Andromache (I, iii, 27). He is Hamlet, the Stranger, the reader of Waller, Herrick, and Béranger. He vows like Montrose to make the Fotheringay "famous with his sword and glorious by his pen" (I, vii, 69). He sees himself as Egmont, as Leicester (II, viii, 85), and as Claude Melnotte (II, xxxiv, 329). He vows not to be Faust with Margaret (II, ix, 93).

More usually, of course, the *narrator* sees him in archetypal and of course often ironic terms. Pen is like the love-sick swain in Ovid (I, iii, 26). He rides out in quest of Dulcinea (I, iii, 28). With the laming of his horse he is as frantic with vexation as Richard at Bosworth (I, vi, 54). He listens to his uncle's tales with the avidity of Desdemona (I, ix, 85). He uses Smirke "as Corydon does the elm-tree, to cut out his mistress's name upon. He made him echo with the name of the beautiful Amaryllis" (I, xvi, 142). After the break-up of his relationship with the Fotheringay, Pen "sate sulking, Achilles-like in his tent, for the loss of his ravaged Briseis" (I, xvi, 146). At college, Pen is a "reckless young Amphitryon" (I, xx, 185) and a prodigal son (I, xxi, 194, xxii, 207). In notable contradistinction to Pen's pseudo near-Eastern Byronism, moreover, Thackeray finds a quintessential archetype of human experience in a figure from a masterpiece of the near-East, *The Arabian Nights' Entertainments,* in order to articulate a reality fundamental to all the wanderers in Vanity Fair: Alnaschar (I, xxxii, 317), a naïve dreamer of impossible dreams who destroys them with his arrogant over-reaching. The dreams are as fragile as glass, and the dreamer is a victim of his unwittingly self-destructive fantasies. So too, Thackeray would seem to be saying, are we all.

CHAPTER TWO:

THE ENGLISH HUMOURISTS OF THE EIGHTEENTH CENTURY AND THE HISTORY OF HENRY ESMOND, ESQ.

Having notably articulated his awareness of human behavior as performance in *The Snobs of England, Vanity Fair,* and *Pendennis*—indeed, even before completing the latter novel—Thackeray decided to emerge as an overt public performer by becoming a lecturer. Even before delivering his six lectures on twelve English humorists of the eighteenth century in London between 29 May and 3 July 1851, however, he had privately expressed his acute and uncomfortable awareness of "how orators become humbugs and . . . absorbed in that selfish pursuit and turning of periods" (*Letters,* II, 766). In fact, he even characterized his lecturing self as "Equilibrist and Tightrope dance[r]" (*Letters,* II, 775). Lecturing subsequently in England, Scotland, and finally the United States during the next two years only increased his uneasy sense of performance, until he finally revolted at what he called "the quackery" (*Letters,* III, 193) of constantly repeating the same words in the same way, accompanied by an uncontrollable and unsettling resurgence of the same emotions, and returned—indeed, fled—home.

As this may help to indicate, Thackeray took lecturing very seriously. For him, the lecturer should be a performer who emulates Harlequin—a person who "without his mask is known to present a very sober countenance," for he is "a man full of cares and perplexities like the rest of us."[1] Inevitably, then, his performance is not "merely humourous or facetious," but also "serious, and often very sad" (pp. 1-2)—all of which qualities we perceive in the lectures. In short, Thackeray's model humorist joins mirthfulness with seriousness—which is to say, gravity. For him, true humor is the response of moral awareness, revealing a pious, feeling heart.

As a humorist, Thackeray stresses the underlying community of performer and audience, especially as both recognize and respond to their shared values. For him, therefore, humor arises not merely out of, say, a sense of comical absurdity, but more profoundly out of a fundamental recognition of ourselves as brother and sister participants in the human condition, and as aspirers towards an immortal destiny. Thackerayan humor seeks to draw humans together in sympathetic understanding. The humorous performer appeals to our moral faculties as he seeks to arouse the love, pity, and kindness of his audiences—their "scorn for untruth, pretension, imposture," and their "tenderness for the weak, the poor, the oppressed, the unhappy" (p. 2). Consequently, humor serves as a socially binding as well as a morally prompting force.

As a performer, Thackeray seeks a close personal relationship with members of his audience, in part by testifying to his own thoughts and feelings through the use of "I," "me," and "my" over ninety times. In a similar vein he tells them "we must remember" (p. 11), he reminds them of their common literary knowledge by saying "We have all read in Milton of the spear that was like 'the mast of some tall amiral'" (p. 36), and he calls upon their shared feelings in characterizing their response to Addison, most especially: "It is as a Tatler of small talk and a Spectator of mankind, that we cherish and love him" (p. 95). That concept, in fact, defines Thackeray's own overall role in these lectures, as he seeks to be the responsive Spectator.

He frequently speaks to them directly: "In treating of the English humourists of the past age, it is of the men and of their lives, rather than of their books, that I ask permission to speak to you" (p. 1). "You know, of course, that Swift has had many biographers" (p. 5). "After looking in the 'Rake's Progress' at Hogarth's picture of St. James's Palace-gate, you may people the street, but little altered within these hundred years, with the gilded carriages and thronging chairmen that bore the courtiers . . . to Queen Anne's drawing-room" (p. 231). "Your love for [Goldsmith] is half pity" (p. 294).

In addressing the members of his audience, Thackeray frequently uses rhetorical questions (often comical) to establish a feeling of community among himself and his hearers, and also with his subjects: "Who would not give something to pass a night at the club with Johnson, and Goldsmith, and James Boswell, Esq., of Auchinleck?" (p. 7). "Isn't that . . . a fine image?" (p. 20). "If you were in a strait would you like such a benefactor [as Swift]?" (p. 26). "Who hasn't in his mind an image of Stella?" (p. 43). "Would you have had one of them [Stella and Vanessa] forgive the other?" (p. 52). "Didn't I tell you that dancing was a serious business to Harlequin?" (p. 65). "You laugh? You think it is in the power of few writers now-a-days to call up such an angel [as Addison did in 'The Campaign']"? (p. 91). "Aren't you all acquainted with it [a once popular poem of Prior's]? Have you not all got it by heart? What! have you never heard of it? See what fame is made of!" (p. 162). "Would not you fancy that a poet of our own days was singing?" (pp. 165-66).

At other times he engagingly alludes to himself or to his own experiences: "it seems to me, [Swift] was no more an Irishman than a man born of English parents at Calcutta [like Thackeray] is a Hindoo" (p. 14). "It has been my business, professionally of course, to go through a deal of sentimental reading in my time, and to acquaint myself with love-making, as it has been described" (p. 44). "[Addison] had not worked crop after crop from his brain, manuring hastily, subsoiling indifferently, cutting and sowing and cutting again, like other luckless cultivators of letters" (p. 97) [an apparent reference to Thackeray's frenetic early days of journalistic writing]. In a similar vein, regarding nineteenth as well as eighteenth century school disciplining, he says: "I have myself inspected, but only as an amateur, that instrument of righteous torture still existing, and in occasional use, in a secluded private apartment of the old Charterhouse School [i.e. the flogging block]" (p. 119). "If . . . , as is the plan of some authors (a plan decidedly against their interests, be it said), it is propounded that there exists in life no such being [as a hero], and therefore that in novels, the picture of life, there should appear no such character; then Mr. Thomas Jones becomes an admissible person" (p. 260). More somberly: "A perilous trade, indeed, is that of a man who has to bring his tears and laughter, his recollections, his personal griefs and joys, his private thoughts and feelings to market, to write them on paper, and sell them for money" (p. 283).

He tries overtly to distinguish his inferences from knowable facts, being acutely aware of how isolated we all are from each other and especially from greatness: "What character of what great man is known to you? You can but make guesses as to character more or less happy. . . . And if it is so with those you know, how much more with those you don't know?" (pp. 105-6). Of Swift he says, quoting a remark of Swift's: "I think he was admiring not the genius [expressed in his work], but the consequences to which the genius had brought him" (p. 30). Of the Stella-Vanessa controversy: "most women, I believe, . . . as far as my experience and conversation goes, generally take Vanessa's part" (p. 44). "He wanted to marry neither of them—that I believe was the truth" (p. 50). Of Addison: "when Mr. Addison's men abused Mr. Pope, I don't think Addison took his pipe out of his mouth to contradict them" (pp. 83-84). "I doubt, until after his marriage, perhaps, whether he ever lost his night's rest or his day's tranquillity about any woman in his life" (p.

98). Of Steele: "I have no sort of authority for the statements here made of Steele's early life; but if the child is father of the man . . ." (p. 119). By contrast, he discovers convincing grounds for admiring Addison because, as in his "Evening Hymn," "His sense of religion stirs through his whole being" (p. 104)—in notable distinction from what Thackeray perceives in the being of two ordained clergymen: Swift and Sterne. Concentrating, as Thackeray does, upon the literal or imaginable details of biography, he does not therefore, as in his fictional narratives, evoke the richness of archetypal allusion, but of course he does not abandon his fundamental assumptions about the nature of human behavior: Vanessa is an Ariadne (p. 50); English undergraduates giddily seek to emulate Horatian Olympic contestants (p. 56); Donizetti's *segreto per esse felice* reenacts figures in Congreve and Horace as well as dramatizes a character from *Lucrezia Borgia* (p. 68); Congreve is a "Phœbus Apollo of the Mall and Spring Garden" (p. 77); in the spirit of Restoration and eighteenth century comedy the actual world abounds with counterparts of the fictional Mirabels, Belmours, Millamants, Doricourts (pp. 69-70), Ardelias, Saccharissas, and of course Sir Foplings (p. 99); the eternal Horatian goddess "Fortune shook her swift wings and jilted [Gay]" (p. 170), but the Duke and Duchess of Queensberry emulate their predecessors in *Don Quixote* by harboring him (p. 174). Speaking of Pope writhing with anguish at a libel directed against him, Thackeray comments: "How little human nature changes! Can't one see that little figure? Can't one fancy one is reading Horace? Can't one fancy one is speaking of to-day?" (p. 213).

The world of Congreve's comedies re-presents the appearance of "Sallust and his friends and their mistresses . . . crowned with flowers, with cups in their hands" (p. 67), engaging in a protracted revel. Indeed, Thackeray's most extended metaphor grows out of this awareness, as the recollection of Sallust's pleasure house and gardens generates the characterization of memory itself as a recovery of buried human presence—the disinterring of a Pompeii. Rereading these plays of Congreve's produces in Thackeray feelings similar to those of a contemporary spectator of those ruins looking at

> the relics of an orgy, a dried wine-jar or two, a charred supper-table, the breast of a dancing girl pressed against the ashes, the laughing skull of a jester.... We gaze at the skeleton, and wonder at the life which once revelled in its mad veins. We take the skull up, and muse over the frolic and daring, the wit, scorn, passion, hope, desire, with which that empty bowl once fermented. We think of the glances that allured, the tears that melted, of the bright eyes that shone in those vacant sockets; and of lips whispering love, and cheeks dimpling with smiles. (pp. 65-66)

Congreve's muse may be "dead, and her song choked in Time's ashes" (p. 66), but memory reanimates his and Sallust's "temple of Pagan delights" (p. 67). Memory articulates the knowledge of evanescence but also the awareness of enduring vitality in bones and skulls—in Thackeray's case, wittily but decorously. Memory manifests the shudder of loss and yet embodies a paradigm of the resurrection of life.

Besides giving expression to his playful or ironic sense of human reenactments, however, Thackeray frequently speaks of his individual feelings and musings in terms like the following: "I fear" (p. 7), "I am glad" (p. 14), "I wonder . . . I suppose" (p. 17), "I can't fancy" (p. 32), "I fancy" (p. 67), "I can't but fancy" (p. 81), "I can hardly fancy" (p. 103), "as I fancy" (pp. 214, 249). Correspondingly, of course, he often encourages the members of his audience to use *their* imaginative powers: "See!" (p. 66), "Look . . . Look!" (p. 68), "Cannot one fancy . . . ?" (p. 125), "Can't one fancy . . . ?" (pp. 126, 213), "Can't one see . . . ?" (p. 213).

Such imaginative participation feelingly joins together lecturer and audience, and helps to reanimate the human subjects of the lectures. In reenacting prototypical roles we certainly articulate a connectedness to our predecessors, historical or mythic, but we thereby also maintain an isolation from those of our contemporaries who fail to understand that they are doing so, or who because of their pettiness cannot emulate certain roles, or who because of their gentle or appalled bewilderment cannot do so. At one point, for example, Thackeray sees Swift as someone like "Abudah in the Arabian story [a major source of Thackeray's archetypes], he is always looking out for the Fury, and knows that the night will come and the inevitable hag with it. What a night, my God, it was! what a lonely rage and long agony—what a vulture that tore the heart of that giant! It is awful to think of the sufferings of this great man" (pp. 31-32).

Prometheus we mortals are not, but we can imaginatively respond to his and Swift's sufferings, as Thackeray does here—*a model for our response.* In the "Drapier's Letters," Thackeray sees Swift as a pathetically maddened Samson "rushing on his enemies and felling them: one admires [obviously in the Latin sense of "wonders at"] not the cause so much as the strength, the anger, the fury of the champion. As is the case with madmen, certain subjects provoke him, and awaken his fits of wrath" (p. 33). Addison receiving Pope's "Epistle to Dr. Arbuthnot" can be imagined as a "St. Sebastian, with that arrow in his side" (p. 202). Bolingbroke's losing of his voice in tears while responding to news of Pope's failing last days is like Timanthes' picture "which hides the grief and heightens it" (p. 211). Imaginative responsiveness is precisely what can lead us, temporarily at least, to overcome our human isolation. Indeed, *that*, in Thackeray's eyes, is the quintessential aspect of the humorist's role: momentarily to overcome our sense of separateness by prompting in us an ability to participate—or at least seem to participate—in another human being's thoughts and feelings, and thereby to fulfill our greatest human capacity—the ability to sympathize and to love.

As he says in his introductory remarks, "If Humour only meant laughter, you would scarcely feel more interest about humourous writers than about the private life of poor Harlequin." But the audience's mere presence, Thackeray reminds them, "shows that you have curiosity and sympathy . . . . The humourous writer professes to awaken and direct your love, your pity, your kindness—your scorn . . . —your tenderness . . . . Accordingly, as he finds, and speaks, and feels the truth best, we regard him, esteem him—sometimes love him" (p. 2). Thackeray assumes that we love them—indeed, expects that we love them—because love is a recognition and a liberation: at its best, "a liberal education," as Steele so memorably wrote (p. 134).

* * * * *

It is of course not surprising that Thackeray's reimmersion in late seventeenth and early eighteenth century history and literature (already a favored period for his private reading) in preparation for his lecture series would lead to the writing of an historical novel set in those times. Readers have long noted how his identification in his lecture on Steele of Lord Mohun as a "fast" nobleman of the 1690's, and his detailed account of Mohun's two trials for murder, reemerged as major events in his swiftly ensuing fictional narrative, *The History of Henry Esmond* (1852). Indeed, Thackeray's careful redesignating for fictional purposes of Mohun's first name prompted Thackeray's annotator of the *English Humourists* (1853), James Hannay, to insert the playful comment that "This amiable baron's name was Charles, and not Henry, as a recent novelist has christened him" (p. 113n). And, of course, readers have also noted Thackeray's evocation in *Esmond* of historical personages like

Pope, Addison, and Steele, as well as his wonderful mimicry of a *Spectator* paper in that novel.

But one can also see *Esmond* as a fulfillment of Thackeray's exuberant evocation of the earlier period in a brilliant, elaborately and knowledgeably detailed, and yet thoroughly imaginative passage like the following from the lecture on Steele:

> As we read in these delightful volumes of the "Tatler" and "Spectator," the past age returns, the England of our ancestors is revivified. The May-pole rises in the Strand again in London; the churches are thronged with daily worshippers; the beaux are gathering in the coffee-houses; the gentry are going to the Drawing-room—the ladies are thronging to the toy-shops—the chairmen are jostling in the streets—the footmen are running with links before the chariots, or fighting round the theatre doors. In the country I see the young Squire riding to Eton with his servants behind him, and Will Wimble, the friend of the family, to see him safe. To make that journey from the Squire's and back, Will is a week on horseback. The coach takes five days between London and the Bath. The judges and the bar ride the circuit. If my lady comes to town in her post-chariot, her people carry pistols to fire a salute on Captain Macheath if he should appear, and her couriers ride ahead to provide apartments for her at the great caravanserais on the road; Boniface receives her under the creaking sign of the Bell or the Ram, and he and his chamberlains bow her up the great stair to the state-apartments, whilst her carriage rumbles into the court-yard, where the Exeter Fly is housed that performs the journey in eight days God willing, having achieved its daily flight of twenty miles, and landed its passengers for supper and sleep. The curate is taking his pipe in the kitchen, where the Captain's

man—having hung up his master's half pike—is at his bacon and eggs, bragging of Ramillies and Malplaquet to the town's-folk, who have their club in the chimney-corner. The Captain is ogling the chambermaid in the wooden gallery, or bribing her to know who is the pretty young mistress that has come in the coach? The pack-horses are in the great stable, and the drivers and ostlers carousing in the tap. . . . I would have liked to travel in those days (pp. 107-9).

In the *English Humourists* Thackeray also, of course, passionately and elaborately responds to the visual world of Hogarth, whose paintings evoke from him the remarkable comment that "these admirable works . . . give us the most complete and truthful picture of the manners, and even the thoughts, of the past century" (p. 228). In response to such pictorial stimulation, and to the detailed articulations of favorite period authors, he goes on to people for his hearers the eighteenth century London streets and countryside of Hogarth, Smollett, and Fielding with another vibrant evocation of thronging literal and yet imaginative presences (pp. 228-31). Similarly participatory recreations of the period do not intrude into Esmond's very personal autobiographical narrative, or disturb its austerity, but the minute and extensive historical awareness that these recreations had articulated in the *English Humourists* suffuses his later narrative, after having undoubtedly demonstrated to Thackeray his capacity to write a novel that would in its own way allow—indeed, necessitate—the imaginative recreation of a life immersed in those realities.

When Steele reappears in the novel, telling young Esmond about the death of his father—an experience that Thackeray had cited in the *English Humourists*—and exhibiting the same minor but real flaws of character, we again see Thackeray's appreciation of basic human goodness, however sullied by experience and by weakness. Quoting from Ovid,[2] Steele acknowledges that he sees and admires the better, but follows the worse. He thereby contrasts with Esmond, who has a basic core of integrity whatever inconsistencies may be revealed in his conduct.

As the mature Henry Esmond looks back at the first major crisis of his life, which has been brought about by the death of his father, he defines for the us the central problem and quest of his life: the uncertainty of his identity and his attempt to define it satisfactorily. To answer the question "Who was he and what?" the boy must decide how he will pursue the quest and where he will do so—in what ways and amid what people and circumstances: "Why here rather than elsewhere?"(I, vi, 52). Sometimes he will wait passively "and abide his fortune" (I, vi, 53); sometimes he will seek it by active pursuits. Finally, however, he comes serenely to see the impotence of human desire as revealed by the developments of personal, familial, and national history.

Esmond discovers that he is what he was, but what he was can be recovered only through memory, which quietly preserves and connects whatever has been deeply experienced. As he recalls his feelings on that early night of sleepless sorrow, he captures for himself and for us the boy's sense of loneliness and the need to love: "he sickened to think how . . . he was now quite alone. The soul of the boy was full of love, and he longed as he lay in the darkness there for some one upon whom he could bestow it" (I, vi, 52). An investigation, therefore, of this dual attempt to discover himself, and to find fulfillment in a truly self-expressive love seems fundamental to an understanding of the novel. The fusion of Esmond's history with the religious, political, and military history of his day,[3] moreover, requires that his growth be seen in the illuminating context of those larger developments.

The pattern that memory imposes upon experience begins unchronologically with Esmond's first sight of Rachel, where his need to love is enacted before us. Even here, however, he is what he was. By the time of his arrival at Castlewood from his fatherless and motherless condition at Ealing, he has already inherited a loneliness and a permanent melancholy, like his creator: "The unhappiness of those days is long forgiven, though they cast a shade of melancholy over the child's youth which will accompany him no doubt to the end of his days." At Castlewood he finds not so much a father as a *"parrain"* (I, iii, 19), a languid "godfather" (I, iii, 21)—a word whose meaning he soon learns with a shame that is not overcome by occasional gestures of kindness.

He finds himself estranged even more from his step-mother, who is both an odd spectacle and an ill-natured tyrant. By virtue of her eventual discovery of her false position, but also by her very nature, she is a most theatrical person who appears to the young Esmond as awful as the Empress of Ealing, and causes him to stare at her "as he had stared at the player-woman who acted the wicked tragedy-queen, when the players came down to Ealing Fair" (I, iii, 22). He soon learns, however, that like his father "she had many qualities by no means heroic" (I, iv, 28), and it is a heroic figure to love, worship, and emulate that he seeks.

Father Holt, who alone calls him "my son" (I, v, 34), becomes "his friend and Master" (I, v, 35). "By love; by a brightness of wit and good humour that charmed all; by an authority which he knew how to assume; by a mystery and silence about him which increased the child's reverence for him; he won Harry's absolute fealty" (I, iv, 27). Subtly accompanying his instruction with delicacy and kindness, Holt instills in Harry a strong devotion to himself and to the Jesuit order of "martyrs and heroes . . . ; so that Harry Esmond thought that to belong to the Jesuits was the greatest prize of life and bravest end of ambition" (I, iii, 25). Here is

Harry's first association of love for a human being with service to God and to a political cause.

Because the boy's eager willingness to serve can find no adequate form of expression, however, this largely unconscious attempt at self-definition essentially fails. Harry announces himself ready to go to the stake for Holt, but the Jesuit just wishes him to hold his tongue and suppress evidence for the Catholic and Jacobite cause, which attracts far more of Holt's interest than does the boy. Holt's remaining legacies to Harry at this time are the *"botte de Jesuite"* (I, xiii, 116) that he and his Cambridge successor teach the young swordsman, his fatal involvement of Harry's father in a plot against King William, and his suppression of evidence of Harry's legitimacy.

As a result, Harry can only acknowledge his father in secret and with mortification; he has "a father and no father" (I, vi, 52). Until he knows his mother, he can neither love nor revere Thomas Esmond, but he can at least feel gratitude for the protection of "his patron" (I, vi, 51). With the death of the third Viscount, therefore, he feels more isolated than ever before in his life. Filled with shame, grief, and loneliness, he thinks for the first time in his life of beginning a quest to discover who he really is—by going to Ireland to learn more about his father's death-bed confession.

He remains passive, however, being counselled by his new friend, Corporal Steele, to remain at Castlewood and await what fortune brings. Meanwhile, he continues to be highly conscious of his ambiguous, unprotected state "in the hands of Heaven and Fate" (I, vi, 52). He welcomes Steele's love and kindness, but soon learns of their limitations. Pious but drunken, kindly but unfaithful, Steele can neither accomplish anything for the boy nor serve as someone to worship. Harry accepts the confidences of Steele about his passion for Saccharissa and the boy keeps his vow of secrecy "religiously" (I, vii, 54), only to find that everyone knows the "secret." This betrayal, a comic epitome of the way of the world in *Henry Esmond,* serves as the final negative preparation for Harry's positive response to the next person he meets: one who is not a bibulous corporal, an evanescent priest, a supine patron, or a gaunt, scraggy woman whose wigs, washes, and rouge-pots comprise her cestus (I, vi, 44), but seemingly the goddess herself—a *Dea certè* (I, i, 6) whom he instinctively worships.

She is not only a Vergilian Venus but also a Christian one, recognizable by the "golden halo round her hair" (I, i, 7) and by her gestures of loving kindness and protection. Like her later treatment of him, the initial kindness is followed by a brief repudiation but then by increased affection, so that his "shy obeissance" (I, i, 6) becomes an act of adoration: "the boy, who had never looked upon so much beauty before, felt as if the touch of a superiour being or angel smote him down to the ground, and kissed the fair protecting hand as he knelt on one knee" (I, i, 7). The instinct that motivates his reaction to this "fair apparition" soon becomes "a devoted affection and passion of gratitude"; it "cannot be called love, . . . but it was worship" (I, vii, 55), a life-long worship, in fact, that contrasts notably with Beatrix's habit of always forsaking an old friend for a new one. As Beatrix had mockingly observed when Harry first knelt before her mother, he is indeed "saying his prayers" (I, i, 7) to Rachel.

He comes, moreover, to change the outer form of his religion by replacing his worship of Holt with worship of her; in the words of Herrick, he ceases to be a Catholic, "Thy Protestant to be." First joining the household at prayers, he then becomes a convert, his "inclination prompting him to be always as near as he might to his mistress, and to think all things she did right"; indeed, "the boy loved his catechizer so much that he would have subscribed to anything she bade him." Towards the end of his life he takes pleasure in the thought that he has been faithful to the early vow of permanent attachment, but in the meanwhile his self-knowledge, his knowledge of her, and the nature of that attachment have to develop significantly.

For a time "the young mother, with her daughter and son, and the orphan lad whom she protected read and worked and played, and were children together" (I, vii, 56). With the passage of time and the development of other relationships, however, this simple intimacy diminishes. Harry's idol not only has "idols of her own," but three increasingly unworthy ones, especially her husband. "Jove and Supreme ruler" (I, vii, 55) though the Viscount seems for a time to to his naïvely adoring wife, he grows weary of the "gentle bonds" of idol worship and like "the Grand Lama of Thibet . . . yawns on his altar as his bonzes kneel and worship him." Partly because Rachel's worship as "chief priestess" (I, vii, 57) is more devoted than Mrs. Tusher's grotesque conduct as "fair Priestess of Castlewood" (I, iii, 22), or than Tusher's as obsequious clergyman, it is also very jealous and demanding. The fault of jealousy therefore becomes both tiring to its object and apparent to Harry as "a fault of character, which flawed her perfection" (I, vii, 59), though he will not allow another boy to say so, and assaults him with a furious and comic chivalry.

Harry's intellectual development, furthermore, inevitably takes place to a considerable degree in isolation. Here too, Rachel responds "with her usual jealous watchfulness of affection" (I, vii, 57)—just as she does later when Harry greets the news that he is to attend the university with a wish to begin immediate preparations for his journey. Finally, the simple intimacy diminishes also with his increasing physical maturity, especially as it reveals itself in his "magnetick attraction" (I, viii, 62) towards Nancy Sievewright. Though Harry feels both grief-stricken and outraged at the injustice of Rachel's jealous taunts, the cruelty is only a momentary one that his worship easily survives. Rachel's discomfort, however, at her discovery of her own jealousy leads to her resolution that their intimacy must be modified.

Consequently, "her page" (I, vii, 59) becomes "Mr. Tutor" (I, ix, 77) and she decrees that he is to leave for Cambridge to study for a vocation that will make permanent his formal relationship to the family, keeping him close yet distant. He in turn prepares to enter the Church "for a livelihood and from obedience and necessity rather than from choice" (I, ix, 79). Wishing, like a chivalric courtly lover, to be "her true knight" (I, ix, 83), he finds that his sole way of serving Rachel is by making submission to her wishes his chief duty, even when it seems that she rejoices to see him go. Before he leaves, however, she has identified for him an important role: friend and protector to her children and her husband. This trust constitutes his *"viaticum"* (I, ix, 82).

At the university, by virtue of his age, his circumstances, and the traits of character they have developed, he finds himself largely cut off from his classmates. As his nickname of "Don Dismallo" (I, x, 87) suggests, he resembles the knight of La Mancha not only in his melancholy temperament and countenance, but in his quixotic willingness to undertake an impossible pursuit. Lacking the necessary seriousness and devotion, he finds himself "at the end of one month a Papist, . . . the next month a Protestant . . . , and the third a sceptic" (I, x, 88). He at last begins to define himself, however, by his spirit of inquiry and rebelliousness that contrasts favorably with Tusher's religious and political servility. Esmond's own worldly ambition, like his politics and religion, expresses itself largely within the context of his personal devotion to Rachel; for himself, he has only a very limited desire for public distinction. Reading, writing poetry, and winning a few victories over his tutor help to make the university less of a prison for Esmond, but his devotion to Rachel seems to offer him permanent servitude: "as he was bound, before all things in the world, to his dear mistress at home, and knew that a refusal on his part would grieve her, he determined to give her no hint of his unwillingness to the clerical office" (I, x, 89).

He still instinctively feels the impulse to worship her, being ready "to fall on his knees, and kiss the skirt of her robe, so fond and ardent was his respect and regard for her" (I, xi, 90), but her coldness holds him in check. So does her marital unhappiness, which he finds himself unable to relieve, as the failure of his peace-making embassy makes especially clear. He finally manages to serve her when he composes the quarrel between Viscount Castlewood and Mohun, as a result of which she almost falls on his shoulder, kisses his hand, and calls him "brother" (I, xiii, 111). But his fundamental helplessness appears again when both his confession that he loves Rachel as a mother and worships her "as a devotee worships a Saint" (I, xiii, 116), and his plea that Mohun leave her fail to achieve their intended effect. His only reward is a second kiss from Rachel, who now addresses him as a son. Soon afterwards, when the dying Viscount leaves Harry and Rachel as the children's guardians, the mingling of roles is extended still further.[4] Once more Esmond has tried to act in a preventative way; this time the failure extends even to himself, for by participating in the duel he makes a clerical career impossible. He is saved from it, therefore, by blundering rather than by choice.

Ashamed as a young boy of the aspersions cast upon his birth and ready to fight at being called "a bastard" (I, iv, 31), Esmond has gradually come to terms with his alleged ancestry: "Though there might be a bar in Harry Esmond's shield, it was a noble one" (I, vi, 53). "Bastard or not," he is ready to stand up to a challenge "as a man" (I, vii, 60). "I can not help my birth, Madam" (I, viii, 65), he tells Rachel when she is unkind to him, and later he himself can refer to it when she gives him his *viaticum* and her blessing: "What matters whether or no I make my way in life, or whether a poor bastard dies as unknown as he is now? 'Tis enough that I have your love and kindness surely: and to make you happy is duty enough for me" (I, ix, 82). When he enters new surroundings at Cambridge and feels as alone as he once had at Castlewood, he suspects that he is being slighted because of his birth, but gradually here too he gains a greater sense of poise.

The Viscount's deathbed confession, undermining as it does the position of Rachel and her children at the same time that it astonishes and strengthens Esmond, produces "an immense contest of perplexity." No sooner has he learned of his legitimate birthright than he must renounce it, lest he bring yet further "misfortune on those he loved best" (I, xiv, 130). The outwardly negative gesture, however, being an act of love, is fundamentally positive. He now is in a position to see that pieces of paper communicate merely external truth; only the inner workings of that truth can confer identity. For these reasons, therefore, Esmond has "that in his heart which secretly cheered and consoled him" (II, i, 135).

The death of Esmond's second protector leads to the second major crisis of his life, for it results in his repudiation by an angry, hysterical, and unprotected Rachel, who once again cruelly attacks him. If the first crisis reflected his anguished sense of being left alone at the death of his father, the second represents alienation from the woman who has come to stand for his mother. Even more than at the news of his father's death, the past unrolls within him: "Her words as she spoke struck the chords of all his memory, and the whole of his boyhood and youth passed within him." Once more he reluctantly submits to "Fate": "But Fate is stronger than all of us, and willed what has come to pass" (II, i, 137).

The younger Esmond had conceived his quest chiefly in terms of an exploration of the past, but now he looks to future time and beyond it. Unwilling to take an inherited title and unable to accept a clerical living, he will have to make a name for himself. Even if he fails to define himself by establishing an outer equivalent for his inner worth, however, he counts on the ultimate recognition of his identity that comes from shared heart-knowledge: "If I cannot make a name for myself, I can die without one. Some day when my dear Mistress sees my heart I shall be righted; or if not here or now, why, elsewhere: where Honour doth not follow us, but where Love reigns perpetual" (II, i, 139). To Esmond, "elsewhere" (I, vi, 52) has become eternity. His inner worth has now been established by the secret discovery of his legitimacy and by the loving resignation of his claim. Therefore, if he cannot secure honor—the public recognition of his worth—he will accept such a loss and rejoice in the personal acknowledgment that transcends time: love.

His resignation has been achieved with the help of an optimistic hope for early reconciliation with Rachel; this time the repudiation is more long-lasting and thorough-going, with the result that when Harry discovers Rachel has not only given Tom Tusher the living meant for him but has asked Tusher to inform him that she will never consent to see him again, he is understandably furious. Surprised into passion, he finds he has developed under the stimulus of ill-fortune to the point where he can direct at Rachel not only protestations of fidelity but also a proud irony that rejects her alms and disdains to appeal against her cruelty and injustice. The Vergilian *dea certe* has become the Horatian "cruel Goddess" who shakes her wings and flees, leaving him "alone and friendless but *virtute suâ*" (II, 1, 141). That new sense of his worth, a further *viaticum*, is in part her unwitting gift.

In prison, as at the university, he remains moody, silent, and mostly alone. Now his "disease" becomes metamorphic as well as literal and coincides with his crisis; when his malady of grief and rage is over he realizes there is a great gap "between the old life and the new." He sees that "his early time" was that of "a noviciate," and his term in prison was "an initiation before entering into life" (II, i, 141). Book I dealt with his spiritual apprenticeship; Book II begins with his rites of passage and follows his career as a warrior and suitor. When he emerges from prison, the belief in his dishonorable birth removed from his mind, he has a firm sense of personal and familial identity as "really the Chief of his house" and he feels "an independency which he had never known before" (II, iii, 151); it remains with him for the rest of his life.

Leaving prison he turns back to the aged Venus of Chelsea and reveals in his relationship with her the change in himself: instead of cowering, he finds himself treating her with confident familiarity. Though he now needs her assistance, he accepts it as his right, and in deciding to secure an ensigncy he carries out his resolution "to continue at no woman's apron-strings longer." Here he defines clearly the shortcomings of his relationship with Rachel: he has been too submissive—worshipful to such a degree that he has magnified Rachel and suppressed the growth of his own identity. To a certain extent he has been in a state of "slavery" (II, iii, 154). Now his quest for self-definition overtly seeks what has hitherto eluded him: discovery of a suitable form of active expression.

This contradiction between two sets of values emerges even more clearly when he rushes away from London to Winchester and Walcote. If Don Dismal is allegedly "Don Dismal no more" (II, v, 169), yet Esmond is Esmond still—crucially defined by his love for Rachel—so that even Mrs. Bracegirdle's charms have no lasting effect and merely the rumor of Rachel's impending marriage to Tusher, even from so fantastical a source as the Dowager, is enough to send an astonished and enraged Esmond off on a midnight ride, disguised to himself as an upholder of the family's honor. His active worship of Rachel begins again in a cathedral amid the evening anthem. His "beloved mistress, who had been sister, mother, Goddess to him during his youth," is to some extent "Goddess now no more" and, indeed, his elder no more, for "by thought, by suffering, and that experience it brings," he feels "older now than she." He has long inwardly known her weaknesses; now he admits and accepts them, cherishing her more "as woman perhaps" than ever he had adored her "as Divinity" (II, vi, 173). Now she admits she knew he had no vocation for the Church. Yet, though Esmond feels himself "strong enough to bear my own burthen, and make my way somehow" (II, vi, 174), he intends to do so with the help of patrons in the army "very able to serve him" (II, vi, 175).

For the first time since their initial meeting, when she came back to him after dropping his hand, she genuinely seeks to make amends for her unkindness—and now she verbally apologizes and tenderly calls him for the first time "my dear" and "my Harry" (II, vi, 175). Thackeray has so arranged matters, moreover, that the anthem's force almost justifies her former cruelty, because Esmond feels "a rapture of devout wonder" and has a heart filled "with thanksgiving" (II, vi, 176), thereby emulating the people of the hymn, who have sown in tears but reap in joy as they return from exile. Her love now being, "for the first time revealed to him quite," he asks himself, "Gracious God, who was he, weak and friendless creature, that such a love should be poured out upon him?" He now has the awareness to conclude: "Not in vain, not in vain has he lived,—hard and thankless should he be to think so—that has such a treasure given him." The wish for patronage and prominence dwindles in significance: "What is ambition compared to that? but selfish vanity."

He now affirms the immortality given not by a goddess but by human love: "only True Love lives after you: follows your memory with secret blessing: or precedes you, and intercedes for you" (II, vi, 176). Esmond and Rachel do indeed meet for the first time as adults,[5] and openly express their feeling for each other, but Rachel cannot agree to leave everything behind and go with him to America. Their responsiveness to each other is limited by Rachel's evocation of her duty to her children and to her father, which ironically prepares for the re-establishment of the old confused relationship between herself and Esmond; the scene ends with their embrace as sister and brother, mother and son (II, vi, 177).

When he sees Beatrix his ambition flares again, but he does not deify her as he had done her mother. Though "a paragon," she is no "Goddess in marble, but . . . a woman." Yet, his reaction duplicates that of the foolish Dick Steele, as the Latin tag reminds us; Esmond forgets the mother, "wrapt in admiration of the *filia pulcrior*" (II, vii, 179), just as Steele had done: "Faith, the beauty of *Filia pulcrior* drove *pulcram matrem* out of my head" (II, ii, 148). "Love seemed to radiate from her," but of course it only "seemed"; Beatrix is too much in love with herself to love anyone else. Like the Miltonic lover to whom he alludes (*Paradise Lost*, VIII, 551-53), Esmond is in a rapture that presages ill: "All higher knowledge in her presence falls / Degraded, Wisdom in discourse with her / Loses discount'nanc't, and like folly shows" (II, vii, 179).

A series of misjudgments follows, for Harry's infatuation with Beatrix obscures his insight into Rachel. Even the comment, "My Lady Viscountess looked fatigued as if with watching, and her face was pale" (II, vii, 180), emphasizes this point, for the observation captures merely her outward appearance; only the reader understands the reality within. Esmond also fails to perceive her underlying jealousy when he observes, "My lady said Amen with a sigh," for he believes that Rachel is thinking of her husband, not that she is responding to Esmond's infatuation. From the actress Bracegirdle, Esmond turns to the actress Beatrix, whose coquettish behavior is so pronounced, and instead of abjuring the world of "Lindamiras and Ardelias" (II, vii, 181), he remains deeply within it—though he fails to perceive that fact. Not only does his perception fail, however, but also his memory (II, vii, 182).

CHAPTER TWO 51

If Tusher pursues a young woman with a "portion" (II, vii, 183), Esmond pursues something equally external: the bauble of temporal beauty, as the metaphor identifying Beatrix's eyes with diamonds shows us (II, vii, 182).

Esmond's need to love also makes him a slave (II, vii, 183) to Frank. And though he departs again for the wars, Rachel's refusal to go to America with him, the presence of her marriage ring (II, vi, 173, viii, 189), and her repeated reference to him as her "son," all help free him from his proposal and assist him to think of himself as the lover of Beatrix and the potential son-in-law of Rachel—thereby doubly her "son" (II, viii, 190). If he can actually regard Beatrix's beauty "with much such a delight as he brought away after seeing the beautiful pictures of the smiling Madonnas in the convent at Cadiz" (II, viii, 191), it is because he perceives only her surface appearance. Seeing faults in himself, not in her, he fails to understand the implications of his inner questionings: "Say that I have merit ever so much and won myself a name. Could she ever listen to me? She must be my Lady Marchioness and I remain a nameless bastard" (II, viii, 188).

Beatrix represents a temptation to him because she makes him want to establish his identity by violating his promise to his "benefactor" and *proclaiming* his legitimacy—not *establishing* it, so to speak, by his own efforts. As a result, he decides to make "a brisk retreat," to call the Dowager, not Beatrix or Rachel, his "mistress" (II, viii, 189), to pay "his court to his new general" (II, ix, 192), and to make a military campaign instead of an amatory one. He follows a leader as ruthlessly egoistic as Beatrix, and though Esmond sees "some of the most beautiful scenes of nature which I ever witnessed" (II, ix, 193), he soon encounters, like Barry Lyndon, "another part of military duty" (II, ix, 194)—the self-degrading destructiveness that forms "by far the greater part of the drama of war."

By stressing that Marlborough is "as calm at the mouth of the cannon as at the door of a drawing-room" Esmond calls attention to the constancy of human selfishness that makes such different worlds part of a continuous whole. He fails to see, however, that Beatrix's youthful interest in becoming Marlborough's daughter-in-law foreshadows the emergence of a real kinship between them, for to the degree that Marlborough as a being of pure ego is a "god-like" (II, ix, 195) hero, Beatrix is a godlike heroine who gains admiration from her victims, like Becky Sharp, by her unrivalled ability to use them. Like him too (II, ix, 196), she win's men's admiration in spite of their knowledge.

After his wound and illness, Esmond gives Beatrix the title of "his mistress" (II, ix, 198, 199); clothed in the Dowager's gift lace and in her phrases and values—looking to see whether he had the *"bel air"* (II, iii, 153, ix, 199) and a becoming paleness—"Mr. Amadis presented himself to Madam Gloriana." The military analogy is explicit: "Was the fire of the French lines half so murderous as the killing glances from her ladyship's eyes?" (II, ix, 199). Though he does not know he still suffers from "his complaint" (II, x, 205), on his return to England after Blenheim he spends "his foolish, useless life in mere abject sighs and impotent longing. What nights of rage, what days of torment, of passionate unfulfilled desire, of sickening jealousy . . . !" Demeaning himself by his passion, he seizes on confidants to "ease his selfish heart of a part of its own pain" (II, x, 206), and becomes a cardboard Amadis pouring out verses to Gloriana.

Such verses are like Addison's "Campaign": not "too near the vulgar truth"—"a panegyric . . . and not a satire." Similarly, she adds about as much to her worshipper's honor as Marlborough's "glory and genius" allegedly "contribute to every citizen's individual honor" (II, xi, 212). Though Esmond can argue against Addison and the Duke, as one "who fought on that day" he feels "a thrill of pride as he recalls it" (II, ix, 196). Addison, with his eye on advancement, feels that "in being victorious as he is, I fancy there is something divine. In presence of the occasion, the great soul of the leader shines out, and the God is confessed" (II, xi, 213). At least Addison, however, announces himself capable of puffing the goddess Fortune away (II, xi, 214); Esmond, who has previously applied this allusion (Horace, *Odes*, III, 29) to Beatrix (I, xii, 106) as well as to an angry Rachel (II, i, 141), does not have that capability. Even more, his abject position towards Beatrix contrasts completely with Frank's towards his mother: "I may do what I like and I know she will love me all the same" (II, xi, 216). That is Esmond's actual relationship with Rachel.

Esmond's confusion of roles continues as he terms Rachel an "angel" (II, vi, 177, vii, 180, x, 207, xi, 216) and thinks of Frank variously as "his boy," "the child," Rachel's boy, "his young pupil" (II, xii, 219), and the brother of the girl he loves (II, xii, 220). Esmond shows how he has grown out of one role, however, when he meets Holt in Brussels and, though he instinctively calls him "My Father" (II, xiii, 222) and "dear Father" (II, xiii, 226), and is eventually greeted in "the kind voice of fifteen years back," he sees Holt's comic faults for the first time, gains a more mature knowledge of Holt's character, and smiles "to think that this was his oracle of early days; only now no longer infallible or divine" (II, xiii, 223); divinity is something he reserves for Beatrix. Harry calmly refers to his own father in a show of strength, and the situation suddenly turns martial: "There may have been on the one side and the other just the faintest glitter of recognition, as you see a bayonet shining out of an ambush; but each party fell back, when everything was again dark." This is "dangerous ground, where neither chose to engage" (II, xiii, 224). When Holt learns from the Dowager, however, "that Captain Esmond was acquainted with the secret of his family, and was determined never to divulge it" (II, xiii, 226), he responds much as she did. *"Mais vous êtes un noble jeune homme!"* she had cried, "speaking, as usual with her when she was agitated, in the French language" (II, iii, 152). "The good Father's eyes filled with tears at this speech . . . : he embraced Esmond, and . . . said he was a *noble cœur*" (II, xiii, 226).

Whereas she had adopted him as nephew-son, Holt now furthers the development of Esmond's sense of identity by telling him the story of his mother and of his early life. Memory does not carry Esmond so far back, yet an imagination permeated by awe and pity sees a realm between time and eternity—beyond the earthly cycles figured by a new generation of nuns who "were kneeling at the same stall, and hearing the same hymns and prayers in which her stricken heart had found consolation," but not a realm of fulfillment beyond death. The most he can imagine for her (and for himself) is not an awakening but a sleep. If she has suffered a sea-change, it is not into something rich so much as strange, and for all of his imaginative pity, his final emotion is one of an awe that is the mark of his isolation in an alien world of ruin underlying the earth: "I felt as one who had been walking below the sea, and treading amidst the bones of shipwrecks" (II, xiii, 231).

Esmond now knows his mother as much as he ever can; consequently he is now able to come to terms with his father (I, vi, 52) and therefore more fully with himself, but all this internal action is implied rather than stated—as the indirection of that strangely powerful analogy suggests. The walk below the sea has also been a walk within himself, below the level of ordinary consciousness, amidst the bones of shipwrecked ventures and shipwrecked selves. If he has not reached a fully articulate understanding of these failures, the experience seems, like the simile, to conclude a chapter of his life and to represent a fundamental adjustment in the self he seeks to discover.

The political struggles go on, unconcerned, of course, with the ventures or private discoveries of individuals, but "the earth is the Lord's, as the Heaven is" (II, xiii, 231), and *"afflavit Deus, et dissipati sunt"* (II, xii, 218) applies equally to the

Spanish Armada, the French at Ramillies, Rachel at the loss of her husband's love (I, ix, 75), Esmond repudiated by Rachel in prison (II, i, 141), James II seeing the action of La Hogue (II, xiii, 225), or the Chevalier St. George suffering new shipwreck as "that ill-wind which ever opposed all the projects upon which the Prince ever embarked, prevented the Chevalier's invasion of Scotland . . . and blew poor Monsieur von Holtz back into our camp again, to scheme and foretell, and to pry about as usual" (II, xiv, 233). Subsequently Marlborough's apparent scheming fails at Wynendael, and yet Webb receives inadequate recognition. The only development of a close relationship for Esmond in the army occurs between him and Webb, who treats him "as a friend, and almost a son" (II, xv, 244).

The quarrel and duel with Mohun reverse Esmond's failure during his earlier attempt to challenge him, and mark both a fulfillment of his pledge to Rachel to protect Frank and an implicit, apparently unconscious assumption of the role of head of the family. When he returns to London, Rachel is once more "Esmond's mistress" (II, xv, 248), even though Beatrix remains the chief standard by which he measures his military honors, and though Beatrix occasionally regains the title (e.g. II, xv, 249, III, v, 310). The three women of the family all receive him as a hero—though pointedly not as "the head of our house," yet as "Cousin," as "one of their family" (II, xv, 252). He now enters the third phase of his relationship with the Dowager: as formally adopted "son" (II, xv, 253). To Rachel he is "son" (II, xv, 250) and, on the occasion of her appearing out of mourning (II, xv, 252), a "friend" and "true knight" now formally invested. To Beatrix he is also a "knight" (II, xv, 252-53) who, having earned his sword of honor, is at his most attractive to her (III, iv, 305).

Other people and events inevitably gain her attention, however, for Beatrix, as Esmond knows, is light-minded, flighty, false, and everything that is the reverse of reverence and faithfulness. Through his foolish devotion to her, Esmond insistently defines himself: "'Tis a state of mind that men fall into—and depending on the man rather than the woman" (II, xv, 248). Hence he terms Beatrix his "fate," even though he knows that Rachel is "better," that he should be no happier if he won Beatrix, and that his winning her is most unlikely (II, xv, 250). What is important to him is the sign, not the reality—the glory of acceptance by a brilliantly beautiful and witty woman whose action would confer a cachet of worth, even if the price is servitude: "I'm her slave. I have sold myself for nothing, it may be. Well, 'tis the price I choose to take—I am worth nothing, or I am worth all" (II, xv, 251). He is treated like a dancing-master or music-teacher, and when the song is over he receives his dismissal.

Therefore, the chief motive of his ambition dwindles; he sells his majority and prepares to free himself from the military profession and from his amorous "Battles and Bruises" (III, i, 263). Whereas earlier, Esmond had revolted from a state of "slavery" (II, iii, 154), and gloried in the liberation, now he reverts to another former role, for he is "more the Knight of the Woful Countenance than ever he had been." Just as in prison after his first duel, his moodiness now sets him apart from his acquaintances, "who like a jolly fellow and laugh at a melancholy warrior always sighing after Dulcinea" (III, i, 263-64). In short, though he claims to have "knocked under to his fate" (III, i, 263), he has not done so any more than James Edward, whose race is also "destined" (III, i, 265).

Esmond now receives a formal inheritance when the Dowager leaves everything to him and thereby provides him with an income that makes him comfortable for life. After being freed from prison following recovery from his first wound, he turned to the liberating experience of his first campaign; after his second wound, he returned to England and fell victim to Beatrix; now, after his third wound, he finally leaves the army and again returns to England. When Rachel had asked Frank to care for "his elder brother" (III, i, 269), she wrote in her new awareness of Esmond's legitimacy, for that news had also been the Dowager's legacy. Now Rachel properly calls Esmond "the Head of our House" and he affirms it: "I am the Head of the House, dear lady; but Frank is Viscount of Castlewood still. And rather than disturb him, I would turn monk, or disappear in America" (III, ii, 278). Since Rachel asserts her sympathy with Esau (III, ii, 276), the future is thereby foreshadowed. Now it is Esmond who is the worshipped being, as Rachel "flung herself down on her knees before him; and kissed both his hands in an outbreak of passionate love and gratitude." "Let me kneel—Let me kneel and—and—worship you." *His* worship continues, for she is his "Dearest Saint." Here, as at the end of the novel, he says "'tis for me to be thankful that I can make you happy—Hath my life any other aim?—Blessed be God that I can serve you! What pleasure, think you, could all the world give me compared to that?" (III, ii, 278).

Because of its context, the statement is a complex one, for with Beatrix still unmarried his hopes are not extinct; though her acceptance of him would not bring happiness, it still would provide a supreme pleasure for him. At the same time, however, it is true that "To be able to bestow benefits or happiness on those one loves is sure the greatest blessing conferred upon a man" (III, ii, 278)—especially if there is some return of affection, whether commensurate or incommensurate. Upon Beatrix, however, he can make no satisfying bestowal; only Rachel offers herself as a satisfactory recipient. With Beatrix he can only debase himself, as he does when he kisses her foot. She coolly accepts worship but values it little and shows herself capable of none, having no "sense of devotion." "She was a Princess . . . and one of her subjects—the most abject and devoted wretch, sure, that ever drivelled at a woman's knees—was this unlucky gentleman; who bound his good sense, and reason, and independence, hand and foot; and submitted them to her." His only response to those "who used to rally Our Knight of the Rueful Countenance at his devotion" (III, ii, 283) to Beatrix is a negative one: "'Granted, I am a fool,' says he, 'and no better than you—but you are no better than I'" (III, ii, 284).

He is the "Faithful Fool," and in the role of Eugenio explores his identity by the wishful device of securing Teraminta's partiality and of marrying the virtuous Rosaria, who is what Rachel has often called herself: a person of the country. So too, he is "Cymon Wyldoats" in the Spectator paper: not twenty-eight, spritely, or independent enough to leave Saccharissa-Jocasta, but a dark man who comes from the country, who has had a university education, who has passed some years abroad serving his country, and, most important of all, whose name is unknown and who masquerades under an assumed one. In the paper, as out of it, he defines himself by his "passionate fidelity of temper" (III, iii, 293), for which he claims no justification but fate, and thereby ignores the definition provided by the object of his fidelity. Other men like Ashburnham are able to break away, but Esmond cannot, even though he blushes at Beatrix's question, "Is it Mamma your honour wants, and that I should have the happiness of calling you Papa?"

Still "gloomy, and dissatisfied, and lonely" as at Castlewood (III, iii, 298), he resolves to go to Virginia with "a squaw," a "Mohock" (III, iii, 299): the use of the latter word, which denotes both a London brawler and a savage counterpart across the Atlantic, is as close as he comes to acknowledging a secret irrationality. Esmond is still "a nameless adventurer" (III, iv, 301), but "the proudest" of "all the proud wretches in the world" (III, iv, 304), who worships willingly and will never be happy except with a woman who also worships him. Therefore, when Beatrix accepts the Duke of Hamilton, Esmond accepts the "bankruptcy" (III, iv, 303) of his efforts to have Beatrix affirm his worth, and as he gives her the Dowager's diamonds, he feels like "the guardian of all the family, and an old fellow that is fit to be the Grandfather of you all" (III, iv, 306).

Now that he has lost Beatrix, his true birth is revealed to her; addressed as "the Head of our House" (III, iv, 307) by Rachel and flattered by the Duke of Hamilton, Esmond receives his most thorough acknowledgment yet. With the patronage of Hamilton and "other great friends in power," Esmond can "look forward to as fortunate advancement in civil life at home as he had got rapid promotion abroad" (III, v, 310). As always, Esmond's loyalties center on individuals; he now fights as a Tory writer because "with people that take a side in politics, 'tis men rather than principles that commonly bind them" (III, v, 312). He fights "with more effect as a politician than as a wit" and is "enabled to do good service for that cause which he embarked in, and for Mr. St. John and his party" (III, v, 315)—an unstable group indeed.

Always, of course, he remains Beatrix's courtier and worships his idol—even as he writes the narrative, for memory can raise a passion from its grave: "I invoke that beautiful spirit from the shades and love her still; or rather I should say such a past is always present to a man; such a passion once felt forms a part of his whole being, and cannot be separated from it." The ability of memory to give permanence then becomes the basis for a belief in an immortality of consciousness that can make permanent isolation impossible: "Parting and forgetting! What faithful heart can do these? Our great thoughts, our great affections, the Truths of our life, never leave us. Surely, they cannot separate from our consciousness; shall follow it whithersoever that shall go; and are of their nature divine and immortal" (III, vi, 321).

In this context, as we see from a running title (III, vi, 325), "The glories of our birth and state / Are shadows, not substantial things." After Hamilton's death, "The world was going to its business again, although Dukes lay dead and ladies mourned for them; and Kings, very likely, lost their chances.

So night and day pass away, and to-morrow comes, and our place knows us not" (III, vi, 325). In the apparent absence of any heart of Beatrix's faithful to the Duke of Hamilton, "the fond bridegroom" has indeed pathetically come to rest in isolation from her on the "nuptial deathbed" that is ironically figured by the chased salver, with Venus and the "prostrate Mars" (III, vi, 322), of Mr. Graves.

When Esmond returns to Castlewood he recalls his boyish "vow to be faithful and never desert [Rachel's] dear service," and he reaffirms to himself the constancy of his behavior—once again in religious terms: "Yes, before Heaven; yes, praise be to God! His life had been hers . . . and her children's" (III, vii, 329). Again one sees the dichotomy of change and permanency. As Esmond and Rachel walk hand in hand through the old courtyard and on to the terrace-walk, along with the familiar sights are a thousand memories of their youth, both "beautiful"—in themselves and because they have been hallowed by a dear past—and "sad," by virtue of their nature and because they are past. Yet there is an immortality as well: "We forget nothing. The memory sleeps but wakens again" and thereby gives promise of endless futurity: "I often think how it shall be, when, after the last sleep of death, the *reveillée* shall arouse us for ever, and the past in one flash of self-consciousness rush back, like the soul, revivified." Self-consciousness, as ever, is double-edged: admonitory, unnerving, divisive, yet, together with the soul, the vibrant essence of one's being, the lasting source of one's identity.

In his plot to bring James Edward to the throne, Esmond is once again Rachel's "knight" (III, vii, 131), but he also tries to be Beatrix's as he announces his intention to do her a great "service" (III, vii, 332). Ironically, he begins with a pseudonym, "Monsieur Simon" (III, viii, 335), and as such is disguised from the young viscountess who bears his name. As a dispenser of laces, he has had training in the service of Beatrix. Like her too, he builds with rotten timber and soon comes to doubt not only his scheme but also "the benefit which might accrue to the country by bringing a tipsy young monarch back to it." Speaking to the illegitimate Duke of Berwick, he again ties the winning of his name to the Jacobite cause: "No doubt he should come by his name, if ever greater people came by theirs" (III, viii, 337). Beatrix now says, "why were you not the head of our house? You are the only one fit to raise it." She reiterates that he cannot have the prize he wants, but it seems that "her liking and respect for him" greatly increase as a result of the complementary actions that define him: "to do and to forego" (III, viii, 342).

If Esmond's worship of Rachel is partly religious, so is hers and Beatrix's of the King in anticipation of his arrival; Beatrix kneels and kisses the sheets "out of respect for the web that was to hold the sacred person of a King" (III, ix, 343), while Rachel makes "a curtsey at the door, as she would have done to the altar on entering a church, and owned that she considered the chamber in a manner sacred" (III, ix, 344). Frank, however, has met James Edward and also has learned of Esmond's sacrifice. As Esmond had knelt to James Edward and kissed his hand, so Frank kneels to him and kisses *his* hand. The substitution then continues as Frank says: "He seems to sneer at everything. He is not like a King: somehow, Harry, I fancy you are like a King" (III, ix, 345). It is Esmond who shows himself more regal, while James Edward is subdued by Beatrix descending the stairs, as Esmond had been at Walcote.

Esmond, of course, is still sufficiently subjugated to Beatrix to think her, as he did her mother long before, "like Venus revealing herself a Goddess in a flash of brightness" (III, ix, 348), and he feels rage and jealousy at the glance she gives James Edward. Rachel soon learns, of course, to her deep mortification, that "the hero whom she had chosen to worship all her life (and whose restoration had formed almost the most sacred part of her prayers)" is "no more than a man, and not a good one" (III, ix, 352). Esmond's disillusion grows as Beatrix flirts with James Edward; only then does Esmond acknowledge to himself that his is "a scheme of personal ambition, a daring stroke for a selfish end" (III, ix, 353). He therefore is like all the intriguers around the dying queen, for none has a political aim unmotivated by private and selfish interest. Only Beatrix's willingness to forego her honor and James Edward's eager wish to take advantage of that willingness free Esmond from allegiance to them.

Having continually been addressed as the Marquis of Esmond by the "Pretender" as he is now called (III, xiii, 387), Henry comes to see the necessity of repudiating the empty title, the Pretender's cause, and the basis for any similar claim of his own upon the world. Secure in his awareness that his identity is defined by the testimony given his worth by his own character and actions, he destroys the pretense that anything else can define him. By burning the documents, breaking his sword, and acceeding to the mortified Pretender's empty gestures of self-consolation, he shows that true honor manifests itself not only in positive actions but at least as much in forebearance.

With his judgment of the conspiring Holt as that "poor fellow," "that unquiet spirit" (III, xiii, 387), Esmond's understanding is complete, as we also see in the shift of tone to one of steady calm and in the quiet consistency of a voice now speaking uninterruptedly in the first person. The distractions and irrelevancies, amorous, military, and political, now having been removed, he can devote himself to a love that does not substitute a human being for the Deity but that partakes of religious devotion and expresses to the full man's capacity for "life," both mortal and immortal: "Sure, love *vincit omnia;* is immeasurably above all ambition, more precious than wealth, more noble than name. He knows not life who knows not that: he hath not felt the highest faculty of the soul who hath not enjoyed it. In the name of my wife I write the completion of hope, and the summit of happiness. To have such a love is the one blessing, in comparison of which all earthly joy

CHAPTER TWO 63

is of no value; and to think of her, is to praise God" (III, xiii, 388).

*****

In *Esmond* Thackeray was moving beyond Pen's struggles to discover valid grounds of conduct and of personal commitment, in order that he might in this next novel examine further dimensions of allegiance: personal, of course, but also political and religious. In exploring the complicated question of how one can achieve mature awareness, and mature commitment to the allegiances that one has found or achieved, Esmond, as we have seen, learns that the experience of personal love can lead to a more profound sense of love as a testimony of religious significance.

Esmond also shows how the world of late seventeenth century English politics debases inherited allegiances, and clouds personal relationships—for example, by misleading Henry and Rachel into thinking that they are doing something for the Pretender, rather than doing something for each other. Active engagement with the public sphere in *Esmond* tempts people like the title-figure to participate in a sordid world sustained by no values other than expediency—a world that parodies personal affection. Both Esmond and Rachel are misled, indeed, partly degraded, by superstitious allegiance to unworthy monarchs and to the pseudo-values of such impostors. In moving to America at the end of the novel, Rachel and Henry appear to be acknowledging that they do not seek to break with their past so much as to redefine their future in a new world that seems to offer self-created meaning centrally articulated by personal allegiance.

She, Esmond, and the other characters live, of course, in the context of Biblical, mythological, and literary reenactments, Biblical prototypes being the most frequent. The third Viscountess is Vashti to Lady Dorchester's Esther (I, ii, 15), but Rachel is also a Vashti awaiting her successor (I, ix, 70, 73).

Rachel's "disposition to think kindnesses and devise silent bounties, and to scheme benevolence for those about her" prompts Esmond to think of the Marys who bring ointment for our feet but who receive little thanks (I, ix, 79). He himself is an Esau, as Thackeray's strategically placed Dutch tiles at the bagnio tell us (I, xiv, 130), and as Rachel comes to recognize (III, ii, 276). He tells her that he would leave all to follow her, using Peter's words to Jesus (II, vi, 176); Thackeray thereby helps us to see the profound implications of her refusal. She herself gives moving testimony of her passionate responses to Biblical passages like those in Psalm 91, and of how they sustain her in times of apprehension for loved ones (III, i, 264).

Webb identifies his relationship to Marlborough as a reenactment of Uriah's to King David (III, i, 268). Esmond recalls the admonitory example of Noah's drunkenness as he refuses to pronounce an older man's judgment upon youthful bibulousness (III, i, 269), and unwittingly, but aptly, refers to himself as a Jacob serving an apprenticeship for Rachel (III, iii, 298). The death of the Duke of Hamilton recalls to Esmond Job's moving words: "He shall return no more to his house, neither shall his place know him any more" (III, vi, 325). Meanwhile, the host of milliners, toyshop women, goldsmiths, and mercer's men, crowding into Beatrix's antechamber in anticipation of her marriage to the Duke, manifest the "army of Vanity-Fair" (III, vi, 323). By contrast, the most moving passage evoking Biblical prototypes is, of course, the scene in Winchester Cathedral, where Esmond returns from exile, like the people in Psalm 126, portions of which Rachel lovingly quotes to him, and for which Thackeray provides epitomizing Latin running heads: *"Qui seminant in lacrymis / In exsultatione metent"* (Those who sow in tears shall reap in joy [II, vi, 175-76]).

Aside from Horatian prototypes soon to be discussed, Shakespearean ones are the most numerous, notably Othello. Esmond uses Othello's own words in justifying his wish to tell the truth, "neither extenuating nor setting down aught in malice" (I, vii, 58), and he endorses the belief that neither "poppy nor mandragora nor all the drowsy syrups of the East will ever . . . medicine [Jealousy] away" (I, xiii, 114). When Esmond jealously confronts the Pretender, who has come to Castlewood with Beatrix, Thackeray appends the running head: "Put out the light, and then" (III, xiii, 382). One is not surprised to remember, therefore, that Beatrix should have called him "you little black-eyed Othello!" and referred to *Othello* as Esmond's favorite play (III, iv, 304,306).

Rachel's loss of her husband's love prompts Thackeray to insert, as a running head, an epitomizing reference to the subject of love not running smooth from *A Midsummer Night's Dream* (I, xi, 92). In another running head Thackeray characterizes the Jacobite plots against William III by using the language of *King John* to identify "The curse of Kings" (II, iv, 158). Esmond thinks of Beatrix, in the words of Helena regarding Bertram in *All's Well That Ends Well*, as a "bright particular star" (I, xii, 106). Esmond consoles himself in his adversity with the remembrance of Duke Senior's words in *As You Like It* regarding adversity's sweet uses (II, v, 168), but when he hears the false news that the widowed Rachel is about to marry Tom Tusher, the rage that he feels evokes his recollection of Hamlet's rage at Gertrude's remarriage (II, v, 170).

As is appropriate for an 18th century English consciousness, Esmond repeatedly draws upon prototypes from classical literature and mythology, from the writings of his contemporaries like Addison (II, ix, 193, II, xi, 209, II, xi, 211-12, II, xv, 247), Steele (II, ii, 146), Congreve (II, iii, 153), Prior (I, ix, 71), Pope (I, iii, 19, III, iv, 306), Gay (III, v, 313, III, x, 354), and Swift (II, iv, 159), from those of the immediately preceding age like Milton (II, i, 137, II, iii, 151, II, vii, 179, III, xiii, 388) and Dryden (I, xii, 106, II, xi, 214, III, v, 319), and from newly translated works like *The Arabian Nights' Entertainments* (Alnaschar being a quintessential figure, of course

[I, ix, 83]). Classical mythology provides Baucis and Philamon (I, xi, 92), the composite goddess Diana-Artemis-Luna-Phoebe (I, xii, 106), Niobe (II, ii, 144), Endymion (II, iii, 150), Clotho and Lachesis (II, ix, 195), Eurydice (II, ix, 199), Oedipus and Jocasta (III, iii, 288-90), Prometheus (III, v, 314), and Omphale (III, v, 315).

Aesop, of course, provides permanent archetypes in fables like that of the lion and the mouse (II, x, 202), the fox and the grapes (III, iv, 303), and the two incompatible pots floating down the same stream together (III, v, 313). Homer furnishes Helen (II, vii, 182), Circe, Odysseus, and Penelope (III, iii, 293), Menelaus and Agamemnon (III, viii, 336), and also a passage from the *Odyssey* that Esmond cites to support his generalization that the Stuarts were the chief architects of their failure (II, iii, 156). As one might expect, however, the classical authors most often drawn upon by 18th century sensibilities are Vergil, Ovid, and Horace.

Like Esmond, Thackeray's Addison and other contemporary figures like Thackeray's Steele constantly think in terms of classical archetypes. Thus Steele speaks of his experience in the words of Dido to Aeneas, as someone not ignorant of misfortune who has learned to help the needy (I, vi, 47), and he characterizes himself as one who reenacts the behavior of Medea in Ovid's *Metamorphoses: deteriora sequi* (I see and approve the better; I follow the worse [I, vi, 49]). Esmond first sees Rachel as a Vergilian goddess (I, i, 6, vii, 55), and later as an Ovidian Medea hopelessly foresaken by her Jason (I, ix, 74), and quotes from the *Metamorphoses* to justify his discretion in refusing to offer a detailed description of Lord Castlewood's scandalous behavior (I, ix, 75).

Classical references continue to provide the basis for a more profound understanding of subsequent behavior as another Thackerayan running head, for example, quotes the *Aeneid* by way of calling attention to Rachel's resentment at being rejected by her husband (I, ix, 81): "*Spretæ injuria formæ."* Addison articulates his justification for celebrating Marlborough in "The Campaign" by citing Vergil celebrating Augustus (II, xi, 212), and quotes figures in Ovid's *Heroides* to justify his recounting of the recent war (II, xi, 213). Esmond quotes from the *Aeneid* in anticipating that perhaps someday it may be pleasant to remember even his battles (II, xii, 220), and quotes from the *Tristia*, in which Ovid speaks of only just seeing Vergil, in order to characterize the brevity of his contact with the great Jonathan Swift (III, v, 313).

Most movingly of all, he testifies to the living presence in his consciousness of the ancient words and of the archetypal experiences that they embody as he evokes and even outdoes the great Vergilian language from the *Georgics,* in a passage of remarkable rhythmic beauty (III, vi, 325): "Esmond thought of the Courier, now galloping on the North-Road to inform him, who was Earl of Arran yesterday, that he was Duke of Hamilton to-day, and of a thousand great schemes, hopes, ambitions, that were alive in the gallant heart, beating a few hours since, and now in a little dust quiescent" (*hi motus animorum atque haec certamina tanta / pulveris exigui iactu compressa quiescunt* [All these spirited movements and such great contests as these will be contained and quieted by the throwing of a little dust]).

Rachel, Esmond, and Thackeray, of course, preeminently live under the guiding principles of Horatian awareness, from the opening words of the narrative to the conclusion. As the title-page epigraph testifies, Thackeray seeks to remain loyal to a fundamental precept of the *Ars Poetica: "Servetur ad imum / Qualis ab incepto processerit, et sibi constet"* ([If you create a fresh character,] have it develop continuously from the beginning and remain self-consistent). Rachel's loss of beauty after the smallpox evokes the generalizing Horatian cry: *"Quo fugit Venus, heu! / Quove color decens?"* (Where has your loveliness fled alas! Where your beauty [I, ix, 69-70]). Esmond is characterized as someone like most young men of his age, a person who understands that *"dulce est desipere in loco"* (it is sweet to act foolishly on occasion [II, x, 200]). And, as always, Thackeray feels the presence of the second rider behind one's back, as a running head testifies: *"Post equitem sedet atra Cura"* (Behind the horseman sits black Care [III, xiii, 379])

Notable Horatian awarenesses that frequently recur in *Esmond* find expression especially in articulations of responses to disaster. Thus, when Rachel loses her husband's love, she ventures upon happiness with her children *"indocilis pauperiem pati"* (untaught to suffer privation [I, ix, 75]). Thackeray's acute sense of the pain caused by fortuitous events[6] reflects itself in Esmond's Horatian language communicating his anguished sense of being betrayed by Rachel: "His cruel Goddess had shaken her wings and fled; and left him alone and friendless but *virtute suâ"* (*si celeres quatit / pinnas, resigno quae dedit et mea / virtute me involvo* [II, i, 141]). Esmond's friend Tom Trett faces an analogous bankruptcy, and "when Fortune shook her wings and left him, honest Tom cuddled himself up in his ragged virtue" (III, iv, 303). The capriciously tormenting young Beatrix is *"sævo læta negotio,"* like Fortune, in the same Horatian ode, rejoicing in her cruel work (I, xii, 106). Once again, when Esmond repudiates his misguided loyalty to the Pretender, Thackeray provides a familiar and telling interpretive running head: *"Resigno quae dedit"* (I renounce [Fortune's] gifts [III, xiii, 384]).

Esmond marvellously transforms Horace's personal claim to have achieved poetic immortality into a declaration of the enduring, transforming power of love itself: *"Non omnis moriar,*—if dying I yet live in a tender heart or two; nor am lost and hopeless living, if a sainted departed soul still loves and prays for me" (II, vi, 176). Most notable of all, however, in reminding us of the continuity of the assumptions that sustain Thackerayan narratives, is the fundamental Horatian statement that prominently appears as a running head concluding the introductory remarks of Book I (p. 5), and that serves as the epigraph of Thackeray's remarkable reenactment of *Spectatorship:* "*Mutato nomine de te fabula narratur*" (With a change of name the tale is told of you [III, iii, 288]).

CHAPTER THREE:

THE NEWCOMES

After submitting to the arduous discipline of writing a superb third-person historical narrative that in part articulates his personal anguish of separation from a marital couple of whom he was very fond (the Brookfields, of course), and that movingly generalizes his pain and his awareness of his narrative's personal implications—as readers well know—Thackeray returns to the contemporary world and to more, though not entirely impersonal, considerations in his next novel, *The Newcomes. Memoirs of a Most Respectable Family*. By way of introduction, however, he reiterates his most fundamental assumption about human behavior. In a brilliant short narrative that brings together in amusing interaction and dialogue characters populating the fables of Aesop and La Fontaine, and the tales of Perrault, Thackeray's narrator (Pendennis) concludes with the rhetorical question: "What stories are new?"

A story-teller is like the youthful old-clothes dealer featured in the chapter's vignette initial: "All types of all characters march through all fables.... So the tales were told ages before Æsop: and asses under lions' manes roared in Hebrew; and sly foxes flattered in Etruscan; and wolves in sheep's clothing gnashed their teeth in Sanscrit, no doubt."[1] The wolves and foxes, and even the sheep and donkeys, have their own individuality, and we all emulate many of them at different times in our lives, but the fundamental patterns endure and are reenacted daily, and the younger authors emulate their predecessors in articulating these quintessential awarenesses.

Thackeray, of course, qualifies the patterns even as he reaffirms them. Speaking in the voice of an imagined critic, he points out that in his initial animal fable "the only innocent being . . . is a fool" (I, i, 4), but in the tones of Pendennis he acknowledges that his ensuing narrative will show, for example, that poverty and wealth, ecclesiastical prominence, and even political activities are not *necessarily* corrupting: "It does not follow that all men are honest because they are poor; and I have known some who were friendly and generous, although they had plenty of money. There are some great landlords who do not grind down their tenants; there are actually bishops who are not hypocrites; there are liberal men even among the Whigs, and the Radicals themselves are not all Aristocrats at heart" (I, i, 4-5). Similarly, he comments that although the insight of the preacher of Ecclesiastes appropriately affirms that there is nothing new under the sun, nevertheless the sun "looks fresh every morning, and we rise with it to toil, hope, scheme, laugh, struggle, love, suffer, until the night comes and quiet" (I, i, 4)—in short, we enact the inexorable patterns of life beneath the sun—whether knowingly or not.

As had come to be his habit, Thackeray opens his narrative with a dramatic scene—as the Cave of Harmony becomes a place of discord. The narrative characteristically has a notable tone of reminiscence as Pendennis recalls his introduction to Colonel Newcome in renewing his acquaintance with Clive, and as the Colonel, among other imbibers, recalls former times, former singers, and old songs like the "Bloom is on the Rye," to which the narrator responds with the emphatic recognition that "the bloom isn't on the Rye any more!" (I, i, 6). Accordingly, with light comic irony, he amplifies the chief singer by calling him "the celebrated Hoskins" (I, i, 5), and "Great Hoskins," by placing him, like Timotheus in Dryden's (and Handel's)

"Alexander's Feast," "on high, amidst the tuneful choir" (I, i, 9). and by asking, in a tone of *ubi sunt*, "Where are you, O Hoskins, bird of the night? Do you warble your songs by Acheron, or troll your chorusses by the banks of black Avernus?" (I, i, 6).

As the mature Pendennis recalls this period of his youth, it seems to him "a time when the sun used to shine brighter than it appears to do in [the present]," and as memory reanimates the past he speaks in the language of a favorite poem of his youth, Thomas Moore's *Lalla Rookh:* "the roses bloom again, and the nightingales sing by the calm Bendemeer" (I, i, 5). In this context of the simple pleasures of imbibing and glee-singing, all of the Colonel's natural simplicity manifests itself. Pendennis and Clive are embarrassed by the Colonel's offer to sing, but the performance manifests his endearing, essential qualities, as he introduces himself to us as well as to the assembled company. By choosing "Wapping Old Stairs" (the same song that Amelia sings to George in *Vanity Fair*), he reveals his attraction to quaintness, sweetness, charm, and artlessness, causing Pendennis to think of Goldsmith's Dr. Primrose, and to find "something touching in the naïveté and kindness of the placid and simple gentleman" (I, i, 9). Therefore Costigan's drunken ignoring of Juvenal's injunction, *maxima debetur puero reverentia* (the greatest reverence is due to a child [I, i, 7]), prompts the childlike Colonel's irate outburst at the boozy performer's off-color song, which so jarringly contrasts with the charming old glees sung earlier. As we can expect, later in the narrative the Colonel will continue to show vehement disapproval as well as charm.

As *Memoirs of a Most Respectable Family, The Newcomes* metaphorically represents the social world that Thackeray wishes to depict: ironically, of course, as a family of mankind without the religious awareness that joins them together as equal children of God. Hence the memoirs detail repeated attempts to establish or maintain wealth and social—

even political—status deemed to be necessary. Inevitably, then, we see generations of the family bound to this set of values and pursuing their aims by means of wealth and calculated marriage. After having acquired wealth, they *bank* it, judiciously enlarging it and strategically investing it, having discovered that rank is purchasable property as well as land and other acquisitions.

The first major pattern to which the narrator calls our attention, therefore, is the success story of "Whittington and many other London apprentices," mirrored by Hogarth's Industrious Apprentice (who figures in the second chapter's vignette initial), and by Thomas Newcome, Senior, who also "began poor and ended by marrying his master's daughter, and becoming sheriff and alderman of the City of London" (I, ii, 12). Thackeray complicates the pattern, however, for—as he had commented in speaking of Hogarth in his lectures on *The English Humourists*—Hogarth's "moral is written in rather too large letters after the fable." It is "the fable of Tommy was a naughty boy and the master flogged him, and Jacky was a good boy and had plum cake" (pp. 221-22). Thomas Newcome's plum cake, by contrast, is rather bitter, as is that of his son's, and his grandson's.

In spite of Thomas Newcome's apparent success in winning "the great City prize with a fortune of a quarter of a million," his marriage is a failure because it lacks affection and therefore becomes a relationship dominated by his controlling wife, who is "manager in Threadneedle Street and at home" (I, ii, 14). His hypocrisy in attending a dissenting chapel as a means of pursuing Miss Hobson, and in becoming "an awakened man" (I, ii, 13), leads to a condition of entrapment, for though "he grew weary of the prayer-meetings, he yawned over the sufferings of the negroes, and wished the converted Jews at Jericho" (I, ii, 14), he has to endure them in silence. Instead of enjoying a love relationship, he experiences the misery of having treated marriage as an economic arrangement—a pattern reenacted, of course, by many other people in the narrative.

His son, Tom, the product of his first marriage, which was a love relationship, as a boy rebels against his stepmother, and as a young man seeks to marry a girl whom he loves and who loves him. Such naïve, though appropriate hopes are thwarted—in this case, because of religious and class differences between the controlling families. Although Tom, a Protestant, is willing to marry Léonore in a Catholic chapel (I, ii, 21), his family objects to her religion, while her French aristocratic family objects to his middle-class, mercantile background. Believing in arranged marriages, her family forces her to marry the much older Comte de Florac, after which Tom goes off to exile in India. In fact, both families, for different reasons, conspire to prevent a marriage that fulfills mutual discovery and affection. Both models, then—the commercial English marriage and the contrasting, aristocratic, arranged French marriage—demean personal affection and thwart happiness.

The next marriage of which we learn, Tom's, is once again inadequately motivated, for he marries a penniless widow who had been mistreated by her drunken deceased husband (I, v, 50), Tom having been overcome not by love but merely by his excessively sympathetic sense of her helplessness (I, v, 49). They share no treasures of the heart, just those of the Colonel's bank account, upon which she amply draws. Consequently, they live only "indifferently together," the relationship being "not happy" (I, v, 50). "Emma had not been a good wife to him; a flighty silly little woman, who had caused him when alive many a night of pain and day of anxiety" (I, viii, 73). Hence, after her death he hardly ever mentions her name, evidently trying to blot out the remembrances—unlike those of Léonore, "which he saw in his dreams and thoughts for faithful years afterwards" (I, xv, 145).

A wife's commanding a man to marry her, produces no better result, of course, as the case of the Hobson Newcomes demonstrates. "Here was a vulgar little woman, not clever nor pretty, especially; meeting Mr. Newcome casually, she ordered him to marry her, and he obeyed; as he obeyed her in everything else which she chose to order through life" (I, viii, 68-69). Bagshot, M.P., a former apothecary, "married a woman with money much older than himself who does not like London and stops at home at Hummingham not much to the displeasure of Bagshot" (I, xi, 107). The impoverished, improvident Fred Bayham can only fantasize about someone introducing him to a "nice" girl—"nice" in his vocabulary meaning rich, "one with lands and beeves, with rents and consols" (I, xi, 114).

Old Lady Kew offers a model of a British aristocratic marriage. Having arranged her daughter's match in conjunction with Sophia Alethea Hobson, she bluntly comments on the alleged compatibility of her daughter, Lady Ann, and the wealthy banker, Brian Newcome, who has since gained a title, but in her remarks Lady Kew blithely ignores the economic motives of the arranged marriage: "'Sir Brian Newcome,' she would say, 'is one of the most stupid and respectable of men. Ann is clever but has not a grain of common sense. They make a very well-assorted couple'" (I, x, 97). Like Tom Newcome, when Lady Ann was young she wanted to marry a youthful sweetheart, but was prevented from doing so by her strong-willed mother—in Tom's case, of course, his step-mother, the equally strong-willed Sophia Alethea. Years later, Lady Ann tells her daughter, Ethel, "The Newcomes are honourable: the Newcomes are wealthy: but distinguished; no. . . . Why did I marry your poor dear Papa? from duty" (I, xv, 146). Duty to what? To a false sense of loyalty to her family's economic ambitions.

Thackeray's novel, which overtly identifies its concern as "the world, and things pertaining to it" (I, xxxvii, 353), while taking as its immediate subject "the world and a respectable family dwelling in it" (I, xxxviii, 364), includes not only bankers and impoverished aristocrats but also worldly clergymen—not only the unctuous ecclesiastics of Clapham, but also, and notably, the Rev. Charles Honeyman, clerical businessman and dandy, lavender kidglove dispenser of smarmy treacle and perfumed, theatrical tears. By contrast, Thackeray's narrator emphasizes that his own worldly limitations preclude his assuming "the divine's office," turning "his desk into a preacher's pulpit" (I, xxxvii, 353), or transforming his narrative into "a sermon, except where it cannot help itself" (I, xxxviii, 364). Honeyman, however, being a thorough humbug, "is always in the pulpit," as Barnes Newcome observes (I, viii, 73). At first, his investment in Lady Whittlesea's chapel, which tellingly rests upon Sherrick's wine vaults and counting-house, prospers. Like a dandy, he allows his dainty indulgences to run him into debt, and bobs about in the fashionable social stream, but he is fundamentally a speculator attempting to operate his chapel as a theatrical enterprise, trying to fill up the box seats, as Fred Bayham appropriately comments (I, xxv, 239). Inevitably, when this speculation fails, he seeks to marry a well-to-do widow with social ambitions, but has to settle for his mortgager's daughter.

The Clapham household of Sophia Alethea manifests an analogous kind of hypocrisy: the profession of strict religious beliefs as a cover for the worship of earthly possessions, some of which, it is true, she gives away in meaningful works of charity. She is called "eminent" by her contemporaries, prompting the narrator's ironic aside "(such was the word applied to certain professing Christians in those days)" (I, ii, 12). When she has her somewhat aged eye on a good-looking, youthful widower, she does "not quarrel with [his] innocent child for frisking about" (I, ii, 13) on the Sabbath, however she might abhor such behavior in other children who lack "seriousness."

In actual practice, hers is a "sumptuous table, spread with the produce of her magnificent gardens" (I, ii, 12). Her house is a "palace . . . , surrounded by lawns and gardens, pineries, graperies, luxuries of all kinds" (I, ii, 14)—cared for by a head gardener "only occupying himself with the melons and pines provisionally, and until the end of the world, which event . . . was to come off in two or three years at farthest" (I, ii, 15). In Egypt itself, the narrator remarks, "there were not more savoury fleshpots than at Clapham" (I, ii, 13)—fleshpots much enjoyed by the Clapham clergy, "florid rhapsodists" with "wearisome benedictions" (I, ii, 14), who sycophantically attribute such plenty as Sophia Alethea's to the blessings of Heaven (I, ii, 12).

In such a context, young Tom's rebellion against the self-flattering controller of that "stifling garden of Eden" (I, ii, 16) helps to define his integrity, as does his naïve, loving devotion to Léonore. Sophia Alethea typifies for Thackeray Clapham people of strict beliefs. As he wrote to his daughter in 1852, "When I was of your age I was accustomed to hear and read a great deal of the Evangelical (so called) doctrine and got an extreme distaste for that sort of composition," and he gently spoke to her of "the misfortune of dogmatic belief" (*Letters*, III, 93-94). Unlike Thackeray, parents of strict beliefs, of course, cause their children considerable unhappiness, motivated as people like Sophia Alethea are by prejudice and by a fierce need to dominate those about them.

For wanting to marry a Catholic, she calls Tom "a wretch and a monster" (I, ii, 21), again justifying her need to control a challenge to her authority with a so-called religious appeal. The real issue, of course, is her need for personal dominance—surely the defining trait of her personality—however masked, like Dickens's Mrs. Jellyby, by her addiction to professional philanthropy, by ostensible efforts "to awaken the benighted Hottentot to a sense of the truth; to convert Jews, Turks, Infidels, and Papists; to arouse the indifferent and often blasphemous mariner; [and] to guide the washerwoman in the right way" (I, ii, 14).

Control over a child's marital arrangements inevitably implies, of course, not only an insistence upon subservience, but also a treatment of the participants as pawns in a family game—one that can extend over several generations, as we see in Lady Kew's manipulation of her granddaughter, Ethel. With such people, so-called affection is a commodity. When the Colonel, now a widower and a distinguished officer mentioned several times in the *Gazette*, begins to remit considerable sums of money to the family bank, "the bankers his brethren began to be reconciled to him," thereby emulating the conduct of Joseph's brothers and illustrating a fundamental principle of human nature: "Surely human nature is not much altered since the days of those primeval Jews" (I, v, 45). Similarly, young Clive becomes an "object" prompting what the narrator ironically terms the brothers' increasing "affection." When first he arrives in England and goes to stay with his aunt Honeyman at Brighton, the brothers ignore him. Following the arrival of another large remittance from the Colonel, however, religion is used to mask the real nature of their interest, as the child is "asked by Uncle Newcome at Christmas." Similar events prompt similar regard, causing Pen's mock apology: "they were only pursuing the way of the world, which huzzays all prosperity, and turns away from misfortune as from some contagious disease" (I, v, 46).

The Earl of Dorking and his wife also treat their daughter as an object and sell her to Barnes Newcome (I, xxviii, 266), for whom she is equally an object. As Major Pendennis snobbishly but astutely observes, "Those banker-fellows are wild after grand marriages" (I, xxiv, 225). For the poor victim, Lady Clara, such a marriage is an immolation—like suttee (I, xxviii, 267). She is a sacrificial victim, like Iphigenia (I, xxviii, 267), to her callous father. Though not wanting the marriage with Barnes, she does her "duty" (I, xxviii, 271) to her family and lives in despairing misery. Florac has a similar experience, though in his case *he* is the impoverished titled figure who agrees to marry the wealthy, aged Miss Higg from Manchester. As Lord

Kew would say, she is a mere *sac d'argent* (I, xxxi, 303) for Florac. Looking back on his married life, he utters the appallingly demoralized comment: "ah! it is fifteen years since, and she dies not" (I, xxviii, 260). Such are the dangers awaiting Ethel.

She is the most complex character in the novel—one who faces daunting challenges, and who has the ability to understand the falseness of her position, to rebel, and to perceive, though with difficulty, the possibility of a more meaningful life than that posed by her family and by her own ambiguous ambitions. Ethel's great qualities are her independence of thought and, indeed, her capriciousness, which of course creates a certain rebellious freedom from the patterns being imposed upon her. When Ethel passionately characterizes the society of which she is a member by birth and by family control as a group of people who have outdone all their predecessors "since the world began" in being "so unblushingly sordid," and asks when "this Mammon worship will cease among us," the Countess of Kew's reply—"You belong to your belongings" (I, xxxii, 311)—though telling, defines Ethel's task: to achieve an independence from her belongings and from their control over her mind and spirit. Although she is not one of the brainwashed girls "as keen as the smartest merchant in Vanity Fair" (II, vii, 66), she feels intimidated by "one part of a girl's duty: obedience to her parents," and by the financial welfare of relatives that depends upon her marital choice (II, ix, 95).

Therefore, she tolerates Lord Farintosh, who has not "a great quantity of brains, or a very feeling heart" (II, iv, 40), and submits to the vacuous evening gatherings into which Lady Kew leads her: in Paris the going from hôtel to hôtel, dancing "waltz after waltz with Prussian and Neapolitan secretaries, [or] with Prince's Officers of Ordonnance" (II, viii, 77), and in London "back among the fiddling, flirting, flattery, falseness" (II, xii, 118) of society. Clive, inevitably, poses the central question: "If it is so false and base and hollow this great world:

if its aims are so mean; its successes so paltry; the sacrifices it asks of you so degrading; the pleasures it gives you so wearisome, shameful even, why does Ethel Newcome cling to it?" (II, ix, 94).

In confessing her divided impulses to Mme. de Florac, she reveals an admiration for that gentle, unworldly woman, and reminds us how a difficult life can worthily be led. Mme. de Florac, forced by her father to give up the man she loves and to marry an indifferent, elderly man of her own social class, survives what she has "daily to bear" (II, ii, 17), and gives herself to chosen meaning that survives imposed decisions: "Religion, love, duty, the family"—her notions of duty and the family, unlike Lady Kew's, being "to soothe, to pray, to attend them with constant watchfulness, to strive to mend them with pious counsel" (II, viii, 75). When the Colonel says of her, "I have seen no woman in my eyes so good or so beautiful" (II, i, 8), surely he speaks of a wonderful beauty of character. She is a person who knows the happiness that she has lost, and who, with pain but without bitterness, knowingly characterizes the fashion of imposed marital arrangements as "this evil and misery, this slavery, these tears, these crimes, perhaps" (II, xv, 144). For the narrator (and Thackeray), she is a model of faith, gentleness, and tenderness, whose devotion shows that "Love lives through all life and survives through all sorrows; and remains steadfast with us through all changes; and in all darkness of spirit burns brightly," and gives promise of Immortality (II, vii, 70).

Here on earth, Thackeray's novel, while extensively satirizing worldly, contrived marriages, offers no panaceas. Pendennis reports that Ethel says to Laura, "save you, I scarcely know any one that is happy in the world" (II, xxx, 270), but no reader can fail to see that Laura's happiness is intimately related to her control over the henpecked Pendennis (e.g. II, xix, 186, xxiv, 228). Marrying for love certainly does not guarantee happiness, as the terrible Mrs. Mackenzie's marriage appallingly demonstrates, for she presumably drives her husband to drink, and apparently into debt and an early demise (I, xxiii, 210). As the narrator comments, both marriages of convenience and love matches will be found to fail (I, xxxi, 296-97). Lord Kew remarks that the romantic fantasy of Jenny and Jessamy is nonsense, and that only a few love, marry, and continue to love. "That is the supreme lot: but that is the lot which the gods only grant to Baucis and Philemon and a very very few besides. As for the rest, they must compromise" (I, xx, 287). In discussing Ethel's feelings towards Lord Kew, the narrator offers a non-emotional, analytic proposal—"Warm friendship and thorough esteem and confidence"—and concludes with a playfully ironic metaphor: "[these] are safe properties invested in the prudent marriage stock, multiplying and bearing an increasing value with every year." "For such a union as that contemplated between them, perhaps for any marriage, no greater degree of attachment was necessary as the common cement ... [beyond] regard, and esteem, and affection" (I, xxxvii, 355-56).

Elsewhere, however, the narrator speaks less ironically, as he identifies the crucial importance in human relationships, including marriage, of *generosity*—of giving, not just taking. He identifies the qualities that make Colonel Newcome beloved as "modesty, and generosity, and honour" (I, v, 51). In order to be generous rather than calculating, one has to be young (I, xii, 115, xiv, 133, xxiv, 227, xxx, 285), or able to retain one's youthful simplicity, like the Colonel, who has "an habitual practice of kind and generous thoughts; a pure mind and therefore above hypocrisy and affectation" (I, xv, 146). In Pendennis's eyes, the "humble-minded" Colonel offers advice that "contained the best of all wisdom, that which comes from a gentle and reverent spirit and a pure and generous heart" (I, xiv, 132). The simple-minded and yet profound advice regarding marriage that the Colonel conveys to his son, offers perhaps the most compelling alternative model in

Thackeray's narrative of unhappy and degrading relationships: "A generous early attachment . . . is the safeguard of a young man. To love a noble girl; to wait awhile and struggle, and haply to do some little achievement in order to win her; [was] the best task to which his boy could set himself. If two young people so loving each other were to marry on rather narrow means, what then?" (I, xxiv, 223).

The narrator, however, even though he genuinely admires the Colonel's values, also sees more complexly. If "Worldly Prudence," as Pen calls it—like a character out of Bunyan—has many motives, however, so too does a simple, ordinary, affectionate person like Miss Honeyman and like the narrator himself in his daily life. "Is it gratitude for past favours? is it desire for more? is it vanity of relationship? is it love for the dead sister—or tender regard for her offspring which makes Mrs. Martha Honeyman so fond of her nephew?" Like the author of *The Book of Snobs. By One of Themselves*, Pen goes on to implicate himself: "I never could count how many causes went to produce any given effect or action in a person's life, and have been for my own part many a time quite misled in my own case, fancying some grand . . . [motive, until discovering] the peacock's tail wherein my absurd vanity had clad itself" (I, v, 47).

As such passages indicate, *The Newcomes* can appropriately be read as an extended interrogation of human motives, and as a demonstration that they are infinite. Ethel (together with the narrator) serves as the prime example of a consciousness intensely aware of the purposefulness of these motives, especially regarding marriage, but also of the ambiguity that they induce in a thoughtful person. Hence her characteristic volatility and rebellion. Therefore, of course, also her inability to make a commitment. In this rebelliousness, especially directed against her grandmother, Lady Kew, she emulates young Thomas Newcome appropriately resisting his oppressive stepmother, Sophia Alethea.

CHAPTER THREE 83

* * * * *

After the overture of old fables with which he inaugurates the narrative, Thackeray establishes another fundamental context by beginning his evocation of life—in Emily Dickinson's memorable words—as *a route of evanescence.* Furthermore, by speaking in the voice of Pendennis, he gives the narrative a tone of personal remembrance of past days. Those days were only roughly twenty years previous, but they now seem to him as if they were far distant—indeed, as if in a world apart: "There was once a time when the sun used to shine brighter than it appears to do in this latter half of the nineteenth century . . . ." With a continuing series of nine more "whens," he calls up the old time in an ever-expanding sentence that almost constitutes an entire paragraph before giving way to two brief personal statements: "It was in the days of my own youth . . . . As I recal them the roses bloom again" (I, i, 5). In addition, as we are introduced to the Colonel, we see *him* entering into remembrance, as he recalls his own youth thirty-five years before. Unmistakably, then, the narrative proper begins with a marked evocation of evanescence.

Even more, after recalling the scene in the Cave of Harmony, Pendennis goes back further in time as he recounts the history of the Colonel's and Clive's family with another, though briefer, series of "whens": "When pig-tails still grew on the backs of the British gentry . . . : when ministers went in their stars and orders to the House of Commons . . . : when Mr. Washington was heading the American rebels . . ." (I, ii, 11). By way of contrast to the history of increasing familial success, the narrator makes us acquainted with the moving personal history of the Colonel's youthful sweetheart, Léonore de Blois, now Comtesse de Florac, as expressed in her letter to the middle-aged Colonel: "I hold you always in my memory. As I write the past comes back to me. I see a noble young man, who has a soft voice, and brown eyes. . . . I listen and pray . . . as my father talks to you.... I look from my window, and see you depart" (I, iii, 25). Her love for him remains, but the hoped-for fulfillment has vanished, leaving only the memory.

The memory of one's youthful days is precious, however painful it may be. As Pendennis says in recalling his early days, "Only to two or three persons in all the world are the reminiscences of a man's early youth interesting—to the parent who nursed him, to the fond wife or child mayhap afterwards who loves him,—to himself always and supremely whatever may be his actual prosperity or ill fortune, his present age, illness, difficulties, renown, or disappointments" (I, iv, 31). Even the pains of remembrance, which are inevitable, remain with him and have a special meaning. And in maturer life, as Pendennis memorably testifies, one gratefully recalls someone like Warrington, a "friend and companion of those days, and all days" (I, iv, 34).

Inevitably, therefore, in considering the reader to be a brother-sharer and sister-sharer of experience, and therefore a part of "us," Thackeray, though attempting to speak through the persona of Pendennis, occasionally speaks in what appears to be his own voice. In doing so, however, he seems to be articulating not only intimate but also broader experience—as when he powerfully characterizes the pain of separation from one's parents on being sent home from India to an alien existence in a boarding school in England—as he himself was: "What a strange pathos seems to me to accompany all our Indian story!" "All" certainly brings together, as was Thackeray's wont, the other people involved in experiencing the pain: mothers and fathers, especially. He (more than Pendennis) concludes with private yet generalizing recollection: "most of us who have passed a couple of scores of years in the world, have had such sights as these to move us" (I, v, 48). Here is where personal remembrance and reenacted human history join.

Communal memory manifests itself with special power, of course, in remembered *language—*

notably, for educated people of the nineteenth century, Greek and especially Latin. They understood that their culture had a *history,* that history articulates memory, and that without memory, individuals, like their cultures, have no identity. Mnemosyne, as the Greeks taught us, is our permanent goddess because she is our enduring source of creativity. Remembering the language and therefore the insights of Homer, Horace, Vergil, and Ovid creates in us new awareness.[2]

The narrator certainly thinks so. Doesn't Plato define us by essentials when he calls us unfeathered bipeds (I, i, 4)? Don't Acheron and Avernus (I, i, 6) still testify to our mortal limits? Does not Odysseus continue to serve as an outstanding epitome of human experience (I, xv, 139)? Does not faithful study of the liberal arts, however publicly underfunded, still sensitize men's minds and polish their manners, as Ovid testified (*"Ingenuas dedicisse fideliter artes emollunt mores, nec sinuisse feros"* [I, v, 51])? Isn't it pleasant to rediscover the wisdom of Horace's awareness, *"dulce est desipere in loco"* (it is enjoyable to be occasionally silly [I, viii, 75, xiii, 127])? Shouldn't we follow Horace's advice, and while young insist upon not neglecting either sweet love nor dances (*"nec dulces amores / sperne puer neque tu choreas"* [I, xxii, 206])? Shouldn't we, with Vergil, acknowledge the pressure of need in a life of hardship (*"duris urgens in rebus egestas"* [I, xxviii, 260])? Of course we have to admit—with Horace once again—that the fable surely is told of us (*"de te fabula narratur"* [I, xxviii, 266, xxx, 285]), and acknowledge with him the unavoidable presence of *atra Cura* (black Care [I, xxviii, 269, xxxviii, 364, II, xxv, 235]), and the inevitability of consequences for our deeds, however haltingly (*"pede claudo"* [I, xxxiv, 334]) they may pursue us.

As the narrator implies, we had better live within that language and know—again with Horace—that there are women like Becky Sharp or the Duchesse d'Ivry, who conceal a fish tail under their fine flounces (*"formosa superne"* [I, xxxvi, 344]). We also need to remember, with him, and with Henry Esmond, the comfort of a little angle of earth that we call home (*"ille terrarum mihi praeter omnis angulus ridet"* [II, xix, 179]). Likewise, we need to remember and emulate the courage of our forebears in order to face pale Death (*"pallida Mors"* [II, xxvii, 247]). And above all, we need while living to understand and emulate the stoic wisdom of that most fundamental Horatian and Thackerayan text: *"si celeres quatit pennas, resigno quae dedit et mea virtute me involvo, probamque Pauperiem sine dote quaero"* (If Fortune shake her wings for flight, I renounce her gifts, wrap myself in my virtue, and seek honest, undowered Poverty [II, xxxiii, 297]).

Profound consciousness of Biblical language and wisdom inevitably permeates *The Newcomes* as well, most centrally the awareness of Ecclesiastes affirming that there is "nothing new under and including the sun" (I, i, 4). The most frequently articulated remembrance (perhaps again for reasons personal to Thackeray) is that of the Prodigal Son, who is evoked at least eleven times (I, ii, 18, v, 45, xxi, 192, xxvi, 243, xxvii, 256, xxviii, 258, xxviii, 265, xxxii, 307, xxxiii, 319, xxxiv, 324, xxxiv, 328). At the very start, the narrator promises us "dinners of herbs with contentment and without, and banquets of stalled oxen where there is care and hatred—ay, and kindness and friendship too, along with the feast" (I, i, 4). There are frequent evocations of friendly banquets in Thackeray's fiction, but several times in *The Newcomes* dinners of herbs are cited and usually preferred (I, xxviii, 267, II, xxxii, 286, xxxv, 308), especially when a life like Lady Kew's is characterized by the narrator as "a long feast where no love has been" (II, xvii, 160).

The marvellous remembered language of the Bible reinvigorates our awareness and enables us to understand the inequality of the fact that the sun shines on the unjust as well as the just (II, xvii, 160). The language of Psalm 138 reminds us that "We are fearfully and wonderfully made" (I, xxx, 286). Less piercingly, as one might well expect, Thackeray draws considerably upon the gentlest of the Evangelists, Luke—not only for the reiterated parable of the Prodigal Son and for the moving example of pain and succor represented by the man fallen among thieves and yet helped by a samaritan (I, v, 45, I, xxviii, 264, II, vi, 52, xxxix, 338), but also for the clear-eyed articulation of an incomprehensible division separating Dives and Lazarus on the basis of their material possessions (I, v, 40, II, v, 44), and of the causes that motivate the greed of Croesus and Dives (II, vii, 66). The Colonel and Thackeray nevertheless recall the words of Simeon and look ahead, with Luke, to the hope of a *nunc dimittis:* "Lord, now lettest thou thy servant depart in peace" (I, xv, 148), sustained by Luke's narrative of the woman whose sins are promised forgiveness because "she loved much" (II, xlii, 364).

Cultural memory of course also revivifies the language and insights of more recent awarenesses, which constitute the most numerous of the narrative's allusions. Shakespeare provides several dozen prototypes, notably from *Othello,* with the scheming Iago (I, xxxi, 304, xxxviii, 361, II, iii, 22), the Desdemona who seriously inclines to hear Othello's captivating words (I, viii, 70, II, v, 45), and the suspicious Othello himself (I, xi, 107), as well as from a half-dozen other plays, notably the *Henry IV* series, revealing the prodigality of Hal and Falstaff, and Hal, Poyns, Nym, and Pistol (I, x, 92, xxviii, 268, II, xxv, 234).

Molière's Tartuffe is an extension of Aesopian insight (I, i, 4), Ethel of the Louvre's Diana (I, xxii, 203), and of the Lady in Milton's *Comus* (I, xxviii, 261), Clive of Milton's Adam with his "shoulders broad" (I, xxiv, 227), Bayham of Cooper's Red Rover (I, xii, 117), Clive of Scott's Dick Tinto (I, xvii, 156), Florac of Scott's Edgar Ravenswood (I, xxviii, 259), Clara of Tennyson's Mariana in the "moated grange" (I, xxviii, 269)—just to cite a few examples from this wonderfully evocative work—but these reenactments are typically more playful and, by design, decidedly less profound than their originating sources. Hoskins, "placed on high, amidst the tuneful choir" (I, i, 9) in the Cave of Harmony is not quite Timotheus in Dryden's (and Handel's) great celebration of the power of music; Lady Clara is certainly not a Chimène nor Belsize a Rodrigue (I, xxviii, 278); at the Hôtel de Florac "a broken-nosed damp Faun with a marble panpipe" (II, ix, 82) emulates only in externals Keats's youth piping to the spirit ditties of no tone; and Ethel's tears certainly lack the profundity and resonance of Tennyson's "tears, idle tears" (II, xxviii, 260),

On the other hand, we see that Colonel Newcome reenacts and is illuminated for us by his literary predecessors, Harley and Don Ferolo Whiskerandos in Sheridan's *Critic* (I, i, 6), Dr. Primrose in Goldsmith's *Vicar of Wakefield* (I, i, 9), Don Quixote (I, vi, 60, II, xxviii, 254, II, xxix, 267), Sir Roger de Coverley (I, xix, 174), and Sir Charles Grandison (I, xxii, 204, II, xiii, 120), as well as by the historical figure of Belisarius (II, 34, 300). His father, Thomas Newcome, *did* emulate Hogarth's Industrious Apprentice (I, ii, 11). Baden-Baden *is* one of "the prettiest booth[s] in Vanity Fair" (I, xxx, 293). Count Almaviva and Don Basilio do not simply exist on the stage, for their counterparts enter the lives of women like la Duchesse d'Ivry (I, xxxi, 297). Hogarth's *Marriage à la Mode* is reenacted in contemporary fashionable society (I, xxxi, 301). Lord Kew's misdeeds emulate (in a minor way) the catalogue of conquests trolled by Leporello (I, xxxiv, 323). Lord Farintosh does have friends who will carry the lantern or hold the ladder as he emulates Count Almaviva (II, xxi, 196). Here again we see the marvellous range of post-classical Thackerayan awareness in *The Newcomes:* evoking as it does the tragedies and the comedies of Western literature, music, and painting.

As this rich testimony to the expressiveness of our culture's languages and awarenesses—notably English, French, German, and Italian—indicates, *The Newcomes* is a remarkable *narrative of voices*. No previous Thackerayan novel had so extensively presented individual discourses—the narrator's, to be sure, but also the voices, at remarkable length, of characters within the narrative. His playfulness often articulates the sense of how we can be at home, not only with our languages but also with their emulations, like French-English or Scottish-Italian: *"Quasty peecoly, Rosiny, . . . e la piu balla, la piu cara, ragazza ma la mawdry e il diav—"* (This little Rosey . . . is the most beautiful, the most darling, girl, but her mother is the dev— [II, vi, 61]). Most especially, however, Thackeray poises against the banalities of conventional social discourse, the spriteliness or awfulness of individual voices.

We hear the appalling, aggressive monologues of Mrs. Hobson Newcome and Mrs. Mackenzie, for example, compelling their hearers into dismayed submission, and we hear the vacuous pretentiousness of preachers like Charles Honeyman momentarily lulling their audiences into thoughtless acquiescence. We hear the unmistakably knowledgeable and shallow accents of Major Pendennis: "Nothing could show a more deplorable ignorance of the world than poor Newcome supposing his son could make such a match [revealing word] as that with his cousin. Is it true that he is going to make his son an artist? I don't know what the dooce the world is coming to. An artist! By gad, in my time a fellow would as soon have thought of making his son a hair-dresser, or a pastry-cook, by gad" (I, xxiv, 225).

We hear the delightful Franglaise of Florac, and, best of all, the thoroughly engaging excesses of the impoverished Fred Bayham indulging in the opulence of language and in aspirations motivated by failed achievement. From his entrance line, ironically directed against Honeyman, *"Salve! Spes fidei, lumen ecclesiæ"* (Hail, hope of the faith and light of the church), and his Shakespearean emulation, "by cock and pye, it is not worth a bender" (I, xi, 113), onwards, this "jolly outlaw" (I, xviii, 169) wonderfully enlivens the narrative. A "restless bird of night" (I, xxv, 236), his compass of moods ranges from a "sportive" to "a solemn and didactic vein" (II, vi, 52). For him, "A glass of good sound beer refreshes after all that claret," and assists him—though he denies it—in writing journalistic columns under the pseudonym of "Laud Latimer": "You wouldn't suppose now . . . that the same hand which pens the Art Criticisms . . . , takes a minor theatre, or turns the sportive epigram, or the ephemeral paragraph, should adopt a graver theme on a Sunday, and chronicle the sermons of British Divines?" (II, vi, 53).

Bayham, as an enterprising journalist, partly succeeds in creating a new beginning for himself, but the Colonel's return to England after thirty-four years as a soldier, reveals the enduring power of the past. When his old nurse, Sarah Mason, embraces him, "her boy who was more than fifty years old," she clings especially to Clive, thinking "that he was actually her own boy, forgetting in that sweet and pious hallucination that the bronzed face and thinned hair and melancholy eyes of the veteran before her were those of her nursling of old days" (I, xv, 141). Like all of Thackeray's narrators, Pendennis reiterates the "old saying, that we forget nothing," and emphasizes how the touch of a youthful hand can be a talisman that leads us back to a beloved, departed figure (I, xv, 145).

Such wonderful revivifications, however, inevitably co-exist in Thackeray's narratives with a sorrowful sense of passage. Remembering the fellowship of a cheery voice brings with it the awareness that it "will never troll a chorus more," though "the kind familiar faces rise up, and we hear the pleasant voices and singing" (I, xxv, 234). "Five and twenty years ago is a hundred years off—so much has our social life changed in those five lustres" (I, xxv, 235). Pendennis, like a number of us, recalls wonderful youthful gatherings—in his case where he and they "sang all the way home through Knightsbridge and by the Park railings, and the Covent Garden carters halting at the Half-way House were astonished at our choruses," but he also feels the sadness of knowing that "There is no half-way house now; no merry chorus at midnight" (I, xxvii, 252).

Visiting Pompeii, as Thackeray did while writing *The Newcomes,* inevitably induces memories of transience and suppressed but recoverable experience, and the awareness of how one can and does "excavate your heart" (I, xxviii, 263). The experience of visiting the Eternal City reunites one with central manifestations of Western culture, from the beauty of classical ruins to the intact magnificence of Raphael's and Michelangelo's achievements. The experience of having been in Paris in the days of one's youth can provoke the delightful but ambiguous sense of having "many many hundred years ago . . . seen Taglioni, after a conquering *pas seul"* (II, iii, 25).

More often, however, the recovered memory is not so much a revivification as it is a testimony of loss. "In latter days with what a strange feeling we remember that last sight we have of the old friend; that nod of farewell or shake of the hand, that last look of the face and figure as the door closes on him, or the coach drives away!" (II, iv, 36). When we revisit places where we have been accompanied by grief, "how its Ghost rises, and shows itself again!" (II, xviii, 168). In terms of London society, the leasing of homes testifies to the triumph of material over domestic values, as a family leases a fashionable house to a foreigner: "Strange mutations of fortune; old places; new faces; what Londoner does not see and [with an ironic play upon words] speculate upon them every day?" (II, x, 99).

Most memorable of all, perhaps—at least for those who have similarly experienced them—are Clive's feelings as, trapped in an unhappy marriage, he sees Ethel and recalls "the past and its dear histories, and youth and its hopes and passions, and tones and looks for ever echoing in the heart, and present in the memory . . . as he looked across the great gulf of time, and parting, and grief, and beheld the woman he had loved . . . ; the same, but changed: as gone from him as if she were dead" (II, xxviii, 260). The grief and the death are real, notably for the Colonel, Clive, and Ethel. Only Laura and J.J. offer mitigation: Laura as a well-meaning, though rather insufferable wife and mother; J.J. as a devoted consort of the imagination. He embodies the most convincing alternative to the heartless materialism of the Newcomes, for he is the appropriate model: "the *good* industrious apprentice" (II, xxxvi, 319 [italics mine]). Honeyman, the false preacher performing above a counting-house and wine vaults, indulges in contrived illusion; J.J., responding to the wonders of music and to the suggestive vistas of existence, lives in "Fancy Street: Poetry Street. Imagination Street" (I, xi, 109). Thackeray, the failed art student, celebrates "the enchanting boon of Nature which reveals to the possessor the hidden spirits of Beauty round about him! spirits which the strongest and most gifted masters compel into painting or song" (I, xi, 112).

To Clive, J.J. "seems to see things we don't" (I, xii, 117). For him J.J. is someone to be envied because of his ability to find sustaining spiritual fulfillment: "to have your desire and then never tire of it" (II, xii, 115). The narrator amusingly sees and satirizes the absurd posturing of bohemian life, but he, like Clive (and Thackeray), "avers that his life as an art student at home and abroad was the pleasantest part of his whole existence" (I, xvii, 157). To the narrator, J.J. occupies himself with meaningfully "consoling work," immersed in the alphabet of a "sacred book" (II, xxvii, 253). Similarly, Ethel testifies that J.J. and Clive have taught her to see "pictures and landscapes and flowers with quite different eyes," to see with Ruskin, one might say, "the secret of the Other Life and the Better World beyond ours" (II, xxx, 269).

As this may suggest, archetypes of human happiness (not just their opposites) do exist, as in the fable of Prince Camaralzaman and the Princess of China (I, xv, 143). And even in the everyday world, we can find some examples of happy imprudence, of successful marriages based upon mutual feeling rather than calculation or ignorant acquiescence. But surely Thackeray's narrative invites us to be *sceptical*—to see fables like Aesop's, or fairy tales like Perrault's, with which he begins and concludes his narrative, as articulations of revealing archetypes of human *motives*, but *not* as convincing revelations of readily achieved human happiness. Hence, of course, his insistence upon drawing the line at the end of his narrative, refusing to say that Ethel and Clive lived happily ever after, and genially mocking our temptation to fancy such an improbable illusion.

CHAPTER FOUR:

THE FOUR GEORGES AND *THE VIRGINIANS*

In using Pendennis as the narrator of *The Newcomes,* Thackeray of course created a greater distance between himself and his audience than if he had spoken in an anonymous, implicitly authorial voice. Therefore, although a personal voice continues to address the audience, intimacy occurs less frequently than in *Vanity Fair* and *Pendennis.* We still hear addresses to "our kind readers" (I, iv, 31). "O gentle reader" (I, viii, 68), "the gracious reader" (I, ix, 82), "O gentle and unsuspicious readers" (I, xxxvi, 343), "O friend" (I, xxxviii, 364), "My fair young readers" (II, viii, 79), "my gentle reader" (II, xv, 137), and "friend" (II, xvii, 163), but the incidence of such intimate addresses is much reduced. The duration of narrative commentary in *The Newcomes,* however, is much increased, in keeping with the extended speech of characters in the narrative, for both the narrator and his characters speak at some length.

In *The Four Georges,* inevitably, he is much more intimate. The crucial issue in lecturing, of course, is a close relationship with one's audience as well as with one's subject. Lecturing on an historical subject is and is not a significantly different kind of discourse from fictional narration. In the case of *The Four Georges,* one can see not only a notable increase of intimacy with his audiences, but also a significant replacement of mythological and literary articulations by an appeal to English historical consciousness, and occasionally to Anglo-American historical consciousness. In his lecture on

George I, for example, Thackeray does not evoke those larger imaginative awarenesses until late in the lecture. Aside from a brief quotation from Vergil ironically characterizing the ineptitude of Scottish Jacobites in the rebellion of 1715 (all these spirited movements and such great contests as these will be contained and quieted down by a sprinkle of dust [*pulveris exigui jactu*—an alleged "powdering of the hair" that was in acutality a fatally detaining quenching of the thirst in a tavern]), and two brief references to Hogarth, Thackeray limits himself to a final, intense evocation of Horatian, Biblical, and Shakespearean language, as he speaks of the king's death: "sure enough, pallid Death . . . presently pounced upon H.M. King George I., in his travelling chariot, on the Hanover road. What postilion can outride that pale horseman?"—a guaranteed veto upon George's hopes "to revisit the glimpses of the moon."[1]

Similarly, his lecture on George II draws upon only a few mythological and literary articulations of human experience. A brief allusion to Vanity Fair serves to characterize the governing context of our lives (II, 180). A reference to Madame de Scudéry's Clélie romances also moves towards generalization, as does the immediately ensuing allusion to "Millamont and Doricourt in the comedy," for those two characters originally existed, of course, in separate works—Congreve's *The Way of the World*, and Mrs. Manley's *The Belle's Stratagem.* Here the two join in order to characterize the manners of gallantry: "a mixture of earnest and acting; high-flown compliments, profound bows, vows, sighs and ogles" (II, 182).

A wonderfully comic reference to George's appearance in Turkish dress with his mistress, Lady Yarmouth, leads to the brilliantly ironic characterization of him as a "little old Bajazet [going] on in this Turkish fashion," as a "strutting Turkey-cock of Herrenhausen!," and as a "naughty little Mahomet"

(II, 191). The only extended allusion, however—one that is notably resonant, as it was in *The English Humourists* and *The Newcomes*—evokes Pompeii, in characterizing the exhumation, as it were, of Hervey's dark spirit in his recently released and published *Memoirs* (1848), with their extraordinary revelations: "About him there is something frightful: a few years since his heirs opened the lid of the Ickworth box; it was as if a Pompeii was opened to us—the last century dug up, with its temples and its games, its chariots, its public places—lupanaria [i.e. brothels]" (II, 180).

A similar awareness of evanescence and—inevitably—reenactment leads in Thackeray's lecture on George III to remembrance of sights from his own childhood, and to the sense that Carleton House "exists no more than the palace of Nebuchadnezzar" (II, 258). He also articulates brief awarenesses of how the king's mother (in emulation of Pope's Queen Anne) "sometimes council took and sometimes tea" (II, 265), of how the king's daughters were "pretty, smiling Penelopes,—with their busy little needles" (II, 271), of how the king's parsimonious gifts to his subjects contrast with Haroun al Raschid's generosity, of how George could unwittingly emulate King Alfred turning a spit, and of how this pathetic monarch was flatteringly portrayed in his time as a king of Brobdingnag (II, 273). In a continuing spirit of satire, Thackeray's lecture invokes an anonymous "heroine of the old spelling-book story" (II, 267) in order to characterize Princess Charlotte writing her perfectly spelled, banal, captivating letter to George. Finally, however, Thackeray—seemingly recalling in private his own loss of an infant daughter—concludes his lecture with an extraordinarily sympathetic characterization of George's loss of his daughter Amelia, as if he were a Lear overwhelmed by the death of Cordelia (II, 277).

The lecture on George IV, understandably, almost abandons depth of reference, given such a shallow subject. One of the few that appears wittily mocks with an admonition from Juvenal the adulations of those who treasure and would purchase at Christie's lockets of his hair: *quot libras e duce summo invenies?* (how many pounds will you find in this greatest leader? [II, 386]). Several others briefly characterize George by a Biblical reference to his inability either to toil or to spin (II, 388), and by an ironic Wordsworthian characterization of his appalling consistency from boy to man (II, 389). Another calls up and yet rejects a familiar Thackerayan allusion, as he refuses to "take the Leporello part, flourish a catalogue of the conquests of this royal Don Juan, and tell the names of the favourites to whom, one after the other, George Prince flung his pocket-handkerchief" (II, 390). Thackeray's only other allusion in the lecture—again, as in *The Newcomes*—calls up Hannibal's warriors at Capua, who, in winter quarters, surrendered to luxury and pleasure, as did George: "What muscle would not grow flaccid in such a life—a life that was never strung up to any action—an endless Capua without any campaign—all fiddling, and flowers, and feasting, and flattery, and folly?" (II, 399)—an expressive series of ironic alliterations.

In speaking to his lecture audiences, who are of course immediate presences, Thackeray understandibly forgoes the narrator's appeal to "readers" and—for the most part—even "friends," addressing them instead as "you," asking them to see, fancy, and imagine, while openly acknowledging his own experiences and feelings. He begins with a moving articulation of a personal relationship (with Mary Berry) that brilliantly epitomizes what will be his continuing synthetic mode of presentation, where a phrase from a book, a reported fragment of speech, or a touch of the hand can reopen a whole past world:

A very few years since, I knew familiarly a lady who had been asked in marriage by Horace Walpole; who had been patted on the head by George I. This lady had knocked at Johnson's door; had been intimate with Fox,

> the beautiful Georgina of Devonshire, and that brilliant Whig society of the reign of George III.; had known the Duchess of Queensberry, the patroness of Gay and Prior, the admired young beauty of the court of Queen Anne. I often thought, as I took my kind old friend's hand, how with it I held on to the old society of wits and men of the world. I could travel back for seven score years of time—have glimpses of Brummel, Selwyn, Chesterfield and the men of pleasure; of Walpole and Conway; of Johnson, Reynolds, Goldsmith; of North, Chatham, Newcastle; of the fair maids of honour of George II.'s court; of the German retainers of George I.'s; where Addison was secretary of state; where Dick Steele held a place; whither the great Marlborough came with his fiery spouse; when Pope, and Swift, and Bolingbroke yet lived and wrote. (II, 1-2)

He then consolidates this relationship with his audiences by acknowledging the immensity of his subject and his own inability to encompass it, by defending himself against misunderstandings from critics, and by speaking of his appropriately limited intentions in composing the lectures: "to sketch the manners and life of the old world; to amuse for a few hours with talk about the old society; and, with the result of many a day's and night's pleasant reading, to try and wile away a few winter evenings for my hearers" (II, 2).

Those hearers would appear to have been much more literate than late 20th century audiences might be. Hence Thackeray's freedom to people his lectures with so many figures and to cite familiarly so much personal testimony and historical compilations. In mentioning "Dr. Vehse" (II, 3) and quoting from him, Thackeray evidently assumes that a number of his hearers have read or at least heard of the German historian's *Geschichte der Höfe des Hauses Braunschweig in Deutschland und England*, which had been published two years previously. Similarly, a reference to "Dr. Doran" (II, 11) must have called up awareness of the English historian's *Lives of the Queens of England of the House of Hanover*, which had just appeared (1855).

Instead of making extensive Biblical and mythological allusions, Thackeray freely cites personal memoirs, letters, and biographies. A few of these sources had been published during the 18th century—like the memoirs of Pöllnitz and Gourville—but the majority of them derive from the quarter-century or so preceding the lectures, when a wonderful cornucopia of manuscript material had poured forth into print. Among the dozens of volumes upon which he draws, one can cite such revealing works as Spence's *Anecdotes* (1820), the memoirs of Horace Walpole (1845, 1847) and Hervey (1848), the letters of Lady Suffolk (1824), Lady Mary Wortley Montagu (1837), Walpole (1840), Fanny Burney (1842-46), George Selwyn and his friends (1843-44), and Lord Malmesbury (1844), as well as biographies like Wallace's *George the Fourth* (1832), and Twiss's *Eldon* (1844). These references, moreover, are made to knowledgeable sharers of historical awareness in his audiences.

The Four Georges, although the fact has not been sufficiently emphasized, constitutes the most extensively intimate of Thackeray's engagements with his audiences up to this point in his career, as one can come to understand by realizing how often he offers them personal testimony. The mere use of "I" exceeds 145 instances, not to mention how often he draws his hearers into unison with himself through the evocation of "one," "we," "our," and "us." Obviously one cannot possibly articulate the range and expressiveness of such forms of speech, but some examples may help to suggest their nature.

Recalling Duke Ernest of Celle's mental instability and love of music, Thackeray evokes a memorable connecting awareness: "One thinks of a descendant of his [George III], two hundred years afterwards, blind, old, and lost of wits, singing

Handel in Windsor Tower" (II, 2). Speaking of monarchical selling and purchasing of troops, he draws together the awareness of both English and American audiences: "You may remember how George III.'s Government purchased Hessians, and the use we made of them during the War of Independence" (II, 6). Mentioning the appalling disparity of wealth and well-being in 18th century Europe, he urges his audiences to remember that "A grander monarch, or a more miserable starved wretch than the peasant his subject, you cannot look on. Let us bear both these types in mind, if we wish to estimate the old society properly" (II, 5).

Personally he testifies that "I remember as a boy how a great party persisted in declaring Caroline of Brunswick was a martyred angel" (II, 13). "I remember forty years ago, as a boy in London city, a score of cheery, familiar [street] cries that are silent now" (II, 18). "When I first saw England, she was in mourning for Princess Charlotte, the hope of the empire . . . [and] I remember peeping through the colonnade at Carlton House, and seeing the abode of the great Prince Regent. I can see yet the Guards pacing before the gates of the place" (II, 258). "I remember as a young man how almost every dining-room had [George IV's] portrait" (II, 387). "And now I have one more story of the bacchanalian sort, . . . at the Pavilion at Brighton, [that] was described to me by a gentleman who was present at the scene" (II, 396). (Indeed, Thackeray's accounts of the prodigious guzzling of wine at table remind us that the world had not yet been blessed with the pre-dinner satisfaction of the martini.)

More typically, however, he speaks of his present emotions and imaginative responses to recollections and challenging awarenesses of the past. Duke Ernest was "not, I fear, a moral prince, of which kind we shall have but very few specimens in the course of these lectures" (II, 7). Contemplating the arrival in England of George I, with his two ungainly German mistresses—in English eyes, the Elephant and the Maypole—Thackeray cannot contain his amusement: "I protest it is a wonderful satirical picture." Going on to project himself into an 18th century spectator, as he often invites his audiences to do, he feels himself "a citizen waiting at Greenwich pier, say, and crying for King George; and yet I can scarcely keep my countenance, and help laughing at the enormous absurdity of this advent!" (II, 14).

Most especially, he expresses the imaginative impetus arising from the historical details that he is recalling and relating: "I fancy" (II, 7), or "one fancies" (II, 10), he often says. "I own to finding a pleasure in these small beer chronicles"—e.g. that the entire Court of Hanover had only two washerwomen. "I like to people the old world" (II, 10), he acknowledges, and then he does so with extensive vibrancy. "I would have liked a night at the Turk's Head" (II, 264). "I should like to go into Lockit's with [Addison]," he testifies, "and drink a bowl along with Sir R. Steele . . . . Our business is pleasure, and the town, and the coffee-house, and the theatre, and the Mall" (II, 18).

Evoking what he ironically calls "the wonderful history" (II, 180) of Queen Caroline's death-bed, where her spouse, George II, grotesquely swears fidelity by promising not to remarry, but only to have mistresses (plural), Thackeray understandably resorts to hyperbole: "There never was such a ghastly farce" (II, 181). Even more notably, perhaps, he goes on to articulate his feelings as an imagined bystander of the actual scene, and also as an appalled audience of the historical narrator who so rancorously preserved this awful event for posterity:

> I watch the astonishing scene—I stand by that awful bedside, wondering . . . —and can't but laugh, in the presence of death, and with the saddest heart. In that often-quoted passage from Lord Hervey, in which the queen's death-bed is described, the grotesque horror of the details surpasses all satire: the dreadful

humour of the scene is more terrible than Swift's blackest pages, or Fielding's fiercest irony. The man who wrote the story had something diabolical about him: the terrible verses which Pope wrote respecting Hervey, in one of his own moods of almost fiendish malignity, I fear are true. I am frightened as I look back into the past and fancy I behold that [event]. (II, 181)

His response to the immediate scene, moreover, extends to an awareness of how the ensuing threnodies of clergymen mirror the sycophantic behavior of the rest of Court society: "I say I am scared as I look round at this society—at this king, at these courtiers, at these politicians, at these bishops" (II, 182).

Amid so much pampered folly, what is there, by contrast, to admire? For Thackeray—as for Carlyle, Ruskin, and Morris—dedicated labor: "a thousand times better chance for happiness, education, employment, security from temptation." He celebrates the contributions made to their society by "working educated men," the good clergy, the honest tradesmen, "the painters pursuing their gentle calling, the men of letters in their quiet studies." For Thackeray, the splendor of the age manifests itself especially in the presence and achievements of people like Johnson, Goldsmith, Reynolds, Burke, and Garrick: "not merely how pleasant and how wise, but how *good* they were" (II, 264). For him, they remain permanent models of responsible citizenship.

* * * * *

Having delivered his lectures on the Georges in America, Scotland, and England intermittently between October 1855 and May 1857, Thackeray then turned to the composition of his next novel, *The Virginians*, which appeared in 24 serial install-

CHAPTER FOUR

ments beginning in November 1857.[2] A successor to his narrative of the Esmond family, of course, but also a successor to *The English Humourists of the Eighteenth Century* and *The Four Georges* by virtue of Thackeray's intense interest in 18th century literature and society, *The Virginians* evokes a roughly thirty-five year period from mid-century to several years following the end of the American War of Independence. As in his recent lectures, the Thackerayan speaker is both an imaginative participant in later 18th century life and also a mid-19th century observer. The latter comments to his audiences, for example, on how his title-figures lived in "that Old World from which we are drifting away so swiftly" (*Works*, XV, i. 2), but he also speaks as an actively imaginative participant in that Old World, articulating his vital involvement through his own voice as well as through the narrative voices of Harry and especially George Warrington.

From the very beginning of the narrative the 19th century speaker expresses his sense of how the 18th century words of the Warrington memoirs (the language of which Thackeray has historically emulated and yet seamlessly created as a living discourse) make those personages appear to be alive: "whose voices I almost fancy I hear, as I read the yellow pages written scores of years since." Thackeray insists upon this doubleness of awareness, as he at the same time characteristically modulates between narrative ominisience and—much more frequently—limited awareness: "I have tried to imagine the situation of the writer . . . . I have drawn the figures as I fancied they were" (i, 2). Even more to the point, he imagines himself back in time as a recording witness: as someone standing at the sideboard, so to speak, and reporting what was said (li, 525), as someone who has "set down conversations as I think I might have heard them; and so, to the best of my ability, endeavoured to revivify the bygone times and people" (i, 2-3).

As in his lectures on *The Four Georges,* Thackeray actively *peoples* the English countryside as well as London during the times of George II and George III, evoking historical places like Stratford on Avon, Derby, Falkirk, and Culloden, "Playhouses, Parks, and Palaces, wondrous resorts of wit, pleasure, and splendour," plump landladies at their bars, surrounded by "china and punch-bowls, and stout gilded bottles of strong waters, and glittering rows of silver flagons" (i, 7), and high roads swarming with light post-chaises of the gentry, ponderous coaches of the country squire with bells and plodding horses, busy inns, chamberlains, chambermaids, and even servants drinking their mugs of ale in the inn kitchens. The "high road, a hundred years ago, was not that grass-grown desert of the present time. It was alive with constant travel and traffic" (i, 8).

Inevitably, therefore, Thackeray plays with the contrast and the relationship of past and present. Allegedly greater respect for a parent in preceding days offers a perennial source for pointed commentary that Thackeray does not neglect, as he comically contrasts George's polite behavior towards his mother with "Nowadays," when "a young man walks into his mother's room with hob-nailed high-lows, and a wideawake on his head; and instead of making her a bow, puffs a cigar into her face" (viii, 78). Similarly, Madam Esmond Warrington's neatness and dexterity in preparing certain dishes, and her honoring of the "old law of the table" in pressing "her guests with a decent eagerness, to watch and see whom she could encourage to further enjoyment, to know culinary anatomic secrets," to execute appropriate carving operations, and "to cheer her guests to fresh efforts," wonderfully express her celebration of "this ancient rite of a hospitality not so languid as ours" (ix, 88).

Although Thackeray laments the lessened authority of humane letters in his current "age of economists and calculators" (lxiii, 660), he is willing to acknowledge that the 18th century "was an age in which wine-bibbing was more common than in our politer time" (xxxi, 318) [though he himself did not neglect the grape], that it made a greater "distinction of ranks" (xliii, 442), that the "old world was more dissolute than ours," that there "was a nobility, many of whom were mad and reckless in the pursuit of pleasure," that "there was a looseness of words and acts which we must note, as faithful historians" (xxviii, 290), and that in those days "the finest folks and the most delicate ladies called things and people by names which we never utter in good company nowadays," being "more decent" and "more cleanly" (liv, 562).

Nevertheless, he did not loose his satirical awareness of the primness of mid-19th century manners, and could also speak more charitably of "the frankness which characterized those easy times" (xxxviii, 395) of the 18th century, and could qualify his praise of 19th century manners with ironic endorsement of his contemporaries' avoidance of frankness and devotion to "hypocrisy, which hides unwelcome things from us!" (lvi, 577). Indeed, his emphasis falls upon the exaggerations of current primness (xv, 154, xvi, 158, xx, 206, xxiii, 240, xxvi, 273, xli, 425, lxix, 725), so that when he speaks of how in "those homely times a joke was none the worse for being a little broad; and a fine lady would laugh at a jolly page of Fielding, and weep over a letter of Clarissa, which would make your present ladyship's eyes start out of your head with horror" (lxx, 738), there seems little doubt that Thackeray's ambiguity about this issue often tends to resolve itself in favor of 18th century manners—in keeping, for example, with his preface to *Pendennis*, where he wishes for Fielding's freedom as a writer.

Even more typically, he reiterates his sense of the sameness of human motives and the continuity of their reenactments. The houses on London Bridge may disappear (xxxvi, 375), but the humans who walk across it feel the same promptings. For all the differences between the two centuries, one cannot detect moral progress, as his irony makes clear: "Yes, madam, we are not as our ancestors were. Ought we not to thank the Fates that have improved our morals so prodigiously, and made us so eminently virtuous?" (xvi, 158). "A hundred years ago, people of the great world were not so strait-laced as they are now, where everybody is good, pure, moral, modest; when there is no skeleton in anybody's closet; when there is no scheming; no slurring over of old stories; when no girl tries to sell herself for wealth, and no mother abets her" (xvii, 178).

In a similar ironic vein, he asserts that of "course there are no such people now" as the scheming, selfish, pharisaical Castlewoods, and pretends to argue that "human nature is very much changed in the last hundred years" (xxiv, 253). "There is no conceit left among us. There is no such thing as dullness. Arrogance is entirely unknown" (liii, 550). Then as now, "a proud thing it is to be a Briton, and think that there is no country where prosperity is so much respected as in ours; and where success receives such constant affecting testimonials of loyalty" (xx, 206).

As Thackeray knew from personal experience, the race of parasites is never extinct: "grown men . . . who loved to consort with fashionable youths entering life . . . ; to act as Covent-Garden Mentors and masters of ceremonies at the Roundhouse; to accompany lads to the gaming-table, and perhaps have an understanding with the punters." In the face of basic human evidence, any claim of the moral superiority of "Queen Victoria's reign . . . [over that] of her royal great-grandfather" (xxx, 306-7) is an obvious absurdity, though the toad-eating may not be as blatant as in the older time (xxxi, 316). So too, the human pursuit of pleasure is constant, and if the contemporary fashionable folks spend a little less time at Epsom, Bath, Tunbridge, and Harrogate than formerly, they have migrated, like Thackeray, "to Hombourg and Baden now" (xxxi,

313), where they dance, frisk, gamble, and drink, as before.

The awareness of continuity expresses itself as a renascence qualified by a sense of the partial irreversiblity of past experience: "almost it makes one young to think of [young Harry Warrington]" (i, 8). Thinking back to a hundred or so years of past history is analogous to thinking back to the time of one's youth. "It is ever so many hundred years since some of us were young; and we forget, but do not all forget" (lx, 623). The revivified sense of one's youth is therefore an avenue not only to one's own past self but also to the associates who made up a whole past world that one shared with them, and analogously to those whose language one has read, known, and treasured.

The narrator's reading of the imagined Warrington letters is also analogous to our reading the autograph letters of our ancestors, or the unpublished letters of Thackeray, for example: "As we look at the slim characters on the yellow page, fondly kept and put aside, we can almost fancy him alive who wrote and who read it—and yet, lo! they are as if they never had been: their portraits faint images in frames of tarnished gold" (xii, 119). Here again, every word counts. The experience is quintessential for a Thackerayan narrator: reading the past and recognizing both its dimness and also its enduring presence in our minds, hearts, and motives.

An evocation in a single paragraph of Aesop, the reiterating Spelling-book, Hylas and the Naiads, Odysseus, the Sirens, Telemachus, Horace, and Mozart expresses the enduring resonance of fundamental human experience as articulated in artistic expression. Harry Warrington is like "that silly dog (of whom Aesop or the Spelling-book used to tell us in youth)," an absurd cur snapping at the imagined bone of a love relationship with Maria. Like a "green-eyed Naiad," she inveigles him into the waters of illusion. "'Hither, hither, rosy Hylas!' Pop goes Hylas. (Surely the fable is renewed for ever and ever?) . . . The last time Ulysses rowed by the

Sirens' bank, he and his men did not care though a whole shoal of them were singing and combing their longest locks," but they had to restrain young Telemachus, who "was for jumping overboard."

As "Brother Boatswain[s]" we are invited to join together in repudiating both the "old, leering witches," and also the absurdity of "fashion"—which, as always, merely pretends to be meaningful. Thackeray, for whom Mozart was an enduringly wonderful presence, therefore calls upon us to laugh at the trends of whimsical unpopularity, and to recognize instead an ability like Mozart's to celebrate the fundamental principles of human behavior when he says, for example, 'Women are like that': "Don't you remember how pleasant the opera was when we first heard it? *Cosi fan tutti* was its name—Mozart's music. Now, I dare say, they have other words, and other music, and other singers and fiddlers, and another great crowd in the pit. Well, well, *Cosi fan tutti* is still upon the bills, and they are going on singing it over and over and over" (xviii, 184-85). In short, popularity is sham: *Cosi fan tutti* is enduring reality, whether popularly recognized or not.

Men, of course, are "like that" in their own way, as the examples of Hylas and young Telemachus indicate. Ulysses apparently has fewer descendants, but Aesop and Horace identify a permanent human susceptibility to folly. Horace especially, quoted or alluded to at least 43 times in the narrative, exemplifies the enduring relevance of classical awareness and expression, which manifest themselves on no less than 105 occasions in the novel. The pre-eminence of Horace's language in educated 18th century consciousness, beginning in schoolboy exercises and continuing into mature re-reading, as with Thackeray personally, reflects itself in this frequency and richness of allusion in Thackeray's narrative, as does to a lesser degree the occurence of the language of Vergil (18), Homer (9), Juvenal (4), Cicero (3), Catullus (3), Lucretius (2), and Aesop, Ovid, Menander, Sallust, Euripedes, Persius, and Terence.

Horace's presence manifests itself most fundamentally in the reiterated consciousness of what Horace expressed in *Satires*, I, i, 69-70: *Mutato nomine de te / fabula narratur* (change but the name and the fable is told of you)—the same awareness that Thackeray had articulated at the beginning of *The Newcomes* and before, as he emphasized how often we reenact the patterns of our earlier life, and of the lives of our predecessors. Hence the narrator points out that Harry fails to recognize how Hetty is "narrating a fable regarding him" (xxiii, 236), and observes that the "ghastly commiseration, such as our dear relatives or friends will sometimes extend to us when we have done something fatal or clumsy in life" is behavior that reenacts an old fable *"de te"* (lxi, 633). Lord Chesterfield also uses the allusion (xxv, 261), as do Sampson (xxxiv, 352), and Hagan (lxxix, 839).

The narrator and his characters also retain Horace's acute consciousness of *pallida mors* (pale Death [lxviii, 718]), *Nox et Domus Plutonia* (Night and Pluto's Abode [lix, 613]), *Atra Cura* (black Care [xxxiii, 346, lxxxv, 907]), and the need to wrap one's self in one's virtue, and to woo honest poverty, undowered though she be, should Fortune swiftly fly away in abandonment (*si celeres quatit / pinnas, resigno quae dedit et mea / virtute me involvo probamque / Pauperiem sine dote quaero* [xlii, 439-40, lxxxi, 856]). The narrator, more than the characters, however, has the sense of the hidden fires of treacherous ashes (*cineri doloso* [xxvi, 276]), of gambling as an activity full of dangerous hazard (*periculosae plenum opus aleae* [xxvii, 277]—the basis for a chapter title)—and of the dangers of Love's fiery darts (*ardentes sagittas* [xxxiii, 345]).

But they share with Horace the sense of fine wine as something not only fit for pontifs' feasts (*mero / ... superbo / pontificum potiore cenis*), but also as a precious inheritance that a careless young man will slosh upon the pavement (*tinguet pavi-*

mentum [ix, 86]). Like Henry Esmond, they have an acute sense of how a special corner of earth smiles beyond all others (*ille terrarum mihi praeter omnes / angulus ridet* [xvi, 161]), of how one can serve in Love's battles and eventually, with appropriateness, give up the stuggle (*Vixi Puellis nuper idoneus / et militavi non sine gloria*[xxiv, 247]), and of how one can reluctantly surrender to the awareness of a measure in all things (*modus in rebus* [xliii, 442]), of how banished nature will always hurry back to reassert herself (*Tamen usque recurrit* [lix, 615]), and of how, if we fare ill today, we will not necessarily always do so (*non, si male nunc, et olim / sic erit* [lxxxi, 860]).

They know about the flirting Lalage (lxix, 735)—a prototype of Becky Sharp—and about Glycera's dazzling beauty (*splendentis Pario marmore purius* [lxx, 737]), but, like George Warrington and like Thackeray, prefer to see seated with them, sharing the fireplace, the sweetly laughing, sweetly speaking spouse (*dulce ridentem . . . / dulce loquentem* [lxviii, 719]). They certainly admire steadfastness of purpose. Like many writers, Thackeray—emulated by George—sought *plausus in theatro* (applause in the theatre [lxiii, 669]), wished—however uncertainly—to build with Horace *monumentum aere perennius* (a monument more lasting than bronze [lxiii, 671]), but, through having to endure the broken masts of shipwreck (especially emotional), sought and found in himself the *impavidum ferient ruinae* (the undauntedness that survives being stricken [lxxx, 849]).

Though a narrator of novels without heroes, Thackeray testified to his admiration of at least one figure whom he considered heroic—Washington—and acquired a plaster copy (now in the Grolier Club in New York City) of Houdon's bust. Extending into *The Virginians* his admiring language for Washington at the end of the lecture on George IV, Thackeray, through the utterance of George Warrington, evoked the superlative words of Horace uttering a dirge for Quintilius: *quando invenies*

CHAPTER FOUR

parem? (When will his peer be found? [lxxxvii, 933]). Certainly not in our time. Vergil, of course, also receives Thackeray's testimony of his having provided Western culture with crucial archetypes of human behavior, from the conduct of *Fidus Achates* (faithful Achates [lxxx, 848]), which Sampson briefly emulates, the anxiety of *pavidae matres* (fearful mothers [xxxiv, 349]), the *facilis descensus averno* (the ease of sinking into tormenting confinement [xx, 198]—emphasized as a chapter title), the ignorant bliss of *fortunatos nimium, sua si bona norint* (happy men, did they but know their blessings [xlii, 434]—again the basis for a chapter title), and the anger of a woman *spretae iniuria formae* (whose beauty has been scorned [lxxiii, 769]). Similarly, Thackeray uses Vergilian language to illustrate the willingness of poets to sing of *arma virumque* (warfare and a heroic warrior [lxii, 636]—another chapter title), the resignation of human hopes because of the discovery that *dis aliter visum* (to the gods it seemed otherwise [xci, 974]), even the inappropriateness of British use of *tali auxilio* (such aid) as Hessian mercenaries and *istis defensoribus* (such defenders) as murderous Indian allies against the American colonists (lxxxvii, 932), and—as the words of Vergil and Sallust join—the awareness of Fox as a man motivated by *auri fames* (hunger for gold) and *alieni appetens* (covetousness of others' possessions [lviii, 595]).

Like most authors—including Vergil—Thackeray warms to the idea of a sympathetic audience, as he cites in successive chapter titles Aeneas's attentive listeners in Books II and III of *The Aeneid: Conticuere omnes intentique ora tenebant* (all fell silent and their faces were attentive [li, 525, lii, 540]). Most notably, however, Thackeray responds to Vergil's characterization of Dido, evoking her response to Aeneas's tale as a moving way of conveying Baroness Bernstein's sympathetic engagement with Harry's narrative (xiv, 138-39), and twice drawing upon Vergil's wonderfully understated rendering of Dido's painful experience, first, to convey the Baroness Bernstein's ability to sympathize with Maria ("Old Dido, a poet remarks, was not ignorant of misfortune, and hence learned to have compassion on the wretched" [lvii, 588-89]), and second, to render George's suffering when he is separated from Theo, being, like Dido, *haud ignarus mali* (not unacquainted with misfortune [lxxvii, 818]).

Homer provides an occasional weighty utterance, as George recalls and endorses (lxxviii, 824) Henry Esmond's quotation from *The Odyssey*, where Zeus tells the gods, "O how vainly do mortals blame the gods, for they say evil comes from us but it is they who by their own recklessness win sorrow beyond what is ordained"—an utterance that Esmond had applied to the Stuarts, and that George applies generally. In *The Virginians*, however, Homer tends to provoke more comic treatment, as we have seen in the example of Odysseus rowing by the bank of the Sirens (xviii, 184), who represent an enduring temptation (lxxxv, 906-07). Similarly, the narrator mocks George and Harry Warrington's unwitting emulation of Achilles sulking in his tent (ii, 18, vi, 62)—like young Pendennis—and the narrator also responds to his Homeric inheritance by comically speaking of "the folks in Polyphemus's cave" (lxx, 736) as he jokingly comments on the female cannibalism that feasts upon susceptible men.

For 18th and 19th century sensibilities, of course, post-classical articulation resonates especially with Biblical and Shakespearean language. Evocations of the Bible occur at least 70 times, an additional 16 coming from *The Book of Common Prayer*. Micah's wonderful image of contentment—"they shall sit every man under his vine and under his fig tree"—certainly captured Thackeray's allegiance, being thrice alluded to (viii, 82, xci, 977, xcii, 979 [see also the equivalent Horatian language, *sub arta / vite bibentem* (drinking beneath the thick-leaved vine [*Odes*, I, xxxviii, 7-8],) in *Letters*, III, 114, IV, 254, *Letters [H]*, 534, and 998]. The appropriateness and subtlety of the image derive also, however, from the fact that sitting under one's vine and fig tree was a reiterated evocation of ideal retirement by Washington himself (viii, 82; *Annotations*, II, 316), whose final happiness George Warrington's history emulates, the fulfillment of which is expressed by the title of the novel's final chapter: "Under Vine and Fig-Tree."

Biblical phrases, of course, have historically furnished cues for bullying other people, as Rachel Esmond Warrington demonstrates near the begining of the narrative, for example, with her pontificating use of the phrase from the *Book of Common Prayer* that characterizes all of us as "miserable sinners." Feeling significant ambiguity about the phrase, the narrator distinguishes between the meaning of what is enunciated in church each Sunday (iv, 35), and on the other hand what is dismissed by Madam Warrington outside of church, lightly parroted by Sir Miles Warrington (xliii, 445), seemingly contradicted by the image of a "Good Old Country Gentleman" (l, 512), and even directly challenged by Hetty, as she denies its applicability to her father (xxiii, 241).

Thackeray's charity responded to the *Book*'s implicit injunction to welcome a stranger within one's gates—mocked by the cynical Lord Castlewood (xv, 153), but acted upon by the Virginia gentry (v, 44), and notably by Colonel and Mrs. Lambert (xxi, 217), who take in the stricken, unknown stranger and later discover in him not only the son of her old friend but a young man who is to become a part of their family. Thackeray apparently felt even more strongly the power of the *Book of Common Prayer*'s Litany, with its prayer for all travellers by land or by water, which is uttered by Harry as he prays for George (xii, 118), recalled by Hetty as she prays for Harry on the military expedition to Cancale Bay (lxiv, 674), and repeated by Colonel Lambert when Harry sails with Wolfe on the expedition to Canada (lxviii, 716).

Thackeray's testimony of the prayer's meaning to him also appeared as he cited it in his correspondence just prior to his departure for America in 1852 and for the Continent in 1861 (*Letters*, IV, 253 and *Letters [H]*, 486). Similarly, he evoked the marvellous passage in Psalm 107, which speaks of the turmoil experienced by those who "go down to the sea in ships" and thereby discover the possibility and the meaning of haven—a meaning not consciously articulated by the people who use that phrase, however: Rachel Esmond Warrington (liv, 557) and George (xc, 969), who think primarily of the dangers.

Naming one of his characters Rev. Sampson, Thackeray, like his characters, plays with references to the worldly prelate's Biblical predecessor, as the clergyman launches only verbal assaults on the Philistines (xv, 149), but on stepping down from his pulpit is captured by them in their more modern roles as money-lenders and bailiffs (xxxviii, 392 [chapter title]), or is rescued from them (xliii, 449), at least temporarily. Similarly, the Baroness Bernstein, having herself played the role of a purposeful temptress, playfully characterizes Lady Maria as a Delilah for wanting to coax from Sampson the letters that he has intercepted (xxxvi, 372). The narrator, however, generalizes further, as he speaks of Harry, even after having been freed from subjugation to Lady Maria, finding himself under renewed female domination in the person of Fanny Mountain, and thereby reenacting the same role that, under the thralldom of Omphale, Delilah, and their like, Hercules, Sampson and others had played before him (lxxxiv, 900), as depicted in a chapter initial, and which a chapter title identifies as "The Common Lot" (lxxxiv, 885).

Even more satirically, Jezebel serves as a prototype for George II's mistress, Madam Walmoden, who has became Countess of Yarmouth. She may privately be called a "painted High Dutch Jezebel" (xxxii, 329) by Colonel Lambert, but unlike her Biblical predecessor meets no harsh fate (2 Kings 9:

30-37). Instead, a bishop of 18th century England cringes before her, a descendant of the Hotspurs stops, bows, and smiles with hat in hand (xxxii, 329), and Lady Warrington, who with undaunted self-righteousness constantly enunciates Biblical maxims, gives a great entertainment for Lady Yarmouth, presents her boy to her, and places "poor little Miles under her ladyship's august protection" (lxxviii, 828). Though Colonel Lambert ironically calls the Countess a "vice-queen" (also the title of an ironic illustration), she finds many fashionable English people willing to lose their money to her at cards, and—as Thackeray had pointedly mentioned in his lecture on George II—is cynical enough to accept a clergyman's bet of £5,000 on a bishopric, to receive his payment on losing the bet, and subsequently to reward him with the appointment (xxxiv, 355, 357). Accordingly, the narrator mockingly pretends to emulate the corrupt and sycophantic people who surround her as he declares that "I . . . am determined never to speak or write my mind out regarding anything or anybody. I intend to say of every woman that she is chaste and handsome; of every man that he is handsome, clever, and rich; . . . [and] of Jezebel, that her colour is natural" (xxxv, 364). Thackeray bitingly satirizes Lady Yarmouth's toadies in English society, clearly reveals her willingness to sell ecclesiastical preferments, and mocks her German accent, but he also humanizes her by dramatizing her good-natured and kind behavior towards Harry, partly because he reminds her of her son in Hanover (lxxxiv, 354), Johann Ludwig von Walmoden, who was born before her divorce from her husband, and was given his last name in spite of having been sired by George II. The response to Lady Yarmouth's extra-marital conduct, therefore, serves to demonstrate a worthy 18th century departure from a Biblical prototype, for the narrator and Colonel Lambert pointedly refuse to make a polemical issue of her adultery, quietly drawing upon the example of Jesus, who implicitly characterized the metaphorical as well as the literal stoning of an adulteress as an act not only of cruelty but of hypocrisy. A jealous and snobbish Baroness Bernstein may mockingly contrast the ancient wish to stone such a woman, with the sycophancy of her contemporaries (lxxxiv, 350), but Colonel Lambert offers an appropriate alternative: "I shall fling no stones at the woman; but I shall bow no knee to her, as I see a pack of rascals do" (lxxxiv, 357). By contrast, the corrupt, worldly, selfish Castlewood family members just smile, shrug their shoulders, and pass on. "These were no Pharisees: they professed no hypocrisy of virtue: they flung no stones at discovered sinners." Empty of all ethical values whatever, they simply "took their share of what pleasure or plunder came to hand, and lived from day to day till their last day came for them" (xxiv, 253). Unlike the Castlewoods, even hypocrites like Lady Warrington would seem to have some residual consciousness of the values they pretend to honor. Rev. Sampson, though not altogether hypocritical, nevertheless also indulges in excessive moralism as he mounts his pulpit and from that vantage "whipped Vice tremendously; gave Sin no quarter; out-cursed Blasphemy with superior anathemas; . . . dragged out conjugal Infidelity, and pounded her with endless stones of rhetoric." The narrator, however, seeks to follow the New Testament example: "I, knowing the weakness of human nature, . . . and, quite aware of my own shortcomings, don't intend to be very savage at my neighbour's" (xli, 427).

Thackeray and his better characters respond especially—and not surprisingly—to the gospel of Luke and its gentleness. The different conditions of Dives and Lazarus (xvi, 167, lxix, 722, lxxv, 799) remain an inexplicable mystery, and the rich man's responsibility to take the stranger within his gates remains a conscious challenge, but the redemptive possibilities of appropriate human behavior communicated by Luke especially attract Thackeray's sympathy, as he responds so unmistakably to the parables of the Prodigal Son—an image of himself (xl, 421, xliv, 458, xlvi, 484, liii, 549, lxxxvi, 916, *et passim*)—and the Good Samaritan (xxi, 212 [chapter title], 1, 511 [chapter initial], 1, 514, lxviii, 719, lxxxi, 860)—an image of what he tried to be and *was* to any number of needy people.

Inevitably, the use of Biblical awareness significantly defines character. Horace Walpole, in Thackeray's brilliant pastiche of a Walpolean letter to Henry Seymour Conway, jokingly refers to Lady Yarmouth's having succeeded the Baroness Bernstein in royal favor, by terming them Esther and Vashti, respectively (xl, 422). The Baroness herself satirically characterizes the fashionable people at Tunbridge Wells by telling Harry that when he goes to church he will "see how the whole congregation will turn away from its books and prayers, to worship the golden calf in your person" (xxiv, 251). She shares their values, of course, as she reveals, for example, when Harry's discomfort at the kind of conversation carried on by his aunt and her associates causes her to call him a simpleton, like Joseph failing to respond to the liberated behavior of Potiphar's wife (xviii, 289).

By contrast, we see how Thackeray suggests that George's ability to understand Lydia's hatred of him derives in part from his remembrance of how Potiphar's wife treated Joseph when he failed to respond to *her* advances (lxxiii, 769). We also perceive how George—when confronted with Colonel Lambert's willingness to sacrifice Theo's happiness—comes to see Jepthah's sacrifice of his daughter as an act of extreme and selfish defensiveness about his so-called honor (lxxxvii, 817). More especially, however, through Mrs. Lambert and George, Thackeray recalls the language of Ruth's moving pledge to Naomi that became a prototype of marital commitment—"those sweet words of Ruth that must have comforted myriads of tender hearts . . . , that whither I would go she would go, and that my people should be hers" (lxxviii, 834), and that became an implicit part of the marriage ceremony, together with the spoken pledge to forsake all others (xxxiii, 339). So too, he has Colonel Lambert and George use the example of the ravens feeding Elijah as a justification for young lovers to marry without abundant money (lxxix, 841).[3]

Thackeray also made prominent use of proverbial utterances, often deliberately mundane so as to emphasize their universality. Gumbo is admired because of his master, Harry: "like master like man," as the people in the servants' hall emulate people in the drawing room (xvi, 162). Similar utterances also survive into our time, with enduring persuasiveness: "At Rome, you can't help doing as Rome does," Lord Castlewood proclaims, however cynically (xx, 202; see also xxix, 301, xxxi, 311). Harry confusedly wonders whether his nasty English Warrington relatives "were not so bad as they were painted" (lvi, 578), and finds himself both—as a chapter title testifies—in a "Pretty Kettle of Fish" (lx, 617), and also a "fish out of water" (lxvi, 692). People like George defensively, but with a certain belief, say that "marriages are made in Heaven" (lxix, 732), but also ambiguously acknowledge that "There is no accounting for tastes" (lxix, 728; see also xx, 205).

The Baroness Bernstein, though wittily inventive, also thinks in terms of proverbial expressions, as she wonders whether Harry's passion for Maria is "a mere fire of straw" (xvii, 178), tells Maria (making us recall ladies of shattered virtue like Madame de la Cruchecassée in *Vanity Fair*) that "When a pitcher is broken, what railing can mend it?" (xxxvi, 370), that people worship the golden calf, and that therefore—as Tennyson's speaker in "Locksley Hall" also testifies—"the gold key will open most of [the world's] doors" (xxiv, 251).

By means of chapter titles Thackeray also emphasizes the necessity of our understanding the validity as well as the banality of proverbial wisdom: an "old namby-pamby motto, so stale and so new!" (lx, 624). George, freeing Harry from debtor's prison, demonstrates that a friend serving one in need is a friend indeed (xlix, 503), and—in a play upon the usual—Harry, by enlisting as a volunteer in a misguided enterprise, partly in order to flee from his social perplexities, "Lives to Fight Another Day" (lxiv, 673)—literally. In another variation upon this theme, the British find that their ineffectual strategy in Virginia and elsewhere requires them "[First to] Fight and [Then] Run Away" (xc, 955).

Naturally, proverbial wisdom does not confine itself to English and American awareness and expression, but also articulates itself in other languages of our Western culture. French, for example, offers proverbial insight parallel to English knowledge that marrying an old woman for her money is a game *ne valant guères la chandelle,* as the Baroness Bernstein testifies (xli, 433), that the virtue of patience reveals itself in the ability of those *pour qui sçait attendre,* as George demonstrates in his love for Theo (lix, 615, lx, 627), and that when one is among human wolves, one had best howl with the pack (*hurlant avec les loups* [xxix, 301]). Latin, of course, defines fundamentals, though typically the Latin proverbs are qualified by ironic Thackerayan awareness: *hodie mihi, cras tibi* (today me, tomorrow you), where Thackeray plays with the comic applications of such a grim utterance (lxx, 736), and where the banal quotation of George Warrington to George Washington—"*Tempora mutantur, et nos mutamor in illis*" (Times change, and we change with them)—is effectively reinterpreted by Washington with the compelling authority of his experience (xcii, 985).

Biblical language, of course, has often become proverbial—further testimony to the meaningful reiteration of epitomizing human experience. Among literal Biblical proverbs, however, Thackeray reponded especially to the assertion of Chapter 15, verse 17: "Better is a dinner of herbs where love is, than a stalled ox and hatred therewith," which occurs eight times in his novels. It appears in *The Virginians* when the narrator utters his cry, "Happy! Who is happy?" (xiii, 137), in commenting on the difficulties of living at the Virginian Castlewood, and cites the proverb, using it to pose the rhetorical question: "What good in a stalled ox for dinner every day, and no content therewith?" The latter utterance then introduces more complicated narrative speculation in the form of a demanding interrogative: "Is it best to be loved and plagued by those you love, or to have an easy comfortable indifference at home: to follow your fancies, live there unmolested, and die without causing any painful regrets or tears?" (xiii, 137).

At least 56 references draw upon Shakespeare, a dozen of which cite *Othello*, which Beatrix Esmond had identified as Henry's favorite play, and which is a notable presence in *The Virginians* as well—though, typically, in comic fashion. George himself unconsciously appears in the guise of Othello, as the title of chapter viii, "In Which George Suffers from a Common Disease,," emphasizes (viii, 76), and as the chapter initial also points out, with its depiction of George as Othello witnessing and jealously misinterpreting a conversation between George Washington (Cassio) and Madam Esmond Warrington (Desdemona). The influence of the play upon George himself, however, is suggested by Dr. Johnson's detection of something in George's play, *Carpezan*, that reminds him of *Othello* (lxiii, 661), and by George's wish that yet another George (the monarch) had dismissed General Howe after the battle of Long Island with Othello's words to Cassio: "Never more be officer of mine" (xc, 965).

The narrator jokingly uses Cassio's words to characterize the similar weakness of the boozily self-indulgent Harry "prostrated by an enemy who has stole away his brains" (xxxi, 324), and arranges to have Parson Sampson, though also drunkenly "cut," lament moralistically "that a man should put an enemy into his mouth to steal away his brains" (xxxiv, 359). The narrator also plays upon Othello's compelling adventures among the "Anthropophagi" in order to convey the comical dangers of social exposure to female cannibals (lxx, 736), as we have seen. More ardently, Colonel Lambert expresses the intensity of his love for his wife by uttering Othello's passionate words to Desdemona in typical Thackerayan fashion, so as to convey the mock-heroic reality of domestic romance: "Perdition catch my soul! but I do love thee, Molly!" (xxxiii, 339). Less comically, the narrator articulates, through the words of Iago, the fundamental change that a stirring, unforgettable emotional experience can bring, in memorable lines that Thackeray cited in three other novels—here, as Hetty feels her hopeless attraction to Harry: "So have many besides: and poppy and mandragora will never medicine them to the sweet sleep they tasted yesterday" (xxxv, 362).

The language of *Hamlet* also appears on a dozen occasions. Colonel Lambert, for example, spontaneously uses Hamlet's words on first seeing the ghost, when he starts back on seeing George for the first time: "Angels and ministers of grace! who are you?" (xlix, 506). Parson Sampson, while obsequiously agreeing with Lord Castlewood about the desirability of Harry's marrying Maria, at the same time wittily turns Hamlet's words about death as a fulfillment into a literal consummation: "'Twere a consummation devoutly to be wished!' cries the chaplain" (xx, 205), but the final implication—that a coming together of Harry and Maria would be truly death-like, seems to be Thackeray's awareness more than Sampson's.

The Baroness Bernstein uses Hamlet's bitter words—"a little more than kin and less than kind"—in only a lightly admonishing way when she addresses Madam Rachel Esmond Warrington (xli, 432), while the Duchess of Queensberry wittily trivializes Shakespeare's tragedy, as she claims to see Harry as a fashionable, lady-killing Hamlet: "With a star and ribbon, and his stocking down, and his hair over his shoulder, he would make a pretty Hamlet . . . . And I make no doubt he has been the death of a dozen Ophelias already" (xxx, 305). George, on the other hand, sees himself as the amorous captivator of Miss Van den Bosch, not understanding that he is only one of the minor performers, like "Rosencranz and Guildenstern" (lxix, 735)—"an attendant lord," as Eliot was later to put it, not Prince Hamlet—and that the play in which he is performing is a comedy, not a tragedy.

In actually using the language of *Hamlet*, George treats it as essentially proverbial, seeing his prominence as an elder son and his unwished-for return to Virgina as events revealing that "The time is out of joint" (lv, 567, lxxxvii, 927). By contrast, when the narrator uses the same phrase, he creates an ironic context for it, by pretending to believe that although Maria "had lost her heart ever so many times before Harry Warrington found it," as he comically puts it, "that, bewailing mischance and times out of joint, she would yet have preserved her love, and fondled it in decorous celibacy" (lxx, 737). Similarly, the narrator offers ironic apology for the remarriage of Hamlet's mother, relating it to common experience: "The truth, very likely, is that the tender, parasitic creature wanted a something to cling to"—like Amelia, perhaps, of whom similar words are used at the end of *Vanity Fair*—"and, Hamlet senior out of the way, twined herself round Claudius. Nay, we have known females so bent on attaching themselves, that they can twine round two gentlemen at once. Why, forsooth, shall there not be marriage-tables after funeral baked-meats?" (lxx, 736).

Language from a dozen and a half other Shakespearean plays also appears, especially *Macbeth*, which inspires part of a chapter title, a chapter initial, and an account of Garrick and Mrs. Pritchard performing the play (lx, 617, 618-21), with special reference to the dagger scene, the vision of apparitions (see also lxxix, 836), and the thundering knocks at the gate, fit to awaken Duncan. The narrator, of course, playfully domesticates "Lord and Lady Macbeth concocting a [social] murder" (l, 513), as he had transformed Hamlet's slings and arrows of outrageous fortune into "the stings and arrows of outrageous Fortune" that can be soothed only by the "gentle unguents and warm poultices" of a soft-hearted woman (lxii, 637). *A Midsummer Night's Dream* inevitably calls forth memories of Pyramus, Thisbe, and the separating Wall—in this case Colonel Lambert—in a chapter title, chapter initial, and a reference in the text (lxxviii, 823, 825). The narrator responds to memory of the play with an ironic request that Puck annoint his eyes, so that he, like Harry, can emulate the ability to persist in considering "the Beloved Object a paragon," and to annoint hers as well "so that my noddle may ever appear lovely to her, and that she may continue to crown my honest ears with fresh roses!" (xvi, 162)—an enduring example of perpetuated illusion. Once again Shakespearean language takes on the quality of a proverb—"The course of true love never did run smooth" [another chapter title (lxxv, 791)]—as such language does in the three citations from *Twelfth Night*, all of which endorse Toby's proclamation of the enduring pleasure of cakes and ale, and Feste's responsive evocation of enjoyable taste (xxx, 311, xl, 421, lx, 624).

Nursery rhymes also recall proverbial awareness, especially in revealing the limitations of kings and lesser men, as George emphasizes in breaking a cup of his hen-pecked grandfather's as an act of rebellion against his domineering mother, and in saying "all the king's horses and all the king's men cannot mend it" (v, 54). In a similar vein, the narrator mocks the absurdity of all the king's men literally marching up the hill, only to march down again (lvii, 1005, lxi, 629 [chapter title]). Analogously, the *Arabian Nights' Entertainments* define for Westerners such crucial archetypes as the nightmarish old man of the sea clinging to Sinbad's shoulders (xxii, 222 [chapter initial])—a figure of the fate clinging to Harry in the person of Lady Maria— and the socially not altogether infrequent Barmecide dinner (li, 528) of a stingy host, or in this case a recalcitrant story-teller.

In Thackerayan narratives, fairy tales, even more than nursery rhymes, define quintessential aspects of human awareness and behavior—notably in the "Bluebeard" of Perrault. George characterizes himself both as a loving warder of his wife, though without having any "other heads in the closet" (lxxxv, 905), and as someone who has survived the calumny of his neighbors about his jealous Bluebeardian treatment of her (lxxxv, 908), but he also mocks the prying behavior of Mrs. Mountain as conduct worthy of a "Mrs. Bluebeard [who] thought it was her duty to look through the keyhole" (vii, 74). The narrator—as usual, a figure of notable playfulness—offers a wonderfully extended series of mock justifications for human misbehavior, as he includes a defense of Bluebeard that claims the man was a husband who "really was most indulgent to his wives, and that very likely they died of bronchitis" (xxxv, 364)—a defense that no doubt would seem plausible to the likes of an O.J. Simpson jury.

George, like most of us, carries within himself the wonderful, implausible wish to make sense of absurdity; consequently, when snubbed by his relative, Sir Miles, he comically invokes the sense of his having "worn the Fairy's cap, and been invisible" (lxxxiii, 873). Lady Castlewood claims that "Every woman would rather be beautiful, than be anything else in the world—ever so rich, or ever so good, or have all the gifts of the fairies" (lxxxiii, 876), but Theo, by contrast, has the awareness of being in "a life-partnership," and can bear her "poverty with such a smiling sweetness and easy grace, that niggard Fortune relented before her, and like some savage Ogre in the fairy tales, melted at [her] constant goodness and cheerfulness" (lxxxiii, 874).

As such language suggests, a Thackerayan narrator, however responsive to unfulfillable romantic need, and however aware of "instinct . . . [and] season," must acknowledge that "I never spoke for my part to a fairy princess, or heard as much from any unenchanted or enchanting maiden" (xxii, 232), and that a Fatima must free herself from her own illusions. With this awareness, understandably, classical memory takes hold and leads though rhetorical question to new enlightenment and open assertion: "When she lighted the lamp and looked at him, did Psyche find Cupid out; and is that the meaning of the old allegory? The wings of love drop off at this discovery. The fancy can no more soar and disport in skyey regions: the beloved object ceases at once to be celestial, and remains plodding on earth, entirely unromantic and substantial" (xxii, 233).

Thackeray makes many references to people, places, and customs of the 18th century, so as to give an appropriate historical texture to his narrative. Preachers like George Whitfield, pugulists like Sutton and Figg, artists like Sir Joshua Reynolds, paintings by Hogarth, music by Handel, and especially works of prose and poetry by authors like Fielding, Richardson, Smollett, Bishop Ken, Gray, Swift, and Sterne, frequently enter the lives of the characters. Even more notably, however, Thackeray seeks to provide verisimilitude by giving speaking parts to a number of historical individuals, including George Washington, General Braddock, Governor Dinwiddie, Benjamin Franklin, General Wolfe, Lord Chesterfield, Freiherr von Pöllnitz (also quoted in *The Four Georges*), Lord March, Samuel Johnson, David Garrick, the Duchess of Queensberry, Lady Yarmouth, King George II, the Duke of Cumberland, Governor Dunmore, General Henry Clinton, General Howe, Patrick Henry, and—through letters that Thackeray, with wonderfully responsive mimicry, composes for them—Horace Walpole[4] and George Selwyn (both also, of course, quoted in *The Four Georges*).

We have seen how often and emphatically Thackeray called attention to the contrast of manners and verbal expression in the 18th and 19th centuries, as well as to the enduring similarity of human motives persisting though the centuries. Though predominantly offering a dual perspective, typically realized through the contrast and continuity of "a hundred years since" and "in our time," he not only sought to stir the imaginative participation of his audiences in former times, but also to remind his contemporaries of their grounding in 19th century life—not always to its advantage. He and his audiences can welcome the improved illumination offered by Price's Patent Candle Company, and comfort themselves "by thinking that Louis Quatorze in all his glory held his revels in the dark, and bless Mr. Price and other Luciferous benefactors of mankind, for banishing the abominable mutton [candles] of our youth" (xxv, 255). Promulgators of Vegetarianism and Temperance, however, do not represent an improvement, except as they prompt one to a renewed appreciation of British beef, and to a celebration of wine and the "friendly caves of [a wine dealer], where the dusky flasks lie recondite!" (xxxi, 319).

Lady Maria Esmond had a fine figure and a dress that "showed a great deal of it," but her hoop was less grotesque "than the iron contrivances which ladies of the present day hang round their persons" (xxvii, 280). Science and book-learning may have advanced, but Gibbon remains "mighty" (xli, 424), while state censorship of the press and the susceptibility of Mudie's Select Library to the prudery and squeamishness of contemporary readers (especially female) have become unpleasant restraints (xli, 425). Stanley, Gladstone, and Lytton occasionally evoke classical "rites, divinities, worship" (like Thackeray, as we know), but love of letters seems to have diminished and great authors seem to have lost their authority during the ensuing one hundred years—in public discourse, at least (lxiii, 660).

The political arena, of course, invites profound scepticism. The "delicate question" of whether the members "of Mr. Disraeli's House of Commons . . . has every one of you his price, as in Walpole's or Newcastle's time" (xli, 424) remains open. O'Connell's windy injunction that "Hereditary bondsmen . . . *strike the blow*" receives an ironic deflation by being placed in the mock-heroic context of marital discord (xxxv, 360). Elsewhere, however, in his allusions to contemporary life and writers, Thackeray speaks genially and personally. As a result of his experiences in the United States, he challenges the comments of visitors like Frances Trollope and her successors about "transatlantic manners" (xxxi, 314). Joining his countrymen in appreciating the American comic song, well-known in England, "Possum up a Gum-Tree," he uses the possum's resignation at being cornered to characterize Sampson's willingness to give himself up to pursuing bailiffs (xxxviii, 401).

The increasing disappearance since 18th century times of "that noble old race of footmen," prompts him to see their American analogue in literature as well as life: "So have I seen in America specimens, nay camps and villages, of Red Indians. But the race is doomed. The fatal decree has gone forth, and Uncas with his tomahawk, and Jeames with his cocked hat and long cane, are passing out of the world where they once walked in glory" (xxxvii, 383). The allusion is partly self-referential, of course, as Thackeray himself had given up writing of Jeames.

Thackeray also pays tribute to his friend Peter Cunningham's edition of Horace Walpole's correspondence, as he comically explains why his simulated Walpole letter did not appear in the collection, the editor "doubting possibly the authenticity of the document" (xl, 421). Characteristically declining to write in detailed fashion about military life, he praises "the skill of my friend Lorrequer," but contents himself with offering mere "hints and outlines" (lxvi, 693). Even more, he warmly praises his friend Carlyle's *Frederick the Great*, the first volume of which had appeared in 1858, and gives amused thanks that Harry Warrington did not take part in Frederick's battles (as though Harry had a will of his own), thus relieving Thackeray of the responsibility for competing with Carlyle—"that master" (lxii, 637). Alluding to the yellow covers of his monthly installments, Thackeray comically asks:

"Could my jaunty, yellow park-phaeton run counter to that grim chariot of thundering war? Could my meek little jog-trot Pegasus meet the shock of yon steed of foaming bit and flaming nostril?" (lxii, 636). Uniquely in his writing career, Thackeray chose to mediate his narrative of *The Virginians* to his audience through the use of two main narrators: the usually anonymous, sometimes omniscient, more often limited Thackerayan speaker, and the limited, overtly autobiographical George Warrington, who narrates the final one-quarter of the novel, though other characters make brief, supplementary narrative contributions throughout. For the most part, Thackeray's chief narrator speaks as a 19th century biographer/editor who has been given access to the letters and private papers of George and Harry by a descendant of theirs (i, 1)—George Warrington of *Pendennis* (lxxxi, 864), another agent of continuity.

It seems plausible to infer that Thackeray's direct addresses to the tangible presences that made up his lecture audiences encouraged his continued and perhaps more frequent and lengthier addresses to his readers in *The Virginians* than in earlier novels. Indeed, aside from often talking of "you," "I," and "we," he speaks to readers on approximately 40 occasions, seeking audiences who are kind, gracious, friendly, amiable, benevolent, candid, and patient, who will accept his narrative summaries of lengthy experiences, who are not prim or censorious, suspicious, or for that matter excessively simple, tender-hearted, or sentimental. Equally overtly, after comically disassociating his fictional narratives from the historical discourses of Carlyle, the Thackerayan speaker confesses his love of the intimacy that he had first overtly sought to achieve in *Vanity Fair:* "stepping down from the stage where our figures are performing" (lxii, 636), and talking with the reader.

Hence, he confides that "There are few things to me more affecting in the history of the quarrel which divided the two great nations than the recurrence of that word Home, as used by the younger towards the elder country" (i, 7). At times his confidences emerge as parenthetical observations, frequently ironic (e.g. xi, 140), and at other times as apologies for not going into greater detail about matters like Harry's feelings for Lady Maria, which would require him to reveal "that utter depth of imbecility into which the poor young wretch was now plunged. . . . I say, it is not fair to take down a young fellow's words when he is raging in that delirium" (xix, 195).

Still more playfully, he generalizes that "All of us want to forget something or somebody," and then, while apologizing for Lady Maria's epistolary indiscretions, asks his individual female readers whether or not each recalls those letters "which you may remember you wrote to your Edward, when you were engaged to him, and before you became Mrs. Jones. Would you like those letters to be read by any one else?" (xxxv, 363). Claiming that "flirting is like drinking," he offers a classical excuse for Maria and her counterparts in his audience to turn to whatever partner is available: "the brandy being drunk up, Glycera, . . . who has taken to drinking, will fall upon the gin" (lxx, 737-38). As for himself, he confides his wish only that "If, in some paroxysm of senile folly, I should fall in love to-morrow, I shall still try and think I have acquired the fee-simple of my charmer's heart;—not that I am only a tenant, on a short lease, of an old battered furnished-apartment, where the dingy old wine glasses have been clouded by scores of pairs of lips, and the tumbled old sofas are muddy with the last lodger's boots" (lxx, 737).

His commentary in *The Virginians*, however, can be quite terse and pointed, as we see when he conveys the coldness of Lady Maria's eyes by saying: "Two fish-pools irradiated by a pair of stars would not kindle to greater warmth than did those elderly orbs into which Harry poured his gaze" (xviii, 184). With similar brevity he pretends that hen-pecked husbands constituted a now-extinct species "of which sort there were a few specimens still extant a hundred years ago" (iv, 35), and amusedly observes that "to compress, bottle up, cork down, and prevent your anger from present furious explosion, is called keeping your temper" (v, 50). The Baroness Bernstein's ability to respond to Harry, at least for a time, calls forth the grim observation: "There were not many fountains in that desert of a life" (xiv, 139). Since her nephew is a master at concealment, he prompts the narrator to explain that "When [Castlewood] adopted that frank tone, there was no fathoming his meaning" (xvii, 171). As the narrator was to say elsewhere, "I declare we know nothing of anybody" (xxvi, 275), but we learn it repeatedly.

Apparently speaking from personal experience, the narrator responds to the terrible little mistress of the Virginia Castlewood by observing: "The satire of people who have little natural humour is seldom good sport for bystanders" (xiii, 135). With equally clear-eyed awareness, but without ironic understatement, he rhetorically queries: "if some people were to do penance for telling lies, would they ever be out of sackcloth and ashes?" (xl 415). Even more disturbingly, he asks: "Have you ever been amongst insane people, and remarked how they never, never think of any but themselves?" (xliv, 463)—an observation having pointed implications for determinedly egoistic, so-called sane people. With sardonic bepuzzlement, he remarks: "I never know whether to pity or congratulate a man on coming to his senses" (lvi, 583). One thoroughly doubts that he reflects Thackeray's own experience, however, when he offers the generalization: "At some period before his marriage, it not unfrequently happens that a man actually is fond of his mother-in-law!" (lxvii, 706).

Although a few of these utterances extend themselves by a reinforcing phrase or sentence, they remain succinct and especially effective because of their brevity and wit. Thackeray is also known, of course, for his longer passages of narrative commentary, which can become extensive in

The Virginians, as his encomium on wine illustrates. Arising from a narrative passage about the frequency of the 18th century practice—not subsequently altogether unknown—of "the filling of bumpers and the calling of toasts" (xxxi, 318), and from an acount of how Sampson and Harry "were just warm enough with the claret to be able to talk with that great eloquence, that candour, that admirable friendliness, which good wine taken in a rather injudicious quantity inspires," his celebration of memorable nights ensues, in spite of the recollection of subsequent racking mornings. As George Saintsbury testified (*Works,* XV, xxvii), this passage of Thackerayan narrative commentary thoroughly justifies itself by achieving an enthusiastic articulation probably surpassed by no one else among the reponsive multitude of oenophiles who know full well the exhilaration as well as the evanescence of such experience:

> O kindly harvests of the Aquitanian grape! Oh sunny banks of Garonne! . . . May we not say a word of thanks for all the pleasure we owe you? . . . After the drinking of good Bordeaux wine, there is a point (I do not say a pint) at which men arrive, when all the generous faculties of the soul are awakened and in full vigour; when the wit brightens and breaks out in sudden flashes; when the intellects are keenest; when the pent-up words and confined thoughts get a night-rule, and rush abroad and disport themselves; when the kindest affections come out and shake hands with mankind, and the timid Truth jumps up naked out of his well and proclaims himself to all the world. . . . I say, in the face of all the pumps which ever spouted, that there is a moment in a bout of good wine at which, if a man could but remain, wit, wisdom, courage, generosity, eloquence, happiness, were his; but the moment passes, and that other glass

somehow spoils the state of beatitude. (xxxi, 319)

With similar conviction, the narrator—though amazingly energetic, like his creator—responds to Harry's *otium sine dignitate* with a deification of idleness that carries obvious conviction, and no doubt reflects satisfied experience: "O blessed idleness! Divine lazy nymph! Reach me a novel as I lie in my dressing-gown at three o'clock in the afternoon; compound a sherry-cobbler for me, and bring me a cigar! Dear, slatternly, smiling Enchantress! They may assail thee with bad names—swear thy character away, and call thee the Mother of Evil; but, for all that, thou art the best company in the world!" (xxix, 298-99). Here again, the narrator challenges primness and sanctimonious morality, presenting instead the twenty-year-old Harry's ease as not only normal and harmless, but as a youthful state of being that ought to activate the sympathetic memory of older people. Indeed, the passage also serves to introduce an account of how Harry's "shrewdness and honesty" kept him largely "clear of the snares and baits which are commonly set for the unwary." Similarly, it leads into an explanation of how his relaxed mode of life helped to gain him other appropriate worldly knowledge, like his ability to learn the fashionable language of French, and to develop "a very elegant and decided taste in wines," that enabled him, for example, to "distinguish between Clos Vougeot and Romanée with remarkable skill" (xxix, 299).

We have seen part of the narrator's commentary on governmental and social censorship, but we ought to recognize as well that the passage is not a gratuitous utterance, but serves to prepare us for his effort to characterize what belatedly-serious grandmothers and aunts have not told younger members of the family about their 18th century life. As he points out, grandmothers as well as grandfathers sowed wild oats: "When she was young, she was as giddy as the rest of the genteel world." As an archetypal woman of the period, she flirted (at the least) with Colonel Tibbalt (who later "married Miss Lye, the rich soap-boiler's heiress"), had her card tables set out twice a week for guests, and gambled "Every night of her life . . . for eight, nine, ten hours. . . . She lost; she won; she cheated; she pawned her jewels; who knows what else she was not ready to pawn, so as to find funds to supply her fury for play?"

By this point in the narrative/commentary (indistinguishable here), he has effectively dramatized the censorship of 19th century prudery, for he can only hint at what such 18th century women were ready to pawn, and propose it merely in the form of a speculation—though a telling one. Similarly, he asks: "What was that after-supper duel at the 'Shakespeare's Head' in Covent Garden, between your grandfather and Colonel Tibbalt: where they drew swords and engaged only in the presence of Sir John Screwby, who was drunk under the table?" [To be "screwed," of course, is to be drunk.] Finally, the narrator offers a more generalizing picture of 18th century privileged male disorderliness in the form of a direct address to the reader: "I tell you those gentlemen in powder and ruffles, who turned out the toes of their buckled pumps so delicately, were terrible fellows."[5] Then his discourse begins to darken: "Swords were perpetually being drawn; bottles after bottles were drunk; oaths roared unceasingly in conversation; tavern-drawers and watchmen were pinked and maimed; chairmen belaboured; citizens insulted by reeling pleasure-hunters" (xli, 426). In concluding this complex passage, he refuses to claim superior virtue—only to give personal thanks "that my temptations are less, having quite enough to do with those of the present century" (lxi, 427). As usual, the revelation is in the details—and so is the fun.

The commentary of Thackeray's chief narrator in *The Virginians*, as we have seen, is not only frequently entertaining but is also typically well integrated into his narrative, though Thackeray evidently came to feel that five moderately substantial passages from the last three-fifths of the novel could appropriately be deleted from the 1863 edition (see *Works*, XV, 1003-5). We have to recognize not merely the frequent, splendid effectiveness of the commentary, however, but also the fact that a significant portion of the novel consists of dramatic and semi-dramatic scenes. In actuality, at least sixteen chapters of the main narrator's portion of the novel are predominantly dramatic rather than narrative in nature,[6] and many of the others have a lively interchange between dialogue and commentary, as the following brief example may illustrate:

> If the sight of youthful love is pleasant to behold, how much more charming the aspect of the affection that has survived years, sorrows, faded beauty perhaps, and life's doubts, differences, trouble!
> In regard of her promise to disguise her feelings for Mr. Warrington in that gentleman's presence, Miss Hester was better, or worse if you will, than her word. Harry not only came to take tea with his friends, but invited them for the next day to an entertainment at the Rooms, to be given in their special honour.
> 'A dance, and given for us!' cries Theo. 'Oh, Harry, how delightful; I wish we could begin this very minute!'
> 'Why for a savage Virginian, I declare, Harry Warrington, thou art the most civilized young man possible!' says the colonel. 'My dear, shall we dance a minuet together?'
> 'We have done such a thing before, Martin Lambert!' says the soldier's fond wife. Her husband hums a minuet tune; whips a plate from the tea-table, and makes a preparatory bow and flourish with it as if it were a hat, whilst madam performs her best courtsy.

CHAPTER FOUR

> Only Hetty, of the party, persists in looking glum and displeased. 'Why, child, have you not a word of thanks to throw to Mr. Warrington?' asks Theo of her sister.
> 'I never did care for dancing much,' says Hetty. 'What is the use of standing up opposite a stupid man, and dancing down a room with him?'
> '*Merci du compliment!*' says Mr. Warrington. (xxxiii, 342-43)

The anonymous main speaker had begun his narrative/commentary in the familiar Thackerayan fashion: a lively scene (several of them here, taking up chapters i and ii), followed by an explanation of what had led up to the scene—in this case, Harry's account to the Baroness Bernstein of what lay behind his trip to England. In Chapter lxxii, the first chapter of serial number 19 for May 1859, however, George replaces the main speaker and establishes his personal perspective: that of a mature man, sitting with his wife by the fireside and looking back at the experiences of the second half of his life, the thirty years spent mainly in England. Here he emulates the autobiographical mode of his grandfather, Henry Esmond, whom he resembles in his straightforwardness, modesty, loyalty, scepticism, wit, and especially melancholy.

Like Thackeray, he is somewhat "cold and haughty in his demeanour to strangers, . . . [but] perfectly courteous towards women, and with those people whom he loved, especially kind, amiable, lively, and tender" (lxvi, 699). Like Thackeray also, his seriousness and jesting are inextricably intertwined (lix, 609). Like the speaker in *The Book of Snobs*, "Daily in life I watch men whose every smile is an artifice, and every wink is an hypocrisy" (lxxxv, 901), but for all his difficulty in forgiving injuries, he has a keen awareness of his own failings. More than his predecessor's in *The Virginians*, his narration/commentary arises from personal experience that we ourselves have witnessed, so to speak, and has an even greater intimacy as a discourse addressed to his children. Like his immediate predecessor, George can be a master of witty terseness, speaking of Sir Miles Warrington's wife as someone "who had ever one eye on heaven and one on the main chance" (lxxiv, 784). Similarly, he terms Sir Miles and his wife members of a tribe—Pharisees, of course—that was "known [1800] years ago, and [that] will flourish as long as men endure" (lxxxi, 860), and asks "What are relations made for, indeed, but to be angry and find fault?" (lxxv, 792). Hearing that John Home has been attacked by fellow clergymen for writing a play, George responds: "If he has been persecuted by the parsons there is hope for him" (lix, 612).

Like his more distant predecessor, Esmond, he refuses to implicate Heaven in human quarrels (lxxiv, 787, lxxviii, 824), submits to the inscrutable forces of contingency, and yet maintains a loyalty to the losing side (lxviii, 718, lxxxv, 901-2). The Baroness Bernstein, responding to his chivalry and loyalty, speaks of him as "the grandfather come to life" (lvii, 590). Like Esmond also, however, he writes a manuscript that provokes supplementary and sometimes dissenting footnotes by his wife (lxxii, 761), his offspring (lxxxiii, 871), and the anonymous editor (e.g. lxxviii, 828-29 and lxxx, 848-49). None of Thackeray's narrators is completely authoritative, even about his own experience.

As a Thackerayan narrator, George Warrington is perhaps most memorable in his attempt to come to terms with the debilitating effects of time. Hearing the Baroness Bernstein's wish to emulate Adam and Eve's life-span, George and his wife cite the devastating example of Swift's deathless Struldbrugs, who can only grimly anticipate all the usual disadvantages that old age brings along with it (lxxxiii, 877). He has a happy sense of rejuvenation as he comes across a familiar book from his childhood that his grandfather had read to him, *The True Travels, Adventures, and Observations of Captain John Smith:* "I become a child again almost as I take from the shelf before me in England the familiar volume, and all sorts of recollections of my early home come crowding over my mind" (lxxx, 843). He is especially aware, however, of time's passage.

As he comments on the changes that time has brought to memorable locales and especially to human beings, he reminds us that the narrative is *set in a continuous action*. The Green Lane, where he used to walk in the hope of meeting Theo "is built all over with houses now" (lxxvi, 804). Looking at the Baroness Bernstein, George wistfully remarks, "Sure, 'tis hard with respect to beauty, that its possessor should not have even a life-enjoyment of it. . . . I would look in her face, and, out of the ruins, try to build up in my fancy a notion of her beauty in its prime." The sight of that "dilapidated palace" can produce imagined scenes of splendor, music, dazzling light, balls, feasts, laughter, and intrigue, but they all yield to a gloomy homily on "departed glories" (lxxiii, 777).

Perhaps the most notable survivals from the past in both narratives, however, are the family portraits. Depicted so often, they define an irrecoverable and yet influential presence. The Warrington brothers grow up in a house dominated not only by Rachel Esmond Warrington but also by the portrait of her father. When Harry first visits the English Castlewood, the family is absent, but he manages to persuade the housekeeper to let him see "my lady's sitting-room and the picture-room, where, sure enough, there was a portrait of his grandfather in periwig and breastplate, the counterpart of their picture in Virginia," and where he also sees "a likeness of his grandmother, as Lady Castlewood, in a yet earlier habit of Charles II's time; her neck bare, her fair golden hair waving over her shoulders in ringlets which he remembered to have seen snowy white" (ii, 12).

Returning to Castlewood for his first dinner there, he finds himself as much in the presence of "the pictures of the [older] family round the walls" (ii, 19), as in the midst of the present inhabitants.

The family pictures reappear in a number of full-page illustrations, as well, indicating their continuing, hovering presence. So too, family portraits appear in the illustrated initial letters of several chapters. George and Lord Castlewood "often looked at the colonel's grave picture as it still hung in the saloon," George with "an extraordinary interest" (lxxii, 764), the degenerate Lord Castlewood with a puzzled lack of understanding.

The most memorable of all the portrait scenes, however, occurs as young Harry and the Baroness talk in Castlewood's wainscoted parlor—she, with her old lady's knitting needles, sitting in front of Kneller's brilliant painting of "a young lady of three- or four-and-twenty, in the easy flowing dress and loose robes of Queen Anne's time— . . . a quantity of auburn hair, parted off a fair forehead, and flowing over pearly shoulders and a lovely neck" (iv, 42). Poor Harry, however, fails to recognize that the portrait is of *her*, the former Beatrix Esmond, and she can only respond to his failure to see her in the picture with a sighing acknowledgment, "Ah! Here is a sermon!" (iv, 43). George, at least, buys it after her death and keeps it with him (lxxxiii, 882) as an enduring fragment from the past. The novel's final illustration is of course another portrait: Bunbury's rendition of "Sir George, My Lady, and Their Master" (xcii, 1001), the aged Gumbo.

* * * * *

One might speak of the 19th and early 20th century as a time fragment energized by humans seeking the enduring meaning of resonant, articulate shards of experience, as one recalls Wordsworth leaving the ruins of Tintern Abbey and, on the banks of the Wye, discovering "in this moment . . . life and food / For future years;" Coleridge, uttering the wonderous achievement of his fragmentary vision in a dream, "Kubla Khan;" Byron, conscious of Venice's crumbling palaces but capable of seeing "from out the waves her structures rise," and, standing at night in the ruins of the Coliseum, feeling how "in this magic circle raise the dead"—as his predecessor, Gibbon, had felt while standing before the ruins of the Forum. One recalls Shelley, amid the tumult of autumnal commotion perceiving the reanimating force of the west wind; and Keats, in front of the Athenian marble fragments, feeling like "a sick eagle looking at the sky" as he experiences the magnitude that they shadow forth.

One recalls Tennyson, lamenting in memoriam and discovering how "The eternal landscape of the past" shall bloom; Browning, succumbing to a banal sense of love among generalized ruins, but able to discern in the specifics of the Campagna the infinite passion as well as "the pain / Of finite hearts that yearn;" Carlyle (like Pound) articulating in *Sartor Resartus* an intuited understanding that can arise from jotted fragments of writing recovered, so to speak, from a paper bag; Ruskin (again like Pound) proclaiming the enduring spiritual meaning of the loosening stones of Venice; Rossetti, rescuing in enduring memorials the painful fragments of a ruined relationship; Hopkins, discovering permanent spiritual significance in the wreck of *The Deutschland.*

One thinks of Arnold, after an arduous journey to the desolation of the Grande Chartreuse, and to the ultimate existential question—"what am I, that I am here?"—responsive to and yet appalled by the image of "a dead time's exploded belief," resisting the forces of anarchic dispersal, and attempting to articulate renewed grounds of meaningful human belief and conduct; Pater, a darker and more languid Arnold, accepting the "moments as they pass," valuing chiefly "the poetic passion, the desire of beauty, the love of art for its own sake"; Yeats, much more energetic, envisioning the lineaments of eternity in the dance of time; Eliot, in "The Waste Land" shoring the fragments of his inherited culture against his ruin, but finally able to proclaim in the "Four Quartets" that "history is a pattern / Of timeless moments;" and Pound, passionately struggling to make the radiant fragments cohere.

Thackeray, of course, was not a visionary poet and would never have claimed with Pound: "I gather the limbs of Osisis"; only Isis can do that. It takes a god to resurrect a god rather than to project a simulacrum. But Thackeray shared with his visionary kin the awareness of how past human experience can live in us, can be a continuing human presence—the awareness of our ability to reanimate, convey, and participate in that ongoing life, whether we are standing in the silent ruins of Pompeii, or in the turbulent wilderness of contemporary London.

Therefore Thackeray insists upon the reiterated nature of human experience and awareness. One thinks of Tennyson's father having the boy recite the four books of Horace's *Odes* on four successive mornings before permitting him to enter the world—a painfully exaggerated emphasis on repetition more than on responsive appreciation, but an emphasis that was presumably motivated by the wish to provide his son with a basis for perceiving and understanding what he would encounter in the world. In a chapter of *The Virginians* entitled "An Old Story," Thackeray asks "Are not [stories] all alike? What is the use, I say, of telling them over and over?" (xviii, 186). Of course, he then immediately goes on to answer his own question, by articulating the promptings of the human heart and imagination that beget and sustain the patterns of reiteration. The fable is told of us because, as Thackeray points out, we "renew . . . [it] for ever and ever" (xviii, 184).

The renewal animates our *personal* memories, to be sure, and when Harry Warrington "pulled out those faded vegetables [i.e. wilted "love" flowers] just now," the narrator acknowledges that he himself, like any "man or woman with a pennyworth of brains, or the precious like amount of personal experience, or who has read a novel before" [a telling claim], fell "to musing on former days when, etc." (xviii, 185)—a wonderfully expressive "etc.," with its sense of incompletion and yet inevitable extension. Even more, however, reiteration connects us with the *rest* of the human race. That is the ultimate, insistent meaning of the various languages of our culture: *"Kai ta loipa"* [and so forth] (xl, 419), "Et cetera, et cetera, et cetera" (lxvi, 699), *"Wir auch* have tasted *das irdische Glück;* we also have *gelebt und—und so weiter"* (xxxiii, 345-46), *"Und so weiter, und so weiter"* [and so forth] (xl, 419). Human nature is *not* "very much changed in the last hundred years" (xxiv, 253), or the last thousand. Customs may be different, but behavior is essentially the same, he implies.

The novelist, therefore, "depict[s] men *out* of their business"—not in the everyday details of "law, stock-broking, polemical theology, linen-drapery, apothecary business, and the like," but "in their passions, loves, laughters, amusements, hatreds, and what not" (lix, 604). A narrative, like human life itself, is *a continuous pageant of reenactment.* Consequently, an historical novel like *The Virginians* is an almost inevitable discourse for Thackeray, and even when evoking contemporary and near-contemporary experience, as in *The Newcomes,* he does so by remembering with advantages "general law[s] . . . not as old as the hills, to be sure, but as old as the people who walk up and down them" (xviii, 185).

Memory is not an indulgence, but an awakening—and an articulation of new as well as of reiterated speech. Some human beings—most of us, probably—"lose it," as the saying goes, increasingly experiencing the death-in-life that loss of memory brings, but there are the Thackerays and Nabokovs, who successfully call upon memory to speak the beloved and the new-found language (treasured in its own way, of course), and who can articulate how we sound the common ground-tone of our humanity even as we attempt to sing the princeliness of our hoped-for individuality. Memory gives us the gift of ourselves, as well as of those who have participated in our lives, and who have created the culture that we share. To *rejoice* in what we have *communally* been given by those whose awareness and language have enriched our lives, and yet to *accept* the temporality of what we have *individually* been given—as George Warrington and, of course, Horace assert (*resigno quae dedit*)—may well be greater than to *dare* (xcii, 989), and most probably will be less destructive, not only to us, but especially to those around us, as so much history testifies.

CHAPTER FIVE:

LOVEL THE WIDOWER

Lovel the Widower, as we know, took its origin from a dramatic comedy called *The Wolves and the Lamb* that Thackeray had written during the composition of *The Newcomes*—specifically between his return from Paris at the end of November 1854 and 17 March 1855, when he sent it off to receive what became the first of several refusals by London stage managers (*Letters*, III, 430, 450, IV, 148). *The Newcomes* includes a number of passages of extensive dialogue sustained by brief narrative phrases, but at this very time Thackeray also wrote several explicitly dramatic scenes consisting of unbroken dialogue introduced, as in a play, by italicized names of the speakers. Four of these overtly scenic conversations, chiefly involving Clive and Ethel, appeared in Volume II, chapter ix, pp. 82-96 (part of Number 15 for December 1854), while a similar passage of stage dialogue between Pen and Laura occurred in Volume II, chapter xi, pp. 105-7 (part of Number 16 for January 1855).

The Virginians does not emulate these passages of stage dialogue, but, as we have seen, it offers a considerable number of dramatic and semi-dramatic scenes. *Lovel the Widower*, however, in spite of having taken its origin from a stage comedy, gives special prominence to the narrator, who indeed becomes the chief personage by virtue of his foreground presence as a registering sensibility. He may be the chorus rather than the hero,[1] but he alone is always present: observing, explaining, commenting, as he overtly appeals to our experience as well as to his own. Evolving from a minor character,

Captain Touchit of the play, into a brief manuscript presence as Pendennis, and finally into the published form of a middle-aged, jilted, but still emotionally vulnerable, unmarried man, the narrator became a developed figure in his own right: Charles Batchelor.[2]

Correspondingly, as the narrator comes to take on such prominence, the scenic aspect of the narrative considerably diminishes. In fact, only about eight percent of the stage directions and dialogue of *The Wolves and the Lamb* appears in *Lovel's* narrative. The play's language does not manifest itself at all in chapter i, where the narrator elaborately establishes himself, only once in chapter v, and four times in chapter iv. The main appearances, therefore, occur in chapters ii (six times), iii (eleven times), and vi (six times).

We can also understand these developments by observing that only after nine pages of narration, much of which concerns Batchelor's life and feelings, do we hear dialogue: an exchange of merely four utterances between him and Elizabeth (I, i, 53). These brief phrases, moreover, are especially meant to characterize *him* (and indeed wonderfully articulate what we later come to recognize as his characteristic freezing of about-to-be-expressed emotion), as well as to help us understand his later failure to enact his desire for her:

"My dear—dear child," says I seizing her hand, "you don't suppose I fancy you—"
"No—no!" she says, drawing the large hand over her eyes. "No—no! but I saw it when you and Mr. Warrington last 'ad some. Oh! do have a patting lock!"
"A patent lock, my dear?" I remarked. "How odd that you, who have learned to pronounce Italian and French words so well, should make such strange slips in English? Your mother speaks well enough."

> "She was born a lady. She was not sent to be a milliner's girl, as I was, and then among those noisy girls at that—oh! that *place!*" cries Bessy, in a sort of desperation clenching her hand. (I, i, 53)

Thackeray's wonderful ability to convey Batchelor's dismayed awareness of her large hand, and Elizabeth's accomplished ability to emulate "a sort of" feeling make the exchange tellingly—and, indeed, foretellingly—expressive, however brief it may be.

The only other emergence of dialogue in the entire chapter, moreover, does not occur until the final page, where a little scene of eight utterances, reflected in a full-page illustration ("I Am Referred to Cecilia"), provides an amusing conclusion, notably as it articulates the reinstalled presence and pompous, stupifying language of a domineering mother-in-law (a misery that Thackeray well knew from personal experience), and the revelation that Elizabeth has become the governess of Lovel's[3] two children:

> "You seem surprised to see me here, Mr. Batchelor!" says her ladyship, with that grace and good breeding which she generally exhibited; for if she accepted benefits, she took care to insult those from whom she received them.
> "Indeed, no," said I, looking at Lovel, who piteously hung down his head. He had his little Cecy at his knee: he was sitting under the portrait of the defunct musician, whose harp, now muffled in leather, stood dimly in the corner of the room.
> "I am here not at my own wish, but from a feeling of duty towards that—departed—angel!" says Lady Baker, pointing to the picture.

"I am sure that when mamma was here, you were always quarrelling" says little Popham, with a scowl.
"This is the way those innocent children have been taught to regard me," cries grandmamma.
"Silence, Pop!" says papa, "and don't be a rude boy."
"Isn't Pop a rude boy?" echoes Cecy.
"Silence, Pop," continues papa, or you must go up to Miss Prior." (I, i, 60)

Here at the very end of the chapter, the dramatic principle briefly triumphs, with its clear expression of the past's overbearing influence upon the conflicts of the present, and also with its witty, largely concealed, and yet hinted-at promise of final resolution.

Inevitably, however, one needs to examine the remaining ninety-nine percent of Chapter i, and attempt to understand its special qualities as a Thackerayan narrative. It characteristically lacks a hero or a heroine (though the infatuated narrator uses the latter term to describe Elizabeth), but even more than its predecessors, *Lovel the Widower* presents a world without social or literary extremes. The initially anonymous narrator promises the familiar human experiences of love and marriage, grief and disappointment—but all in a context of flawed, not villainous behavior, without high life or low life, where servants and masters exist "on the same [human] level." Lady Baker may be a baronet's widow, but her behaviour thoroughly identifies her meanness—i.e. however awful, still not verging upon extremes. In spite of her pretenses, she is just "an abominable selfish old woman . . . ; an old sponger on other people's kindness . . . ; an old swindler of tradesmen, tyrant of servants, bully of the poor" (I, i, 44).

Indeed, after identifying the principal personage as a "muff," the narrator introduces a long passage of commentary intended to demonstrate that the mediocrity of muffdom characterizes most human beings, however relectant they may be to acknowledge it. This reluctance, moreover, prompts the narrator to identify a number of examples, extending from literary heroines to the clergy, the army, members of parliament, members of the peerage, and of course literary writers and their audiences: "Yes; perhaps even this one is read and written by—Well? *Quid rides?*" (I, i, 44-45). Here, of course, he mockingly clinches his argument with the familiar Horatian allusion: "Why do you laugh? Change the name and the tale is told of you" (*Satires*, I, i, 69-70).

The satire is, of course, genial, as befits the subject: human weakness—here comically provoked by a metaphoric "irresistible dish of temptation." Drawing members of his audience together with him in joint recognition, the narrator establishes a basis for addressing the reader as "dear friend": "the chances are that you and I are not people of the highest intellect, of the largest fortune, of the most ancient family, of the most consummate virtue, of the most faultless beauty in face and figure. . . . But we are not altogether brutal and unkind, and a few folks like us" (I, i, 45). With this encompassing passage, therefore, the narrator has provided a context for introducing Lovel, who is good-natured but very susceptible to being hen-pecked, well-off but not rich, good-looking in a sort of way, and has a country house, but only at Putney.

The narrator's idiosyncrasy soon begins to emerge, however, for he not only inserts himself into his narrative as a friend of the title-figure, but also soon displaces Lovel by giving lengthy expression to his own emotions, especially resentment at Lovel's wife and mother-in-law. The brief characterization of Lovel, therefore, turns into a long diatribe against Cecilia and Lady Baker for having taken a dislike to the narrator and driven him away. Part of what he says is delivered with humor, as when he speaks of the cold shoulder as "a joint I never could like" (I, i, 45), or when he directs irony against himself as he makes the seeming mock apology: "Kindnesses are easily forgotten; but injuries!—what worthy man does not keep *those* in mind?" When he succumbs to his resentment, however, he terms Cecilia "a lean, scraggy, lackadaisical, egotistical, consequential, insipid creature," and elaborates upon his prior characterization of Lady Baker. He can even anathematize her, though she is literally absent, as "You old Catamaran" (I, i, 46), testifying to her persistent, disturbing presence in his consciousness.

Before beginning his narrative proper, however, the narrator nervously denies any wish to depict actual people, asserting that though his account is true, it is not literally veracious. The revelation that Lovel has now remarried (though "now" and "then" are hardly ever clearly identified) appears almost as an aside in the midst of the narrator's disclaimers, until it suddenly reemerges as a justification for his alleged lack of literality: "I dine at Lovel's still; his company and cuisine are amongst the best in London. If they suspected I was taking them off, he and his wife would leave off inviting me."

One can understand the triumph of self-interest here, but his ensuing remark is somewhat puzzling: "Would any man of a generous disposition lose such a valued friend for a joke, or be so foolish as to show him up in a story?" (I, i, 47). Does he really believe that he is acting out of generosity, or is the term an expression of playfully ironic self-mockery? Here we are confronted with an issue that Thackeray seems to have presented to us as a deliberate challenge to our understanding—perhaps as a hint to us of the narrator's limited self-awareness.

When the speaker finally begins his narrative of life on Beak Street, he speaks of it as "the curtain of our present drama draw[ing] up," but continues to make direct addresses to the reader: "You will not see," "you will please to suppose," and especially "You are right. Elizabeth is the principal character in this story" (I, i, 48). Having already identified Lovel's present wife as Elizabeth (I, i, 47), with this present statement he has effectively communicated the story's outcome, implicitly asking us to concentrate instead on the comical maneuvering that leads up to it. He also reveals himself as a narrator whose thoughts generally do not fall into a linear sequence so much as they form associative patterns. As a result, he is susceptible to the temptations of digression.

After an account of Elizabeth's theatrical occupation and her use of her money to support her family, for example, the narrator contrasts her behavior with that of Miss Montanville, who fulfills the stereotype of the actress as kept woman, but soon finds himself not just providing an account of Miss Montanville's finery, but being caught up in a long disquisition on her selfishness, a disabling injury that she suffered, and her subsequent career as a box-opener—details that have little to do with the original contrast between a poor virtuous actress and her opposite. Similarly, after providing an amusing picture of Elizabeth as a Cinderella—that prominent Thackerayan motif—who has to leave her finery behind her at midnight every evening at the theatre, the narrator turns to a characterization of the lodgers at her mother's boarding-house, and then goes off into biographical details concerning one of them, Slumley, even alluding to a meeting with the man some years later in a lobby of the opera (I, i, 51).

Again, the details are not quite irrelevant, but are definitely peripheral. By way of a parallel but more relevant procedure, however, the narrator, after having called up knowledgeable memories of a stage "regiment of Sea-nymphs, or Bayadères, or Fairies, or Mazurka maidens (with their fluttering lances or little scarlet slyboots!" [I, i, 52]) prancing in the theatre, evokes a later conversation, one with the impressario, Dolphin (whom we have met in *Pendennis*), but one that testifies to Elizabeth's independence in real life from the Faust-Margaret relationship. In this case, the reiterated procedure provides reinforcing testimony that seems part of a larger narrative pattern, not just an indulgence. Seemingly inexplicable procedure follows as the narrator asks three highly relevant questions, none of which he answers: "why should a poor lodging-house keeper make such a mighty secret of having a daughter earning an honest guinea by dancing at a theatre? Why persist in calling the theatre an academy? Why did Mrs. Prior speak of it as such, to me who knew what the truth was, and to whom Elizabeth herself made no mystery of her calling?" (I, i, 52). All that directly follows these puzzling questions is the first passage of dialogue, in which the narrator and Elizabeth discuss a quite different subject: the leakage from his brandy-bottle down the thirsty throat of her mother, the landlady.

And what narratively succeeds this only moderately heart-rending conversation? Revelation of the great trauma of the narrator's emotional life, as epitomised by old letters, a glove, and an outgrown waistcoat recently rediscovered in a box unopened for fifteen years: "some letters written—never mind by whom—and an old glove that I used to set an absurd value by; and that emerald-green tabinet waistcoat[4] which . . . I wore at the L—d L—t—nt's ball, Ph—n—x Park, Dublin, once, when I danced with *her* there!" Here we have the disabling experience of his life, introduced with what we will come to recognize as his need to refer to its significance, but also his inability to express its pain in other than a repressed, comically dismissive manner. Hence he jokingly speaks of the waistcoat rather than of his emotions ("It would no more meet round my waist now than round Daniel Lambert's"), and then indulges in a sententious observation that utterly belies his feelings: "How we outgrow things!" (I, i, 53).

In what one comes to recognize as a typical psychic gesture, he then circles back—in this case giving a narrative account, not of the failure of his love affair, but of how he came to be a lodger at Mrs.

Prior's. It may have been precipitated by the urging of her brother, his old master at St. Boniface's (Pen's college), Oxbridge, but we soon see that the primary reasons are emotional. He has *already* indicated his need to be cared for, even if just by "that mutton broth which Elizabeth made so well" (I, i, 52)—once again told to us out of temporal narrative sequence because the patterns of juxtaposition are more important than linear discourse.

Similarly, he *now* confesses himself to be "a confirmed invalid," but we most especially see his emotional invalidism in his *initial* attraction to the Prior children and to Elizabeth ("then only just emerging from childhood") because of his rejection by that "some one" in Dublin, who *now* has children of her own. From that *past* debacle he *now* announces that he takes his permanent identity: "Mr. Batchelor" (I, i, 54). In short, the movement of the narrative up to this point now reveals itself to have been a *collage* of self-definition. The modernity of *Lovel's* technique is unmistakable.

* * * * *

In what we now recognize as a characteristic impulse, Batchelor, after identifying himself to us by "name," recalls how he learned quadrilles in order to dance with "her" during a long vacation, and then represses the emotion: "Be still, thou foolish heart!" (I, i, 54). When he next speaks—of having misspent his time as an undergraduate and having left Oxbridge without a degree (like his creator)—we understand that for him the emotional and academic failures are fundamentally linked. As he then returns in thought to the university years, he presents what he seems to think of as a contrasting experience: the beginning of his continuing friendship with Lovel, though he also admits to having then shared the "flattery, worldliness, [and] mammon-worship" of his fellow undergraduates, and now acknowledges that "it was very base and mean of us to like a man chiefly on account of his money."

Like a true Thackerayan narrator, he calls it "an old story about parasites and flatterers" (I, i, 55), but here again in Batchelor's account we see the juxtaposition of his current with his youthful attraction to the enticements of Lovel's table: "I dine at Lovel's still; his company and cuisine are amongst the best in London" (I, i, 47); "it [was] pleasanter to come to [him] and have good dinners, and good wine, than to go to Jack Highson's dreary tea and turnout, or to Ned Roper's abominable Oxbridge port." As a result, one questions whether the mammon-worship has ever ceased.

Like a number of Thackerayan predecessors, Batchelor finds himself imprisoned for debt by a bailiff ("at Mr. Shackell's horrible hotel" [I, i, 55]), but in spite of his release by Lovel, he creates for himself a new imbroglio by emulating another unfortunate model, Moses Primrose, as he entangles himself with two unsavory characters from *Pendennis*, Honeyman and Sherrick, in buying a newspaper (like his creator). Here again the basic human patterns and the Thackerayan articulations join, even more so as Batchelor rationalizes his folly by attempting to implicate the reader: "I daresay I made a gaby of myself to the world: pray, my good friend, hast thou never done likewise?"

Recollection of the newspaper and its deadlines prompts remembrance of a character new to the narrative, teen-aged Dick Bedford, Batchelor's printer's devil, infatuated with Elizabeth, and therefore a counterpart of the narrator. What distinguishes Bedford from the narrator, however, is his quality of being "touching" (I, i, 57)—his ability to evoke affection—a quality to which Batchelor can at least sympathetically respond, even if he cannot prompt it in other people, except for Lovel. By contrast, of course, we see Elizabeth, who is defined by her ability to attract affection, but more especially by her chilling inability to love others: "she said he was a strange child" (I, i, 58). Once more the narrative principle is that of juxtaposition, not sequential unfolding.

CHAPTER FIVE

After having avoided answering several significant questions six pages earlier, Batchelor (now admitting to the Christian name of Charles), raises and answers these and others—as the installment nears its conclusion—by providing exposition concerning Elizabeth's and especially Lovel's family background. Batchelor also returns to earlier material, however, notably the cold shoulder given him by Lovel's wife that keeps him away from Lovel's home for a period now identified as eight years, which ends with her death. The concluding scene then takes place—in the oppressive presence, however, of Cecilia's portrait and her now only nominally silent harp: "'The harp that *once*' indeed! the accursed catgut scarce knew any other music, and 'once' was a hundred times at least in *my* hearing" (I, i, 59). It will sound again.

Chapter Two's title, "In Which Miss Prior is Kept at the Door," expresses Batchelor's characteristic hesitation, as he follows the brief dramatic scene at the end of the first chapter, revealing that Elizabeth has become the governess of Lovel's children, with an articulation of the memories erupting from that sudden juxtaposition of past and present. What we need to follow, therefore, is the conflict-ridden movement of his awareness—a movement that of course constantly returns upon itself in an immobilized need to confess its anguish. He reveals the inescapability of his memory as he acknowledges how, a week before the scene at Lovel's house, he had revisited his former lodgings at Beak Street—unable to forget the intensity of his confessions to Elizabeth about his devastating rejection by Glorvina.

The bizarre new inhabitants of the boardinghouse define his alienation from his past, and its irrecoverability, except in memory. Most especially, however, by assimilating the denizens of Beak Street and Leicester Square, some blocks to the east—always for Thackeray an area of shabby continental bohemian exile—Batchelor feels himself prompted to speculate about the possibilities of their lives, however preposterous, and thereby to express his sense of the confinements of his own existence. Most amusingly of all, Thackeray has Batchelor succumb to the appeal of another new inhabitant, the proprietor of an entirely novel science—photography. He agrees to "Step in, and 'ave it done. Your correct likeness" (I. ii, 234). That, of course, is what we have been seeking.

What is a "correct likeness"? A shadowy image upon a photographic plate, with a head and body rigidly held in place? (Thackeray had had many occasions to ask this question, both in England and America.) A formal oil portrait like Cecilia's, suspended upon the wall of a family house? A quickly sketched drawing by a responsive friend like Maclise or Laurence? A brilliant passage of imaginative writing? A satirical challenge to unworthy behavior? An expression of a man's loving regard? A responsive tribute to his humanity? An insightful joke at his expense?

For poor Batchelor, the "likeness" provides just a reiterated sense of his loss, of his absurd hope that he might still mean something to "her" (the impossibility of which is suggested by the image of his "forehead as bare as a billiard ball" [I, ii, 234])—an appropriate simile, considering that she never seemed to consider the relationship as any more than a game. In retrospect, Batchelor seems unable to decide whether his is a tragedy or not, though it is an easier decision for us. As he recalls his confessions of pain to a seemingly compassionate and love-abandoned Elizabeth, his reiterations seem to declare the reality of "our tragedy," but as usual he soon flees to the opposite emotional viewpoint, pretending to call it "RUBBISH," and seeking to emulate Horatian indifference to the slights of Fortune (*si celeres quatit / pinnas, resigno quae dedit* [I, ii, 235]).

In a very real sense, one could argue that Batchelor's unrecognized search is to discover his actual "likeness." The full-page illustration accompanying Chapter ii, "Bessy's Spectacles," depicting

Batchelor holding up Elizabeth's disguising eyeglasses in an interrogative way, certainly raises the issue of perspective, and certainly does not reveal a Batchelor with a billiard ball forehead, but, rather, an appropriately hirsute, though notably susceptible young man—one strangely at odds with his earlier verbal self-portraits. "Do you mean that I am painting a portrait [i.e. of a "muff"] which hangs before me every morning in the looking-glass when I am shaving?" (I, i, 45). "I am a confirmed invalid." "I am a steady, a *confirmed* old bachelor" (capable still of wishing to propose marriage, however [I, i, 54]).

Another early passage suggested that university life especially prompted absurd illusions: "Those prints we ordered *calidi juventâ;* those shirt-studs and pins which the jewellers would persist in thrusting into our artless bosoms; those fine coats we would insist on having for our books, as well as ourselves" (I, i, 55). His writings for *The Museum*, as we have also seen, constituted another foolish attempt to construct a likeness. With a little more maturity, however, he can assert a sense of identity by recognizing what he is *not:* one of the shabby inheritors of Beak Street, especially the current occupant of his former chambers, who has the appalling name of Plugwell (I, ii, 234).

Batchelor convincingly defines himself by his tolerance of Mrs. Prior's extortionate bills, her guzzling of his sherry and brandy, and her slanderous comments about his assertion of her indebtedness to him—as well as by his kindness in securing employment for Elizabeth and a brother, and in helping to place another brother at a charity school. He also defines himself, however, by the literary and historical models that he evokes in order to characterize himself—not only the Horatian example already cited, but also by his typically Thackerayan evocation of Dido's sympathetic understanding of human suffering (in this case the privations of the widow Prior and her children): "I was not ignorant of misfortune, and knew how to succour the miserable" (*Non ignara mali miseris succurrere disco* [I, ii, 243]). More amusingly, he proclaims his understanding of wrongful accusation on the basis of having heard Rossini's opera, *La Gazza Ladra* (1817), and his knowledge of siren-singing from having read *The Odyssey* and having heard Bellini's *Il Pirata* (1827). Most comically of all, he self-mockingly calls his desolate heart a Persepolis, a Tadmor, a Palmyra (a telling redundancy), deserted by its destructive Zenobia, its shattered columns left alone in cold, marmorean stillness (I, ii, 246). These are the thoughts—he would have us believe—that rushed through his mind as he beheld Bessie's spectacles, and as he then heard the voices that erupted to constitute the scene suspended for almost the entire second serial installment, devoted as it has been to retrospection, and drawing upon the dialogue of *The Wolves and the Lamb* only in the most fragmentary way. In short, his discourse constantly plays between the touching and the ludicrous, the grandiose and the reductive.

For much of the third installment, Batchelor sets about discovering "the secrets of the house" (I, iii, 344) and loosely narrates the experiences of his first and second day there, but again his main recurring subject is his rejection by Glorvina, who is mentioned a half-dozen times. As a means of consolation, he evokes the pleasures of being a bachelor guest at Shrublands, and unknowingly imitates the attitude of Aesop's fox after having been unable to reach the grapes. He also consciously and amusingly inverts the celebratory language of Horace and Vergil. The *"domus et placens / uxor"* (home and pleasing wife) praised by the former appears in Batchelor's version as a nagging wife, a grey mare, while the child in her palace (*parvulus aulâ*) tenderly longed for by Dido (to whom Batchelor had compared himself in the previous serial installment), who could have given her some solace after Aeneas's departure, emerges in Batchelor's imagination as "a roaring baby" (I, iii, 331) who keeps a poor father up all night. Though he comically diminishes *The Bible's* Ruth, by terming the scavenging Mrs. Prior a Ruth gleaning in the household of Lovel (I, iii, 338), he also comically inflates Bedford by likening him to Swift at Shene serving as Temple's secretary (developed at some length in Thackeray's lecture), and to Spartacus before his rebellion. Horace's Black Care, however, appears in his usual troubling guise, though comically described as being "not only behind the horseman, but behind the footman; and not only on the footman, but on the buxom shoulders of the lady's maid" (I, iii, 333). Such universality reappears in yet more familiar form as "an old story told over again" (I, iii, 335) between Bedford and Mary Pinhorn, and between Elizabeth and Bedford: "'It's the old—old story,' says Dick. 'It's you and the Hirish girl over again, sir'" (I, iii, 341).

Batchelor, morever, in sympathizing with Pinhorn can cite and, at least momentarily, endorse a favorite Thackerayan quotation from Schiller: "*Ich habe genossen das irdische Glück—ich habe—geliebt!*" (I have enjoyed earthly good fortune—I have—loved [I, iii, 335]).[5] As a more distant observer of the struggles and passions going on at Shrublands, however, he becomes capable of uttering a choric observation first articulated by Vergil: "*hi motus animorum atque haec certamina tanta / pulveris exigui iactu compressa quiescunt*" (all these passions and such great struggles as these will be contained and quieted down by the throwing of a little dust [I, iii, 340]).

Aside from this richer texture of allusion, the third installment is also notable for the increased frequency and the extensiveness of its dialogue. Thus we hear not only bits of breakfast and dinner conversation, but witness an emotional scene between Bedford and Pinhorn, and most especially a scene involving Bedford, Mrs. Prior, Pop, Cissy, and Lovel. The latter scene not only appears in the form of a theatre text, with italicized identifications of the speakers, but also contains language (I, iii, 335-38) used in *The Wolves and the Lamb*. Indeed, though the speech headings come to disappear, most of the rest of the chapter consists of dialogue. Accordingly, language of the theatre brings it to conclusion, as Batchelor refers to "one or two little comedies going on in the house" (I, iii, 344), and finally announces that he will draw the curtain on the final quarrelsome "scene" with Lady Baker, which concludes "this absurd little act" (I, iii, 345).

A moderate occurrence of dialogue, though without as much relatedness to *The Wolves and the Lamb*, characterizes the fourth serial installment, which also lacks the wit and audacity of the previous chapter's playful allusiveness. Allusions to the enduring attractions of Batchelor's remembered image of Glorvina, and to his "namby-pamby" subservience to those sentimental memories continue to define him, while his major Horatian reference pointedly serves to introduce another of his exaggerated images of middle-aged decline: "the fugacious years have lapsed, my Posthumus! [*Eheu fugaces, Postume, Postume / labuntur anni*] My waist is now a good bit wider than my chest, and it is decreed that I shall be alone!" (I, iv, 395)—just before he mumbles an incoherent proposal of marriage to Eliza (I, iv, 402). An allusion to Bluebeard provides a final connective image, as the second installment's reference to semi-attachment and to a mutual locking-up of that terrible secret room "where the skeleton was" (I, ii, 246), joins with the dread of what we don't know about about our marital partner (I, iii, 331), and with Batchelor's request to be recognized as an appeasable Bluebeard (I, iv, 401).

Referring to himelf as a "stout elderly man, short in stature and in wind" (I, v, 583), who could not possibly have responded to Captain Baker's affont to Eliza—again, a verbal image totally belied by the youthful illustrations of his face and figure drawn by Thackeray for installments two and five— Batchelor reveals his circumspection, otherwise known as cowardice. From here until the end of the comedy he acts in a continually bifurcated way, romanticising himself as an Ivanhoe capable of rescuing Rebecca (Eliza) from Sir Brian de Bois Guilbert (the drunken Captain Baker), and then quiveringly withdrawing from the terrifying image of himself as "a bullied father of ten children. (Eliza has a fine high temper of her own)" (I, v, 584). Similarly, he imagines what a horrific life he would lead with Eliza's family preying upon him (I, v, 589-90), only to yield to a soporific notion of safe conduct through such a minefield that prompts a renewed proposal of marriage (I, v, 592-93).

Batchelor's feebleness is all too apparent, but his saving grace of witty self-mockery comes to manifest itself, of course, not only in his discomfort with his pathetic marital proposals, but also in the recovery of a larger, though thoroughly comic sense of dismayed absurdity. He *is* not only an inept Ivanhoe but also an ineffectual Fortinbras (I, v, 586), a ludicruously suffering Othello (I, vi, 654), a permanent Wandering Alien, an unrescuable Robinson Crusoe, a permanently frustrated ghost witnessing the union of his former love with his successor (I, vi, 655), and a seeker of Stygian forgetfulness (I, vi, 656). Like a typical Thackerayan speaker, he exists in that indeterminate realm where the permanently recurring enactments of human conduct and the bizarre individuality of human ludicruousness join. Inevitably, for the intertwining represented by *Lovel the Widower* and *The Wolves and the Lamb*, the comedy ends with a mixed metaphor: not just a descent of the curtain, but also a parting of narrator and reader (I, vi, 668).

CHAPTER SIX:

THE ADVENTURES OF PHILIP

Thackeray's next long novel, as its title immediately tells us, focuses on the history of a single chief character, not a family like the Newcomes. Like that earlier novel, *The Adventures of Philip* concerns itself with attempts to establish or maintain wealth and social status, but it narrows its social scope in order to concentrate especially upon the relationship between Philip and his parasitical father. In doing so, it evokes the larger, characteristically Thackerayan contexts of individual and communal memory. Though a darker novel than *The Newcomes*, beginning with the literal and metaphoric issues of death and survival, it also celebrates the revivifying powers of memory and the supportiveness, not just the numbing indifference, prompted in other people by the harshness of one's own experience.

Beginning with a remembered conversation among people some of whom are now deceased and some still surviving, it immediately speaks of the sickness of a young boy whose parents are absent, the possibility of transmitting a potentially fatal disease, and of our inevitable descent "towards the valley of the shadows."[1] As its full title emphasizes, *The Adventures of Philip on his way through the World; Shewing Who Robbed Him, Who Helped Him, and Who Passed Him By*, the novel's central metaphor expresses human life as a journey (not a quest), where one is assaulted and passed by, but where one also finds Samaritan assistance to provide succour—a word that, like "Samaritan," occurs very often to help lighten the novel's darkness.[2]

CHAPTER SIX

The journey begins in history and literature as the narrator in chapter ii re-animates the streets of eighteenth century London, even while being conscious of the ensuing "decline and fall of city sovereignties" not altogether unworthy of a Gibbon's attention, and being aware that the "lives of streets are as the lives of men" (III, ii, 14): their history is a narrative of disappearance held only, and only partly, in memory. The portraits of Pen's and Philip's mothers, however precious, may be mere "painted shadows on the wall" (III, i, 7), but the marvellous stage characters, actors, operas, and dramas witnessed by enthusiastic youth—Mirabel, Mercutio, Faulconbridge, Long Tom Coffin, Vanderdecken, Charles Kemble, Fanny Kemble, *Semiramide, La Donna del Lago*, and even *The Bottle Imp* and melodramas of the Adelphi Theatre—constitute an enduringly vital legacy with "a flavour of Elysium" (III, ii, 15). [3]

Remembrances of "this life-journey of ours" (III, ii, 11) also find origins in schoolboy experiences, like those recounted at the beginning of chapter ii, where several mature dinner-companions of the narrator (Pendennis) recall being assaulted by a flogging headmaster. Although memory causes them to "become young again," time has brought stultifying consolation, so that they can converse and laugh for a good hour at the brutality of his conduct, and accept it because they think of him as "a thorough gentleman" (III, ii, 10). Here we first meet the question of how one can deal with victimization when one is in part a willing accomplice—a question that emerges only years later in the lives of these individuals, but that extends throughout the novel and that challenges rigid, conventional pieties, like those of the narrator's wife, Laura.

Clearly, with the revelation at the end of the first serial installment that Firmin, like the Bible's David, is "the man!" (III, iii, 24) appropriately to be denounced for sexually exploiting a woman, the issue of victimization becomes paramount. The circumstances of Firmin's hoaxing and deserting of Caroline in "A Shabby Genteel Story" of 1840 briefly re-emerge, but the immediate and prominent legacy is an understandable, permanent distrust in his son of Firmin's motives and conduct. Even to the youthful Pendennis, who appreciates Dr. Firmin's generosity, he is nevertheless inexplicably yet appropriately to be distrusted, as the old verses regarding "Dr. Fell" (III, i, 8, ii, 12) authenticate: "I do not love thee, Dr. Fell, / The reason why I cannot tell; / But this I know and know full well, / I do not love thee, Dr. Fell."

The journey also begins in fable, with a Bluebeard skeleton in the closet (vignette initial for Chapter iii), emblemizing not only Dr. Firmin's secret, which is to be revealed at the chapter's end, but also—more generally—all the "corpses of our dead loves" [plural] (III, iii, 18). Aesop's fable of the frog wishing to expand to the size of an ox animates the full-page illustration that introduces the second serial installment, "Mr. Frog requests the honour of Prince Ox's company at dinner," and his jackdaw with peacock feathers appearing in the vignette initial that inaugurates chapter iv also typifies the social posturings of the Twysdens, and recalls to us the fables that introduce *The Newcomes*. In Philip's case, his journey has a *new* beginning, as he is rescued from the socially indifferent figure of Horace's *"pallida mors"* [pale Death] (III, iii, 19) by a caring doctor and nurse, during his parents' absence in the Isle of Wight, where Dr. Firmin continues his social attendance upon the Grand Duke of Groningen.

The Twysdens also, of course, emulate the Levite in the Biblical parable, being quite indifferent to anything but their own aspirations, which are as nasty as their entertainments, featuring as they do not only blatantly hypocritical behavior but also the accompanying wretchedness of "feeble champagne; . . . public-house sherry; . . . acrid claret; . . . clammy port . . . [and] horrible meals" (III, iv,

167)—in short, "vinegar and chopped hay" (III, iv, 168). Here Pendennis can speak as an appalled victim of such so-called banquets, but as he is led to speak more generally about gossip, then life-histories, and finally "conscientious history-books" (III, iv, 174), he seems to become Thackeray the novelist as well as Pendennis the narrator, and to express the creative tension between an active participant and a more distant observer. Thus he speaks as a personally knowledgeable biographer, as a novelist who sometimes contradicts himself, and also as an "infallible historian" (III, iv, 175). The nature of this encompassing and unstable expression is, of course, distinctively Thackerayan.

Pendennis' humor, however, expresses itself in grimmer, less buoyant terms than in earlier novels. He indeed advises partakers of Twysden breakfasts not to "ask for a roc's egg, but eat that moderately fresh hen's egg which John brings you" (III, iv, 175), but more usually he ironically advocates, for example, with a rather stern wit, hypocritical submission to arrogant dominance ("as the punishment is one for edification" [III, iv, 168]). Similarly, he mocks youthful infatuation and asks: "Is it that (lean, or fat, or stumpy, or tall) woman with all those children whom you once chose to break your heart about; and do you still envy Jones?" So too, the fable of Cinderella appears not in order to celebrate the ability to discern beauty in narrow circumstances, but to mock the worship of manifested wealth: "Could people see Cinderella's beauty when she was in rags by the fire, or until she stepped out of her fairy coach in her diamonds?" (III, iv, 174).

Partly, of course, he is responding to the nature of his subject, as he reports the hypocritical behavior of the Twysdens and their fatuous conversation. Even more, he uses the sardonic Lord Ringwood to mock their folly with Aesop's fable of the two incompatible pots floating down the stream of life—as Steyne had Becky—and of course with the Horatian alternative to ostentatious living: "a maid and a leg of mutton" (III, v, 181). He also responds to the inexplicably different patterns of human conduct that can prompt in an onlooker-participant both an appalled awareness of evil and a bewildered gratitude for the miracle of goodness.

In doing so, he recalls Biblical language, that of Matthew and Luke, speaking of the obscuring beam in our eyes, of how we bring forth that which is in our heart, of how we "go through life, stumbling, and slipping, and staggering," with a rueful awareness of our "own wretched weakness," and of how we can appropriately, in the words of *The Lord's Prayer*, quietly ask that we "not be led into temptation" (III, v, 183). And then, with a startling change of attitude, he issues a fiercely ironical apology for denigrating worldly success: "I praise and admire success wherever I meet it. I make allowance for faults and shortcomings, especially in my superiors; . . . I trust I don't offend. Have I said anything painful? . . . I recal the expression. I regret it. I contradict it flat" (III, v, 184).

In a lighter mood, marking a brief return of the youthful Pendennis (and his creator), he offers a celebration of Bohemia as a joyful alternative to a life of worldly ambition:

> A pleasant land, not fenced with drab stucco, like Tyburnia or Belgravia; not guarded by a huge standing army of footmen; not echoing with noble chariots; not replete with polite chintz drawing-rooms and neat tea-tables; a land over which hangs an endless fog, occasioned by much tobacco; a land of chambers, billiard-rooms, supper-rooms, oysters; a land of song; a land where soda-water flows freely in the morning; a land of tin-dish covers from taverns, and frothing porter; a land of lotos-eating (with lots of cayenne pepper), of pulls on the river, of delicious reading of novels, magazines, and saunterings in many studios; a land where men call each other by their Christian names; where most are poor, where almost all are young, and where if a

few oldsters do enter, it is because they have preserved more tenderly and carefully than other folks their youthful spirits, and the delightful capacity to be idle. I have lost my way to Bohemia now, but it is certain that Prague is the most picturesque city in the world. (III, v, 186)

The mature, somewhat disillusioned Pendennis, "whose days are already not few in the land" III, v, 185), having an acute awareness that "Yesterday is gone," therefore takes special pleasure in yesterday's being "very well remembered; and we think of it the more now we know that To-morrow is not going to bring us much" (III, vi, 273). Hence his repeated celebration of Bohemia, oysters, smoking, song, and idleness—even the morning after's sodawater—but he also knows, along with Philip and his own creator, that "Man was meant to labour," as well as "to be lazy" (III, vii, 281)—to emulate the workers in the field as well as the lilies (III, vi, 277).

Subsequently reflecting upon labor, he decides (along with Thackeray, it would appear) that "To be a painter, and to have your hand in perfect command, I hold to be one of life's *summa bona*.... Each day there must occur critical moments of supreme struggle and triumph, when struggle and victory must be both invigorating and exquisitely pleasing." He sees J.J. Ridley, therefore, as a model of human happiness. "Black care may have sat in crupper on that Pegasus, but has never unhorsed the rider" (III, vi, 275-76).

For less fortunate mortals, there are nevertheless the pleasures of the inkstand and of genial company—formerly, at least, at places like the Haunt, the memory of which prompts a notable cry of *ubi sunt?*: "Where is the Haunt now? and where are the merry men all who there assembled? The sign is down; the song is silent; the sand is swept from the floor; the pipes are broken, and the ashes are scattered" (III, vii, 282). Having literally disappeared, the Haunt exists only in memory, along with less roisterous customs like a "modest supper": "The homely little meal has almost vanished out of our life now.... I can see friendly faces smiling round such a meal, at a period not far gone, but how distant!" (III, vi, 273). Here again Pen struggles with the problem of the uncontrollable disappearance of innocent pleasure, not only in the form of specific instances, but even more as a custom, indeed as a comfortable and comforting institution.

By contrast we experience the posturings, the tensions, and the imperfectly concealed hostilities of Philip's call-dinner. In a chapter whose very title identifies the old, revivifying wine of *The Aeneid* (*"implentur veteris Bacchi,"*), and which quietly evokes the Horatian pleasures of reposing "comfortably in the arbour under the arched vine" (III, vii, 281), we hear the drunken babble of "young men . . . who quoted their Greek and their Horace glibly" (III, vi, 275), and Dr. Firmin's pedantic citation from Ovid in praise of the liberal arts: *"ingenuas dedicisse fideliter artes / emollit mores [nec sinit esse feros]"* [faithful study of the liberal arts softens men's manners (and makes them civilized)] (III, vii, 284)—but not in his case, except superficially.

The cultural inheritance is wasted upon him, and he, as we discover, will steal Philip's literal inheritance. Meanwhile, the smoldering antagonisms call forth genuine classical articulation in Philip, as he recalls the suspended Damoclean sword (in Horace's language *"destrictus ensis . . . pendet"*), thinks of Horace's fires hidden under deceitful ashes (*"incedis per ignes / suppositos cineri doloso"*), and anticipates in his own life the eruption of Vesuvius over Pompeii (III, vii, 292-93). Fortunately, however, he also has the ability to remember an old German song, "Dr. Luther," and, like his creator, to sing to gathered friends its celebratory verses, culminating in the enduring refrain:

> Who loves not wine, woman, and song,
> He is a fool his whole life long. (III, vii, 289)

His choice of an individual woman unfortunately leaves much to be desired, as he imagines himself to be in love with Agnes Twysden. Pen accurately terms it "only a little brief delusion of the senses" (III, ix, 391) from which he is rescued when Agnes reveals herself to have her eye solely on "the main chance" (III, ix, 393). If Philip is a Corydon piping his music to her, she is a "Phyllis, who, all the time . . . has Melibœus in the cupboard" (III, ix, 391-92)—the pastoral language, of course, mocking the hard-eyed calculations of the contemporary urban marriage-market.

In a similar manner, Thackeray characteristically joins the nineteenth century with ancient history, when he has Pendennis identify the trade as prostitution, seeing the counterparts of the current mercenary London woman as Laïs, Phryne, and Aspasia (III, ix, 394). The implied text, inevitably, is *mutato nomine,* overtly identified a few pages later when Pendennis asks, "Is it of your ladyship this fable is narrated?" (III, ix, 397). In terms of another recurrent metaphor, he remarks: "As in a theatre booth at a fair there are two or three performances in a day, so in Beaunash Street a little genteel comedy is played twice" (III, ix, 399)—once for each suitor.

Immersed, as the narrative comes to be, in the details of Hunt's threatening appearances, larger patterns emerge only briefly in immediately succeeding chapters. Hunt glibly quotes Horace, trivializing his cultural inheritance by proclaiming a common university experience of reading classical literature in order to assert a social equality, and in the process distorting Horace's use of *pallida mors* (III, x, 404), though the clarity of the Horatian language shines to readers through the complacent darkness of Hunt's discourse. Similarly, he fails to obscure the meaning of the parable of the prodigal son by reducing it to the enjoyment of "a good fillet of veal" (III, x, 406)—i.e. fatted calf.

We depend instead on the narrator, so as to participate in the wit of *his* use of Horace—*nunc vinum, cras aequor*—in order to characterize Dr. Firmin's use of wine to stupify Hunt and thereby gain time for a stategic maneuver, or so as to share in the narrator's quiet evocation of Goethe's "Zueignung": "Ah, ghosts of youth, again ye draw near!" (III, xi, 564), or to enjoy the playfulness of his terming Caroline's attempt to distract Philip from the shock of Hunt's accusation of illegitimacy as the act of "the little innocent Delilah coaxing and wheedling this young Sampson" (III, x, 567). Similarly, we question with him the appropriateness of Justice proceeding with the haltingness of a *pede claudo* (III, xii, 572), experience once again the terror of an overhanging sword (III, xii, 568, 576), sympathize with a physician's need to heal himself (Luke, 4: 23 [III, xii, 572]), understand that thoughtless Macheaths wound the Pollys and Lucys they leave behind (III, xii, 573), and participate in the *"quidquid agunt homines"* (III, xii, 579), the diverse acts of human beings that form the subject of his narrative, as well as the narratives of his predecessors.

  The two ensuing chapters (Number 6 for June 1861) even more actively draw together the classical, the proverbial, the Biblical, and the more modern, from figures like Marcus Junius Brutus sacrificing his sons (III, xiii, 644, xiv, 656) as a ironic counterpart of Talbot Twysden attempting to sacrifice his nephew, Philip; Twysden as an Aesopian monkey attempting to use the cat's paw of a lawyer (III, xiii, 642); Agnes doffing the old love and putting on the new (III, xiv, 652); Dr. Firmin as an Abraham sacrificing his son (III, xiv, 665); Agnes pleading the precedent of "the notorious Mrs. Robin Gray" (III, xiv, 656); Agnes hypocritically singing George Peele's wonderful verses of fidelity, "His golden locks time hath to silver turned" (III, xiv, 658); and of course the articulate Horace, whose language appears seven times, speaking of royal ancestors (III, xiii, 645), the universality of fables (III, xiv, 656), the appropriateness of bequeathing valid insights (III, xiv, 662), and—even though pompously conveyed by Dr. Firmin to his son—the neccessity of stoical acceptance, and of the ability to withstand ill-fortune, black Care, and tormenting anxiety (III, xiv, 664-65).

These chapters also present an intermittent debate between Laura and Pendennis about fidelity and fickleness, she of course speaking reverently of engagement and marriage, while he enlivens the discussion with ironic wit and humor that masks and yet expresses his respect, but not his entire acquiescence. For her, "love and truth are all in all here below" (III, xiii, 646), while for him she represents "the exuberant school of philosophers" (III, xiii, 647). She nevertheless pointedly raises the issue of how to express the feelings of the heart.

Chapter xv offers one fundamental answer. Though the chapter enunciates the contextualizing assertion of Ecclesiastes: "All is vanity" (IV, xv, 6), it also emphasizes the mitigating power of human charitableness, dominated as the chapter is by the theme of samaritanism, appearing in its title, the vignette initial, the full-page illustration, and the text (e.g. IV, xv, 3). The following chapter then begins a discussion of liberation, as Pendennis introduces the subject with an ironic play on Byron as parroted by O'Connell: "Hereditary Bondsmen! know ye not / *Who* would be free *themselves* must strike the blow?" (IV, xvi, 10).

More seriously, however, he speaks of Philip's impoverishment as a freedom from the confinements of fashionable living. Like Thackeray remembering his own youthful experience in the Temple living in chambers several stories high, Pendennis celebrates the "happy rooms, bright rooms, rooms near the sky, to remember you is to be young again," and recognizes that for Philip, now no longer attended by "housekeepers, butlers, and obsequious liveried menials," to "be freed from that ceremonial and etiquette of plush and worsted lace was an immense relief." Again, there is a Biblical model: the dinner of herbs, love, and contentment (Proverbs 15: 17 [IV, xvi, 10]). The novel continues actively to explore the question of how one can find freedom from the restrictive contingencies of life, doing so partly through a debate between the worldly prudence that Pendennis expresses and the other-worldly optimism of his wife. Philip joins in the debate as well, denouncing Pen's prudence as "genteel atheism" (IV, xvii, 135). Like Laura, he finds emancipation in faith. She argues that "Heaven will . . . send him help at its good time" (IV, xvii, 132), and Philip cites the Bible: "Isn't there manna in the wilderness for those who have faith to walk in it?" (IV, xvii, 135).

Aside from evoking the nightmare of Philip's having Mrs. Baynes as a prospective mother-in-law, Pendennis conveys to us at some length an alarmed sense of what prospects face an impoverished man "thinking . . . of committing matrimony" (IV, xvii, 134). Terming his wife's views romantic, and speaking of Philip's condition as "a state of happiness so crazy that it is useless to reason with him" (IV, xvii, 135), he advocates honoring the values of "sense and discernment" (IV, xvii, 132) and refuses to make a romantic story out of the love between Charlotte and Philip. And yet, Pen himself has divided loyalties.

For one thing, he acknowledges that *some* human beings, at any rate, can look back in memory to their reenactment of Darby and Joan, or John Anderson and his dear wife: "and yesterday, is not that dear and here too?" For another, he meditates upon the testimony of an acquaintance who recently spoke of his past life and declared "that he would gladly live every minute of it over again." Continuing his questioning of the church service's insistence that we are all miserable sinners, he allows for that possibility, but also thinks of Vergil's fortunate men, and of the double happiness of knowing as well as experiencing one's good fortune.

He also, however, has Hamlet's sense of the thousand "ills to which flesh is heir," and though he comically trivializes some of them, he acutely remembers past griefs. Like Hamlet too, he considers the idea of suicide, but does so with characteristic humor, as he plays with the notion of emulating Socrates cheerfully drinking the cup of hemlock. Yet, even in this instance, he expresses ambiguity, as he imagines toasting those who go on living: "Here's a health to you, my lads!" (IV, xvii, 133).

Like his creator, Pendennis knows that the absense of ravens bringing sustenance and the lack of manna create needy supplicants, and bring into question the meaning of human suffering. At the same time, however, he knows that besides the power of stoical acceptance, we have the gift of renunciation—in Goethean language, as Carlyle emphasized, *entsagen*. A Goethean example, as the title of Chapter xviii makes clear, is to be found in his poem, "Vanitas! Vanitatum Vanitas!" which articulates the joyful liberation of *entsagen*: "*Ich hab mein Sach auf Nichts gestellt. / Juchhe! / Drum ists so wohl mir in der Welt. / Juchhe!*" Committing himself to nothing, instead of to money, possessions, fame, or the gaining of honors, is what makes the Goethean speaker so free, so happy, so capable of clinking the glasses (*anstossen*), chiming in with the songs (*einstimmen*), and drinking the wine of living.

Accordingly, the chapter celebrates joy. The Goethean speaker, at first mistakenly seeking military glory, achieved only the loss of a leg, but the Thackerayan image in the vignette initial conveys the jubilation of an aged figure, legs intact, inspired by a jug of wine that epitomises a sustaining joy, and who raises a crown of what might be vine leaves. The delight of men and gods, Lucretius' "*alma Venus*" is the presiding generative force (IV, xviii, 141) in this "story . . . , however old it may be" (IV, xviii, 146), and "maiden meditation" (IV, xviii, 147), awaits its fulfillment. Even more, as Thackeray's great modern biographer has made clear, sustaining "consolation [is] to be had from [the] sweet uses of adversity" (IV, xviii, 152).

Detailed presentation of shabby genteel life in Paris during the reign of Louis-Philippe, and extended dialogue engage much of the novelist's attention during serial installments 9 and 10, which offer few sparkling allusions to provide relief from the prattle of Mrs. Boldero and Mrs. Bunch, or from the harangues of Mrs. Baynes. After the death of Lord Ringwood in chapter xxii, however, the tone lightens as the narrative "Hover[s] About the Elysian Fields"—the Champs Élysées, of course, where Charlotte and Philip escape the oppressive Mrs. Baynes—and as the narrator moves closer to his audience: "I must own . . ." (IV, xxiii, 513), "You see I am acknowledging . . . ," "Do you . . . ?" In similar fashion, after ironically observing that "Kindness is very indigestible," he makes a direct address to the reader: "O brother! may we help the fallen still though they never pay us, and may we lend without exacting the usury of gratitude!" (IV, xxiii, 514). In raising the subject of love, he asks of a mature female reader: "Have you ever looked at your love-letters to Darby, when you were courting, dear Joan? . . . You scarce need spectacles as you look at them" (IV, xxiii, 515).

Alternating once more, he soon returns to more dramatic presentation as he provides reported conversation, and even goes to the length of italicizing the names of the speakers, simulating a printed drama—as in *The Newcomes.* In effect, he presents a mini-comedy involving young men of the British Embassy in Paris (IV, xxiii, 520-23) that, among other matters, introduces Charlotte's second suitor. An immediately ensuing chapter, with its witty injunction from Horace, *"nec dulces amores / sperne puer neque tu choreas"* (young man, do not neglect sweet love nor dances [IV, xxiv, 528]), highlights a ball at the Embassy. Unfortunately, however, Philip *does* neglect the dance, and retires to the Embassy garden, only to meet his hostile cousin. When Twysden insults him, Philip—his exploding jacket emulating his undiplomatic behavior—tosses Twysden into the Embassy fountain, and as a result of this tumultuous conduct finds himself kept away from Charlotte by her family. In short, the prevailing comic tone abruptly ends.

Suffering, therefore, dominates the two succeeding chapters of Number 12 for December 1861. Introduced by a chapter title with a mock-heroic play upon Aeneas' unutterable sorrows (*Infandi dolores*) regarding the fall of Troy, which he then *communicates* to Dido, the narrator follows suit in speaking of the sorrows of Charlotte and Philip at being separated. Philip, "rolling a dismal cigarette" (IV, xxv, 649)—rather early in the historical cancer-giving process—understandably sees Mrs. Baynes as a Lady Macbeth providing her husband with daggers (IV, xxv, 643). She in fact forces him to violate his basic integrity—making him no longer *sibi constans* (consistant with himself), the Horatian phrase that had articulated a guiding ideal on the title page of *Henry Esmond*, and that had previously defined Baynes (IV, xxiv, 531).

The allusion to daggers also points ahead, of course, to the relieving farcicality of Chapter xxvii, with its comic resolution of the dead-set situation epitomised by Sheridan's *The Critic:* "I Charge you, Drop your Daggers!" (V, i, 1). Thackeray thereby offers a resolution based upon an earlier comic pattern. After Baynes's melodramatic performance, he reverts to his true values—unlike Dr. Firmin, who continues in his role, as we see in the letter to his son.

Typically, Dr. Firmin trivializes classical awareness through glib quotation, like the young men at Philip's call-dinner—degrading, for example, the Lucretian *amari aliquid* that Thackeray had cited in his January 1860 Roundabout Paper, "On a Lazy Idle Boy," as giving an appropriate tartness to his own writing (I, i, 128). Similarly, Dr. Firmin embellishes his letter with unwitting parodies of Horatian awareness, as he pompously and dishonestly claims to have dealt with the blows of fortune (IV, xxv, 652). The telling counter-statement comes at the chapter's end, as the narrator wittily plays with Horace's *de te fabula* in implicitly characterizing Dr. Firmin's "fables" (IV, xxv, 654) as lies. In the narrative, however, Charlotte's and Philip's sufferings go on at some length, prompting the speaker (apparently very close to Thackeray recalling his dire illness of 1849) to accept the experience of pain because of the love that it can evoke from responsive friends: "The world is full of love and pity, I say. Had there been less suffering, there would have been less kindness. I, for one, almost wish to be ill again, so that the friends who succoured me might once more come to my rescue" (IV, xxv, 650).

Inevitably, however, in Thackerayan discourse, a complicating awareness sets in. Dr. Firmin's sinister letter from New York creates a darkness of tone, especially with its announcement of a further theft from Philip. Soon after, the narrator moves towards acceptance of the Prayer-book's characterization of humans as miserable sinners: "acknowledge the sinfulness of our humankind. How long had our race existed ere murder and violence began? and how old was the world ere brother slew brother?" (IV, xxvi, 655). Similarly, he speaks of "miserable sister sinners" (V, xxvii, 2), and of Mrs. Bayne as a "stupid criminal" (IV, xxvi, 656). To the Horatian awareness that "the years slip away fugacious" (IV, xxvi, 657), he adds the consciousness that the memory of sorrow remains.

As for the sleepless, guilty, repentant Baynes, "the past rises up in that wakeful old man's uncomfortable memory. His little Charlotte is a child again .... He remembers the fever which she had, ... [how he] brought her to the river, and parted with her to send her to Europe" (V, xviii, 14), as young Thackeray himself had been sent. Though his deed of agreeing to separate Charlotte and Philip "is done, it is not past recalling" (V, xxviii, 15). Even though he tries to distract himself from the passionateness of his feelings by dining at "one of those luxurious restaurants in the Palais Royal," and then going to see "a ballet at the Grand Opera" (V, xviii, 15), he does not respond to the food or to the ballet, even though "Taglioni, and Noblet, and Duvernay, danced before his hot eyes" (V, xxviii, 18).

Baynes, more than any other character, feels conflicting emotions, but the narrator broadens the scope of memory, as he speaks of how "Our griefs, our pleasures, our youth, our sorrows, our dear, dear friends resuscitate" (V, xxviii, 24). So too he evokes a wider range of human experience, wondering, for example, how universal is the Othello-like impulse to throttle a spouse. Speaking of Baynes and his wife, he recalls Zoffany's painting of Garrick and Mrs. Pritchard as Macbeth and Lady Macbeth, and expressively comments on how "Macbeth stands in an attitude hideously contorted and constrained, while Lady Mac is firm and easy" (V, xxviii, 14). Inversely, Mrs. Baynes' meek behavior towards her troubled husband provides an insight into the Shakespearean play: "After Lady Macbeth had induced Mac to go through that business with Duncan, depend upon it she was very deferential and respectful to her general" (V, xxviii, 15).

Lightheartedness and awareness of the darkness of life prominently intermingle in Number 14 for February 1862. Continuing the playfulness of the previous installment's Chapter xxviii, which—apart from what we have seen—gives expression, for example, to Mrs. Baynes's anxious perception that her husband is speaking in "his Bluebeard voice" (V, xxviii, 15), the two ensuing chapters offer an entertaining collage of classical figures and language, near-Eastern figures, literary figures and expressions in Cervantes, Béranger, Scott, Jonson, Perrault, Milton, Shakespeare, and also contemporary actualities like Smith's *Dictionary of Greek and Roman Antiquities* (1842), *The Cornhill Magazine*, (1860 ff.) and Hoe's gigantic printing presses, which turn out the *Magazine*. In short, Thackeray's method is especially evident here, with its juxtaposition of personal and mythological experience, the contemporary and the historical, the topical and the typical.

Thus, in thinking about Mrs. Baynes brooding over her defeated efforts, the narrator says, "If I contemplate that wretched old Niobe much longer, I shall begin to pity her. Away softness! Take out thy arrows, the poisoned, the barbed, the rankling, and prod me the old creature well, god of the silver bow!" (V, xxix, 130). Teasing his female readers of a certain age who might remember whispering and warbling love-talk like that uttered by Charlotte and Philip, he reminds them that "This . . . is a February number. The birds are gone: the branches are bare" (V, xxix, 132). Together with the memory, such a one has only the sense of Time's passing. For those readers, it is too late to seize the day—at least love's youthful day.

Speaking personally, and also more broadly, the narrator remarks:

> Having myself seen the city of Tours only last year, of course I don't remember much about it. A man remembers boyhood, and the first sight of Calais, and so forth. But after much travel or converse with the world, to see a new town is to be introduced to Jones. He is like Brown; he is not unlike Smith. In a little while you hash him up with Thompson. (V, xxix, 133)

His faulty remembrance of Tours then prompts recollection of Scott's fallacious description of that city in *Quentin Durward* (a rendering that the narrator prefers to the actual city), which in turn leads to a narrative of Quentin Firman and Isabel de Baynes, as the contemporary figures of his narrative briefly join with those of Scott's novel. Observing, however, that the romantic aspect of *Quentin Durward* does not appear in contemporary drawing-room fiction, and that such feats as fighting the Wild Boar of Ardennes will not appear in *The Adventures of Philip*, the narrator nevertheless insists on the reality of present-day domestic boars who attack reputations, and indeed become bores.

With the death of General Baynes, the tone of course becomes more sombre. The narrator offers a mock-excuse for Baynes's hen-pecked behavior by citing the prior example of Marlborough being dominated by the fiery Sarah, but the subject of *ending* induces a solemn and challenging discourse on what might appropriately follow therefrom—or indeed precede it. Almost inevitably, the narrator thinks of Biblical experience, and most appropriately of Job's suffering, his desire for death, and his sense that "[his] place [shall] know . . . him no longer."

Understanding Job's awareness that his days are vanity (Job 7: 16), the narrator asks why "we expect to be beloved, lamented, remembered?" "Is it because we have been so good, or are so wise and great," or because we have forgotten, like Xerxes and Jonson's blustering Bobadil, "how abject, how small, how low, how lonely [we] are, and what a little dust will cover [us]"? Here the Biblical awareness melds with the Vergilian: *"hi motus animorum atque haec certamina tanta / pulveris exigui iactu compressa quiescunt"* (all these spirited movements and such great contests as these will be contained and quieted by the throwing of a little dust [V, xxx, 141]). Here also we must notice that the issue is posed as a question. A man so thoroughly aware of human triviality, as Thackeray was, unmistakably coexists with a man committed to remembrance of human significance.

The narrative then takes on a more matter-of-fact tone as it recounts Philip's career as a journalist, Charlotte's arrival in London, their marriage, and their beginning a family. Only a few non-literal details appear: Philip contenting himself with a dinner of herbs (V, xxxi, 261), young lovers in a garden "talking some such talk as Milton imagines our first parents engaged in" (V, xxxi, 266), and Mrs. Baynes behaving like "some old fairy, who was furious" (V, xxxiii, 391), at not being invited to a christening (that of her granddaughter's), for example, together with the usual glib use of classical quotations by Dr. Firmin in his letters from America. As Philip's struggles with poverty increase, however, so does the presence of Biblical awareness.

Philip is no Job, but the narrator sees something of a precedent in the Biblical figure: "Patient as he was, the patriarch groaned and lamented, and why should not poor Philip be allowed to grumble, who was not a model of patience at all?" (V, xxxiv, 400). The Good Samaritan—so frequently in the consciousness of the main characters—decidedly reappears (V, xxxiv, 403, VI, xxxix, 125, xli, 217, 219, xlii, 224), as do references to *The Lord's Prayer*, (V, xxxvii, 649), especially to the gift of daily bread (V, xxxiv, 403, xxxv, 514), but also to having been rescued from temptation (V, xxxiv, 403), and to the hope of being forgiven for trespasses (V, xxxvii, 649). Tregarvan "sleeps with his . . . fathers" (V, xxxiv, 404) like Jeroboam. Mrs. Woolsey is as "innocent as Susannah" (V, xxxiv, 406).

Recollection of a sunrise seen years before in the near-East makes the narrator think ahead like John to "when the night comes" (V, xxxv, 515). Awareness of his wife's benefactions makes him think of the rejoicing in Luke "When one sinner is saved" (V, xxxvi, 527). Isaac/Philip thinks of his father as an Abraham sacrificing him in stages (V, xxxvii, 643). The novelist ambiguously, but on the whole positively, presents Carolyn as a Judith to Hunt's malevolent Holofernes in the full-page illustration of Number 18.

Classical awareness briefly re-emerges in Number 17 for May 1862, beginning with the title of its opening chapter, which quotes Juvenal's *res angusta domi* (V, xxxv, 513), the final words of an utterance meant here to epitomize Philip's situation: difficult indeed it is for those to emerge from obscurity whose noble qualities are cramped by narrow means at home. Mocking Dr. Firmin's pompous use of the classics, Pendennis redirects the famous Vergilian utterance, *"timeo Danaos et dona ferentes,"* in order to term the Doctor a "wily old Greek" (V, xxxvi, 532).

Number 18 for June 1862 also begins with a classical chapter title, once again redirected, for the leech in this case is not the poet as characterized by Horace in the *Ars poetica,* but Dr. Firmin, who will not let go until gorged with his son's blood: *"Nec plena cruoris hirudo"* (V, xxxvii, 641). An equally emphatic judgment is made as Dr. Goodenough rejoices in Carolyn's chloroforming the leech's agent, Hunt, and her burning of the forged bill of exchange. Using appropriate Horatian language, the Doctor celebrates her glorious deceitfulness: *"splendide mendax,* . . . [whose] robbery was a sublime and courageous act" (VI, xxxix, 123).

Besides drawing so notably upon the cultural inheritance that he shares with his readers, Thackeray in the person of Pendennis moves closer to his audience as the novel nears its end. Besides mentioning the Nile sunrise that Thackeray saw in 1844, and the experience of having "been in a great strait of sickness near to death" (V, xxxvi, 526) in 1849, he addresses his audience with less irony and more affection. The individual member of his audience is a friend whom he wishes well "when the night comes" (V, xxxv, 515).

His reader is addressed as "dear" (V, xxxvi, 526), "kind" (VI, xl, 136, 144, xlii, 239), and "good" (VI, xlii, 225). Using the language of the church service, he terms his audience members (at times, a congregation) "dearly beloved brethren" who, like he, "go on promising to improve, and stumbling and picking ourselves up every day. The pavement of life is strewed with orange-peel; and who has not slipped on the flags?" (V, xxxv, 517). With similar affection tempered by humor, he calls upon "us, dearly beloved," to be thankful that we are "outside the hulks or the asylum" (V, xxxvii, 641).

As he nears the end of his serial novel, he recalls a dear friend whose "kind old eyes used to read these pages, which are now closed in the sleep appointed for all of us. And so page is turned after page, and behold Finis and the volume's end" (VI, xlii, 225). Finally, ending what was to be his last completed novel, he writes: "The night is falling . . . and it is time to go home . . . . Good night, friends, old and young! The night will fall: the stories must end: and the best friends must part" (VI, xvii, 240).

CHAPTER SEVEN:
ROUNDABOUT PAPERS

Concurrently with the appearance of Batchelor as narrator of *Lovel the Widower*, readers of *The Cornhill Magazine* witnessed the emergence of another new personality: someone who, like Batchelor, spoke openly in offering personal testimony, but who also spoke anonymously and without the impress of personal identity. Indeed, the reader as well as the writer was called upon to participate in the discovery and articulation of that speaker's reality—someone who ultimately became identified as "Mr. Roundabout." Hence an understanding of that process requires, at least to some degree, a chronological awareness.[1]

The speaker of "Roundabout Papers.—No. 1. On A Lazy Idle Boy" was clearly distinguishable from the essayists who wrote "The Chinese and the Outer Barbarians," "Studies in Animal Life," "Our Volunteers," "A Man of Letters of the Last Generation," and "The Search for Sir John Franklin," not only because his title promised a continuing series (so did "Studies in Animal Life"), but most especially because he was writing as a representative of the publishers, Smith, Elder, and Co.—from the overt perspective of 65 Cornhill (repeated three times in the essay)—and implicitly as the journal's editor, who was known to be W.M. Thackeray, though he was not identified by the journal itself. Emerging at the end of the essay as the implicit journal editor, he testified to the authenticity of his authors (though without revealing their personal identities), and commented upon their achievements.

Up to that point, however, he had presented himself simply as a man who sought to engage his readers with his notably personal tastes and preferences. (Only two months later did he think to identify his models as Montaigne and Howell.) Most appropriately for an issue of the magazine that contained serial installments of two novels, he implicitly justified their inclusion on the basis of his passionate enjoyment of accomplished story-telling, from Dumas to the *Arabian Nights,* but including English and American contemporaries: Dickens, Ainsworth, Lever, Surtees, G.P.R. James, Bulwer-Lytton, Harriet Beecher Stowe, Mrs. Trollope, and her son, Anthony.

Here again the discourse is that of open secrecy, expressed in a forthright and yet partly disguised manner: "You take the allegory? Novels are sweets. All people with healthy literary appetites love them" (I, 127). Inevitably, the metaphor extends itself into a proclamation of culinary pleasures, whether "jellies," or "wholesome roast." (British "boiled" [I, 128] we can do without.) Most notably of all, perhaps, the anonymous speaker talks of the magazine's Thackerayan novel in terms of its creator's reputation as a dispenser of *amari aliquid* (something bitter), before finally identifying it as the work of *Vanity Fair*'s author (the speaker implicitly being that person), and *Framley Parsonage* as the work of *Barchester Tower*'s author. The mixed reticence and revelation continue, moreover, into the final paragraph, where the metaphor of the *table d'hôte* merges with that of the initiatory voyage, with mention of two hospitable ship captains whose relevance is known only to a few people besides Thackeray: Captain Lang, who took him on his first trip to America in 1852, and Captain Comstock, who brought him back in 1856 from his second and last trip.

Uniquely, the February 1860 issue of *The Cornhill Magazine* began with an anonymous Thackerayan essay, instead of ending with a Roundabout piece. As this indicates, "Nil Nisi Bonum" is not literally a Roundabout Paper, since it does not offer personal remarks that conclude the magazine's issue, and does not proceed in an identifiable "roundabout" manner. Instead, prompted by the deaths of two friends who were warmly admired authors, Washington Irving and T.B. Macaulay, it offers "testimony of respect and regard from a [fellow] man of letters." As such, it is a part of the evolving process that provides discovery and articulation of the personal concern that will come to be an important part of "Mr. Roundabout's" identity.

One of the essay's most notable qualities reveals itself in the writer's emphasis on presenting and having the reader perceive Irving and Macaulay as worthy human beings, not just writers of genius. He terms them "the Goldsmith and the Gibbon of our time" (I, 129), but his discourse takes the form of a "little sermon" (I, 134), whose theme (thrice enunciated) is Walter Scott's injunction to his son-in-law and biographer: "Be a good man." Presenting Irving as an "ambassador" (I, 129), a "messenger of goodwill and peace" between England and America (as Thackeray himself had sought to be, and was still seeking to be in this very essay), the speaker not only offers responsive praise of Irving's qualities as a man, but, even more notably, provides moving personal testimony of Irving's devoted generosity and good-humored charm, including typifying quotations from private talks that they had had.

Even more, besides speaking warmly and admiringly of Irving's family life at Sunnyside on the Hudson, the essayist emphasizes how responsively other people regarded him as well: "I had the good fortune to see him at New York, Philadelphia, Baltimore, and Washington, and remarked how in every place he was honoured and welcome" (I, 130). Hence the Thackerayan speaker rhetorically and climactically asks, "Was Irving not good, and, of his works, was not his life the best part?" (I, 131).

Similarly, he presents Macaulay "not [as] a poet and man of letters merely, but citizen, statesman, a great British worthy" (I, 132). Also in keeping with his remarks about Irving, he draws upon details of personal acquaintance and conversation, and calls attention to Macaulay's generosity. So too, he expresses great admiration for Macaulay's "astonishing memory" (I, 132), his "prodigious intellectual feats," and his extraordinarily energetic scholarship ("He reads twenty books to write a sentence").

Most strikingly of all, however, the speaker evokes Panizzi's great dome at the British Museum Library in order to characterize the great writer's achievement as an open, living contribution to society: "Under the dome which held Macaulay's brain, and from which his solemn eyes looked out on the world but a fortnight since, what a vast, brilliant, and wonderful store of learning was ranged! what strange lore would he not fetch for you at your bidding! A volume of law, or history, a book of poetry familiar or forgotten (except by himself, who forgot nothing), a novel ever so old, and he had it at hand" (I, 133). As this splendid tribute indicates, the Thackerayan speaker is once again engaging in the dozen-year-old debate about the dignity of literature and, as he reveals in his final paragraph, he addresses his words especially to aspiring young men of letters.

By the time of "Roundabout Papers.—No. II. On Two Children in Black," which appeared at the end of the March 1860 *Cornhill*, the anonymous speaker, identifying his models as Montaigne and Howell, writes a discourse characterized by the extensive presence of the personal pronoun, and by a temperate, genial defense of the virtues of egotism: "Their egotism in nowise disgusts me. I hope I shall always like to hear men, in reason, talk about themselves. What subject does a man know better?" (I, 380). Indeed, he directly challenges any disapproving reader by arguing that "I was natural, and was telling the truth. You say you are angry with a man for talking about himself. It is because you yourself are selfish, and that other person's Self does not interest you. Be interested by other people and with their affairs. Let them prattle and talk to you, as I do my dear old egotists just mentioned."

Since it is the last article in the monthly journal, he sees it as a kind of farewell to the reader—even as a kind of night-time reading—"that you can muse over, that you can smile over, that you can yawn over." He also, however, intends it to be an essay containing recognizably truthful human observation and fellow-feeling that shall not put the reader to sleep but arouse him: "I should like to touch you sometimes with a reminiscence that shall waken your sympathy, and make you say, *Io anche* [I too] have so thought, felt, smiled, suffered." In short, third person circumlocutions are not to be part of the roundabout process: *"Linea recta brevissima.* That right line "I" is the very shortest, simplest, straightforwardest means of communication between us" (I, 381).

For the first time he identifies himself as "Mr. Roundabout" (I, 380, 381 [twice]), and comments on the procedure he intends to follow: "these are Roundabout Papers, and may wander who knows whither" (I, 381). He even imagines a satirical friend asking, after reading two of the essay's five pages, why it is called "On Two Children in Black," when there has been no mention af any children, or anything black. He has created the question, of course, in order to emphasize the method, citing the interchangeability of many of Montaigne's titles, and asserting that "I *have* a subject" (I, 382).

Even after making that statement, however, he still needs two more paragraphs in order to explain that the mysterious little anecdote is a treasure like a fine vintage kept in the darkness of one's wine cellar, and requiring appropriately elaborate presentation. Thereafter, for the final half of the essay, he proceeds to tell the story in perfect chronological sequence, but he also recounts numerous complicating thoughts and feelings prompted by the simple tale: memories of parting as a child from one's parents, memories of the hostile experience of arriving at boarding school, and questions arising from various details of the narrative. Since the tale itself is a tantalizing riddle, we are left with a final aspect of roundabout procedure, at least this one: irresolvability.

After speaking in his own voice, identified by his signed initials, "W.M.T.," as he paid final tribute to Charlotte Brontë and introduced her fragment, "Emma" ("The Last Sketch" in the April 1860 *Cornhill*) ("two black jobs will be too much for one number," as he wrote to George Smith, referring also to "Nil Nisi Bonum" [*Letters [H]*, 930]), Thackeray composed his third Roundabout Paper, "On Ribbons," as the concluding piece in the May 1860 issue. Here he seemed to be exulting in the very large sales of the magazine (over 100,000 copies), and thinking of himself as having a podium from which to address national issues. The argument that he sought to make in this lengthy ten page essay concerning the establishment of an award for British merchant seamen seems rather boring at this date, but the opening 4 1/2 pages of his roundabout procedure of getting to his point constitute a matter of enduring amusement and revelation.

Though he goes on in his tedious argument to recite at exhausting length the struggles of British seamen to deal with shipboard fires—making one wish for quenching liquids not exactly of the sort to which he refers—his major achievement is to demonstrate, before that, the absurdity of most public distinctions: notably those between unpretentious, honorable, common people who serve their country without receiving special notice, and pompous generals like Wellington, who flaunt their ribbons, "idiots" who are born peers and are therefore "born legislator[s]" (I, 632), aldermen who job their way to knighthood, royalty who readily accept grovelling behavior, peers who intrigue for yet further honorific distinction, and other squabbling contestants. Thackeray's satiric abilities wonderfully articulate this human absurdity.

Even more successfully, he evokes the narrow-minded politics and jealousy that distort and, indeed, prevent valid perception of human merit, especially in fields of artistic endeavor: "Fancy the claimants, and the row about their precedence!" (I, 633). "Fancy the struggle! . . . Fancy the distribution of prizes!" Telling his reader overtly that the roundabout process is in reality a search for appropriateness, he says: "When I began this present Roundabout excursion, I think I had not quite made up my mind whether we would have an Order of all the Talents or not" (I, 634). After rejecting that idea, however, he then accepts the appropriateness of "Ornamental Classes" and the naturalness of strutting human peacocks. Here is where his irony and therefore his argument fail.

It is *not* "good for Mr. Briefless . . . that there should be a Lord Chancellor, with a gold robe and fifteen thousand a year." It is *not* "good for a poor curate that there should be splendid bishops at Fulham and Lambeth," and one would have thought that a Thackerayan speaker would have said so, rather than have offered the feeble justification that "their lordships were poor curates once, and have won, so to speak, their ribbon." Though appropriately (and wittily) refusing to think ill of someone simply because he has achieved eminence (*"qui mal y pense"*), the speaker arrives very strangely indeed "in my roundabout way near the point towards which I have been trotting ever since we set out" (I, 635), at an attempted justification of awards to merchant seamen simply because other people have won benefits in the lottery of life.

One questions how much "we" are involved, since the roundabout procedure in this specific case seems to convey notable confusion and uncertainty of thought in the speaker, however emphatically he makes his final suggestion. In short, though the proposal is harmless enough, it fails to grow out of the powerful ironies of the previous discourse—indeed, it seems to betray them.

Thackeray's sense of triumphant achievement as editor of an extraordinarily successful new magazine emerged unmistakably in "Roundabout Papers.—No. IV. On Some Late Great Victories," concluding the June 1860 issue and, simultaneously, the first volume of *The Cornhill Magazine*. Here, as the roundabout process gradually revealed, was a joyful, exuberant, and yet comically restrained *crow*. Seeking a contemporary analogue, the speaker began by offering the testimony of personal experience, as he recounted his witnessing the response of readers of popular journalistic accounts of the late, great battle at Farnborough between the English and the American boxing champions: Sayers and Heenan on 17 April 1860—a battle remarkable for the audience's intrusion, which halted the struggle and thereby identified no loser. *That* is an important aspect of Thackeray's celebration of the *Cornhill's* triumphs, as he pointedly refuses to seek polemical triumphs.

The roundabout speaker, with appropriate ambiguity, questions personal violence, but evokes national standards in justifying violent defense of home values, as England was later to do so memorably against Hitler: "In these national cases, you see, we override the indisputable first laws of morals. Loving your neighbour is very well, but suppose your neighbour comes over . . . to rob you of your laws, your liberties, your newspapers, your parliament . . . ?" (I, 756). Here is another crucial aspect of the roundabout process and of the awarenesses to which it can lead: the discovery of fundamental social values defined not according to an absolute code of behavior, but in terms of the appropriateness of a people defending a meaningful way of life.

Typically, and with typical wit, the Thackerayan speaker establishes a context for the triumphs of the devoted templars of the Mons Frumentarius (Hill of Corn) by evoking the protective interventions of Homeric gods (like the British audience at Farnborough), the contests of historical warriors

(Napoleon and Wellington, the *Java* and the *Constitution*), and especially the vulnerability of human efforts, like those of Washington at Valley Forge, and the insubstantiality of human triumphs, as epitomised by Sancho Panza at Barataria—not without remembrance of the actively hostile warriors of the rival Saturnine Magazine (*The Saturday Review*, of course, which had just attacked "On Ribbons").

Appropriately, for the mind and sensibility expressing themselves in these essays, a triumphal assertion, however qualified, inevitably recedes into open acknowledgment of the dismaying experiences that inevitably accompany and challenge ego-fulfilling acomplishments, as "Thorns in the Cushion" [July 1860] demonstrates. Memory evokes the initial metaphor of setting out on a sea voyage (No. 1), and the awareness of having successfully continued the voyage for six months (No. 6), but the roundabout method creates a metamorphosis, turning the voyage into a victorious land procession, with the editor appearing in an epitomizing illustration (II, 122), as an occupant of a triumphal gold coach, much like the Lord Mayor's each year on the ninth of November as he goes to the Mansion House to be installed.

But the procession turns into a recession, as the costumes are doffed and "The Mayor becomes a man," and as the *Cornhill's* editor takes the reader into his "private room" (II, 123), and speaks of his personal cares. As always in these essays, Thackeray moves back and forth between the private and the public worlds, using the one, of course, to illuminate the other. His immediate subject being the bizarre fierceness—as we saw in the previous essay—of critical opinion, he cites the example of a painting by Simeon Soloman at the recent Royal Academy exhibition that he very much liked, but that was attacked by a journalistic critic (from *The Saturday Review*, of course) in crudely dismissive terms.

Before revealing the nastiness of comments directed at himself as a magazine editor, however, he makes a relevant roundabout detour in order to challenge the appropriateness of the whole "attempt to *castigare ridendo*" (II, 124), to mock people in the manner of arrogant, tyrannous, sarcastic schoolmasters, instead of trying to enlighten them. Inevitably, however, the detour also requires a testimony of allegiance to the enlightenment of humor (II, 124), as well as to the appropriate disorderliness of the satiric impulse, with its horns, hoofs, and active shanks (II, 125). As this suggests, the argument is thoughtful and subtle, as well as playful.

The dissensions of opinion are of course not the issue—but the meaningless disorder of Donnybrook clamor, espressing itself in vehement, irrational denunciations, evidently proved to be very unsettling to the editorial bosom. "Ah me! . . . we create anger where we never meant harm" (II, 128). Thackeray now had a public address and had abundant mail sent to him at 65 Cornhill (and sometimes at home, with touching pleas of human need quite unconnected to journalistic merit). His testimony, given his vulnerable responsiveness to individual distress, is very personal and anguished: "No day passes but that argument *ad misericordiam* is used. Day and night that sad voice is crying out for help. . . . Before I was an editor I did not like the postman much:—but now!" (II, 126).

If the essay on Victories can be seen as a roundabout and inevitable way of coming to speak about Thorns, however, the latter unquestionably leads directly to a discussion of subsequent editorial miseries in "On Screens in Dining-Rooms" (August 1860). In "Thorns" the editor had spoken of "the gloomy moral which I am about to draw" (II, 123), but by the time that he writes "Screens" he has discovered an even gloomier reality: the misery of knowing that he has been used as a means of nastily mocking (*castigare ridendo*) his friend and publisher, George Smith. The libel—instigated by a malicious British penny-a-liner, Edmund Yates, with whom Thackeray was subsequently to knock heads because of Yates's later hostile journalism directed against Thackeray himself—had first appeared in *The New York Times* of 26 May 1860, and had then been reprinted, with apparent glee, by *The Saturday Review* (where else?) of 23 June 1860.

Inevitably, the discovery causes a roundabout return to memory—a process that deserves attention. It begins, appropriately, with the comic generalization that importuning, would-be authors and their conspiring advocates seeking to persuade editors are much like bailiffs seeking to mislead and capture their intended victims. The editor then explores the psychology of rejected aspirants, archetypically configured (in Roman terms) by Minerva and Juno, in their indifference to the consequences that others suffer from their anger.

Again, the archetypal reveals itself in the diurnal and the diurnal shades into typicality: an Irish actress angered that a Thackerayan character in *Lovel* could be thought to reflect upon herself (repeated from "Thorns"), and a "man *qui crois toujours avoir raison,*" whose "anger is not a brief madness, but a permanent mania"—which Thackeray expresses with a remarkable sense of pathos for the obsessedly vituperative man: "His rage is not a fever-fit, but a black poison inflaming him, distorting his judgment, disturbing his rest, embittering his cup, gnawing at his pleasures, causing him more suffering than ever he can inflict on his enemy" (II, 254). The context, typically, is that of a sympathetic as well as an appalled understanding of lunacy, not rancorous resentment at having been assaulted.

The major roundabout return to memory, however, occurs as a complex unfolding. Recollection that just after sending "Thorns" to the printer he had read the malicious *Saturday Review* attack—deriving from a New York newspaper—upon George Smith prompted Thackeray to remember not only the Irish actress's assault upon himself but also of an earlier denunciation of himself by an Irish journalist in a New York newspaper eight and one-half years before. This memory then leads back yet further in time, in inevitable roundabout fashion, to the experience of being birched at school, and also to the awareness that the schoolboy indignity was conducted in private, so to speak, and not in the presence of one's wife (here again a generalization made by the metaphorically widowed Thackeray) and children, like a journalistic assault in the morning paper lying upon the breakfast table in full view of all the family members.

Here the public world not only interacts with the private realm, but inflicts its hostility upon family members whom one would wish to protect against malicious intrusion—precisely Thackeray's anguished concern not simply at being personally maligned, but especially at being used by mendacious journalists to fabricate mockery of a respected friend as well as publisher. Clearly, the occasion required and received an articulate statement from Thackeray, who, addressing responsible members of his profession, expressed his sense of the ethical responsibility of those, like himself and his contributors, who write for the public and therefore have a "public duty," and who owe an allegiance "to the honour of your calling" (II, 256). As usual, he defines positive values and appropriate allegiances, even while satirically exposing screened malice— here as he takes up the alleged dinner-table reference to screens and transforms it into an indictment of the journalist who invented it and of those who repeated it.

Memory serves almost entirely as the roundabout path running through "Tunbridge Toys" (September 1860). Only near the bottom of the fourth page of this five-page essay do we emerge into the world of 1860 with the *Cornhill* writer placing himself at his desk in a house overlooking Tunbridge Wells Common, where Thackeray had taken his mother, stepfather, and children. To arrive at his desk, and to enunciate a joint awareness of past and present, the writer had to evoke the memory of a twelve-year-old Thackeray journeying

CHAPTER SEVEN

from Charterhouse to Tunbridge Wells, where his elders were vacationing.
Even before recounting that journey of thirty-seven years before, and explaining what made it painfully memorable, however, the writer has to reveal the origins of his troubled youthful emotions connected with the journey to Tunbridge Wells and with a brief, subsequent period of solitude there. Recalling a specific event, however, is like transplanting it: the process brings along its rooted connections. Extraordinarily, this essay originates in the mini-world of a schoolboy's pocket, and the roundabout journey of the writer's mind and sensibility begins with the mundane fact of his having owned, so to speak, and kept in his pocket one of "those little silver pencil-cases with a moveable almanack [a resonant detail] at the butt-end" (II, 380).

In effect, it was a kind of toy that amused the youth "twiddling round the moveable calendar"—which is what the writer is now doing with that childhood memory, that Tunbridge toy. Partly, however, it also provokes an enduring torment. He had borrowed money from a youthful capitalist in order to purchase it, but couldn't pay his creditor for months, as a result of which he still hears the bullying remarks and "curses, so terrible from the lips of so young a boy" (II, 381), prompting him as an elder into an extended advocacy of tipping school-boys, a practice for which the mature Thackeray was well-known.

The minute financial logic of the boy's impoverished situation and its troubling emotional consequences then unfold, culminating in feelings of guilt at having spent fourpence of his parents' money on a breakfast of coffee and toast—feelings expressed in the present tense: "I am very hungry. ... I pace the street, as sadly almost as if I had been coming to school, not going thence. ... And here am I hungry, penniless, with five-and-twenty shillings of my parents' money in my pocket. ... I remember the taste of the coffee and toast to this day" (II, 382-

83). What a touching evocation of a decent, vulnerable, insecure child!

He had been taught the inappropriateness of prodigality, and had taken it all too much to heart, as Thackeray wittily emphasizes in playing with the Biblical parable (II, 380), and its simple-minded Hogarthian successor, *Industry and Idleness* (II, 383)—here treated as mock-archetypes. By contrast, Thackeray cites the exaggerated novels of his youth, and praises the splendid liberation that these marvellous vacation toys offered from oppressive actuality: "can all the fashion, can all the splendour of real life which these eyes have subsequently beheld, can all the wit I have heard or read in later times, compare with your fashion, with your brilliancy, with your delightful grace, and sparkling vivacious rattle?" (II, 384). Finally, he walks in imagination about the Common, peopling it with figures from the 18th century, losing sight of his manuscript, and then feeling the emotions of his frightened youthful self immersed in the harmless terror of a gothic novel—another liberation.

As the mere title of Thackeray's next Roundabout essay indicates ("De Juventute" [October 1860]), it grows out of the memories of youth articulated in "Tunbridge Toys," and also out of energies released by the publication in the same *Cornhill* issue of Thackeray's lecture on George IV, a prominent monarchical presence during his early days. Notably, it is also his longest Roundabout essay to date—a fact suggesting the power of that double engagement of memory, his attitude towards George, of course, being thoroughly satirical. Indeed, the essay seems to have been written shortly after "Tunbridge Toys," for the writer alludes to "the country-place where I am staying" (II, 502)—which was true of early September 1860, when he first mentioned the essay (in a letter from Tunbridge Wells) and, indeed, because of its length, spoke of it as a possible double number (*Letters* [H], 2: 988).

The essay arises from a conflict between iconic images epitomized by a coin of 1823: on the one side (illustrated by the vignette initial) St. George overcoming the dragon (surrounded by the motto of the Order of the Garter: *Honi Soit Qui Mal Y Pense*—recently played with in "On Ribbons"), and on the other, George IV, whose lazy, fat, self-indulgent nature had been extensively characterized by Thackeray's lecture-essay. Being someone whose life had overlapped with Thackeray's for nineteen years, George IV was an unavoidable image. As Thackeray had written in that earlier piece, recounting the preposterous illusions perpetrated by the egoistic monarch:

> I suppose there were more pictures taken of that personage than of any other human being who was ever born and died—in every kind of uniform and every possible court-dress—in long fair hair, with powder, with and without a pigtail—in every conceivable cocked-hat—in dragoon uniform—in Windsor uniform—in a field-marshal's clothes—in a Scotch kilt and tartans, with dirk and claymore (a stupendous figure)—in a frogged frock-coat with a fur collar and tight breeches and silk stockings—of wigs of every colour, fair, brown, and black—in his famous coronation robes finally, with which performance he was so much in love that he distributed copies of the picture to all the Courts and British embassies in Europe, and to numberless clubs, town-halls, and private friends. I remember as a young man how almost every dining-room had his portrait. (II, 387)

By 1860, George is a largely vanished presence. Though an amusing statue in Trafalgar Square and the extravagant coronation robes at Madame Tussaud's have survived, "Charon has paddled him off," together with Madame Tussaud, "t'other side the Stygian stream" (II, 501). Characteristically, however, the Thackerayan speaker also questions whether the utterly contrasting spirit of St. George survives in 1860—St. George, that epitomizing icon of British 19th century idealism in literature and in art, as for example in Ruskin's Guild of St. George—though the Guild had not yet come into being when Thackeray wrote the essay, and would presumably have provoked his scepticism. His emphasis typically falls upon the feebleness and quixoticism of well-intentioned human aspirations. For him the battle of life is not epitomized by *The Seven Champions of Christendom*, but by humbler attempts to do our duty so far as we can manage to identify it.

That return to the realities of everyday existence inevitably leads to the present, to contemplative life at Tunbridge Wells, to sights of holidaying families, and to the witnessing of a father's laugh that transforms itself into a remembered image of thirty-seven years previous: "I *saw* [my emphasis] that very laugh which I remember perfectly in the time when this crown-piece was coined" (II, 502). Like the laugh, the coin is a talisman—not a tribute to Charon for passage across the Styx, but a magical conjuring of youthful life, with its quintessential conflict between the needs of the imagination and the tyrannous assertion of insensitive, indeed brutal authority, as epitomized by the physical assault upon the boy's head by a schoolmaster after he has been discovered surreptitiously enjoying the liberating experience of reading a work of comic literature (Pierce Egan's *Life in London*—not life in the confines of Charterhouse).

The painful remembrance of that episode then transforms itself into a more generalized expression of the patterns of human life, as the schoolboy becomes a university student, indulges in excesses of alcoholic stimulation, falls in love, marries, has children, and sees that his sylph has become a stout matron. Startlingly, the writer then projects himself as a paterfamilias reading a personal attack upon Dickens and Thackeray (whom he overtly names) by the *Superfine Review* (one has no doubt about the meaning of that pseudonym). He then ironically characterizes this recent attack of 25 August 1860 as another fragile image, like a fading contemporary manifestation on silver bromide film ("The vision has disappeared off the silver").

He denies the *Superfine Review*'s snobbish reading of the present as a falling away from old-fashioned gentlemanliness, and instead asserts that the major difference between the world of 1860 and the entire past has been the emergence of the industrial world, as typified by the mid-19th century's chief mode of travel—the railroad—and therefore its outlook. He jokingly speaks of the transition from the age of chivalry, as expressed by the alleged founder of Charterhouse School (a place of brutality, as we have just seen, emulated by the *Superfine Review*), Sir Walter Manny, to the age of the steam engine, as expressed not only by the railroads, but even more recently by the steamships of Isambard Brunel, engineer not only of railroads but also of immense trans-oceanic vessels like the *Great Eastern*.

The speaker's main assertion, however, emphasizes that a sense of living in both worlds is the crucial awareness of the members of his generation. Memory is more brightly enduring than photographic film (certainly of that date), and "We who have lived before railways were made, belong to another world" (II, 503), but we are also "of the age of steam. We have stepped out of the old world onto Brunel's vast deck," know of extensive new possibilities, and have even met "a man who had invented a flying-machine" (II, 504). We are also, alas, like Father Noah, disembarking not on the slopes of Mt. Ararat but into a railway station, so to speak. The antediluvian hippopotamus, elephant, and giraffe, whom we have brought with us, exemplify our own archaism (II, 505).

The imaginative surge that these metaphors embody then expresses itself in an extended evocation of equestrian entertainment, as a troupe of performers visits Tunbridge Wells, prompting the speaker to invite a young boy to witness the spectacle. Inevitably, the boy's lively response becomes the chief entertainment for the speaker, who remembers, though he cannot emulate, his own youthful enjoyment. Here again is a quintessential Thackerayan configuration: sympathy and separateness.

Thinking of contemporary opera and ballet, and of his own tired, old, fogyfied, jaded, yawning responses, the speaker asks: "about *some* things when we cease to care, what will be the use of life, sight, hearing?" (II, 506). Fortunately for him, the question leads to the discovery of a major resource: the vibrant memories of his admiring responses to the analogous figures of his youth, whom he calls up as thronging, vital, talismanic figures: Pauline Duvernay as the Bayadère, Ronzi de Begnis, Maria Caradori, Maria Malibran, Luigi Lablache, Matteo Porto, Giuseppe Ambrogetti, Alberico Curioni, Domenico Donzelli, Henriette Sontag in *Otello* and *La Donna del Lago*, Miss Chester, Miss Love, Cecilia Serle, Lise Noblet, Marie Taglioni, and Pauline Leroux. (Only a few Britons among this group.)

Naturally his thoughts also turn to memories of such sources of human pleasure as claret and cookery, great red wine being of course an enjoyment from a reasonably distant past, and hence an appropriate metaphor of sustaining inheritance. Moving to youthful pleasures, he recalls indulgence in literal and figurative sweets: tarts and novels. As in the case of ravishing female performers, he recites a magical sequence of works—extending, in effect, the brief list at the end of "Tunbridge Toys"—from Jane Porter's *The Scottish Chiefs* and Ann Radcliffe's *The Italian*, to *Don Quixote*, *The Arabian Nights*, the novels of Smollett and Scott, and of course Pierce Egan's *Life in London* (II, 508-12), together with two literal illustrations, showing how they captivated him.

For Tom and Jerry and their youthful readers, "the game of life proceeds," but for the speaker there is the continuing double awareness of then and now. With his acute sense of evanescence, he inevitably cries out *ubi sunt?* Where has it all gone, the whole world of childhood and of the literal and emblematic stage-coach journeys? This time, however, he remembers not only the painful separation from parents as he travelled to boarding school, but also the return home for the holidays. Being on holiday now, with his family gathered around him, he realizes that he is therefore at home, and so writes a coda expressing his gratitude for the journey from youth to where he now is:

> It is night now: and here is home. Gathered under the quiet roof, elders and children lie alike at rest. In the midst of a great peace and calm, the stars look out from the heavens. The silence is peopled with the past; sorrowful remorses for sins and shortcomings—memories of passionate joys and griefs rise out of their graves, both now alike calm and sad. Eyes, as I shut mine, look at me, that have long ceased to shine. The town and the fair landscape sleep under the starlight, wreathed in the autumn mists. Twinkling among the houses a light keeps watch here and there, in what may be a sick chamber or two. The clock tolls sweetly in the silent air. Here is night and rest. An awful sense of thanks makes the heart swell, and the head bow, as I pass to my room through the sleeping house, and feel as though a hushed blessing were upon it. (II, 512)

As usual, doubleness persists: memory and current awareness, joy and sorrow, continuity and disappearance, expansive joy and subdued gratitude, realization of the human condition as one of sickness as well as health. The prevailing groundtone of these remarkable statements is that of *acceptance*, expressed most notably of all, perhaps, as the tolling of the clock sounds sweetly.

Similar concerns emerge in "A Roundabout Journey," which concludes the November 1860 issue. Though not actually termed a Roundabout Paper, and though literally an account of a journey to the Low Countries, its mode of proceeding indicates that the title applies not just to the holiday trip but also to the act of writing the account. As in his two previous essays, the speaker meditates upon the dual awareness of past and present. Old stories repeat themselves because we can't help but remember. Travelling with his daughters to Belgium and Holland inevitably recalls to him his first journey to the Continent, when he landed at Calais and traveled in a diligence to Paris: "In making continental journeys with young folks, an oldster may be very quiet, and, to outward appearance, melancholy; but really he has gone back to the days of his youth, . . . and is amusing himself with all his might" (II, 624)—as he does here in rich detail.

Again, memory is an awakening. The ample personage of 1860 may be inertly sitting in a railway carriage, but the remembered young man of 1830 is slim, active, and revivifying. Using Dale Owen's *Footfalls on the Boundary of Another World* as a metaphor, the speaker explains that "So, in this way, I am absent. My soul whisks away thirty years back into the past" (II, 625). As he does so, he also wonderfully speculates about the uncompleted experiences of the past, especially one's romantic attachments. Like many of us, he keeps interrogating the meaning of the distant but well-remembered past, and cannot help wondering what might have been, however comically absurd such an inquiry must be.

Being awakened one morning by the tolling of another bell—this one from Antwerp Cathedral—he hears in its sound a shadow dance from a recent Meyerbeer opera, and he hears the emphatic rhyming chimes of history: "*Quot vivos vocant, mortuos plangunt, fulgura frangunt*" (How many living ones they call, how many dead ones they lament, how many splendors they ruin). He becomes conscious of the besieging French in 1832, of the occupying Spanish in the sixteenth century, of the battle of Oudenarde in 1708, and of Waterloo in 1815—

all this history being contained in and evoked by this ancient, tolling bell, which he continues to hear, even in London, sitting and writing at the desk to which he has been recalled.

The memory of journeying—*backwards*, especially, which is what defines him as "old-fashioned" [made in the old manner]—extends itself into the Roundabout Paper for December: "On a Joke I Once Heard from the Late Thomas Hood." Identifying himself as someone who likes to remember more than to prophesy (though he had recently published a prophet like Ruskin in the *Cornhill*), Thackeray comunicates his sense of travelling in a "hobby-coach under Time, the silver-wigged charioteer" (II, 752) with young folks looking ahead, but he emphatically testifies, as he had in "A Roundabout Journey," to his sense of the ability of "an oldster" (though only 49) to see remembered images "with a halo of brightness invisible to [the youngsters], because it only beams out of his own soul" (II, 753).

Acknowledging the source of his essay as the *Memorials of Thomas Hood* (1860) by Hood's children, he speaks of it as a metaphoric book of travel through life, and responds to it as a reawakening of experience, in his case as their two lives touched at a dinner where he overheard a not very witty pun made by Hood. This minor, specific occasion then prompts the larger, general question of how to pay appropriate tribute to a writer whose genius one admires. As so often in Thackeray's essays, the larger question emerges out of his specific quarrels with petty annoyance—whether with the *Superfine Review*, as in preceeding Roundabout pieces, or, as here, out of back-stabbing abuse by a personal "friend."

He therefore refuses to repeat the feeble pun, because to do so seems to be emulating the "friend's" abuse of him, especially because Hood's greatest ability seems to Thackeray not to have been expressed in the comic mode, but when Hood "put the motley off, and spoke out of his heart" (II, 755) and genius. Here, as in "Nil Nisi Bonum," Thackeray seeks to articulate appropriate celebration of a recently deceased literary figure, and does so by praising him as a good person with the ability to touch human hearts. And, as at the end of the June 1860 issue, Thackeray makes another return by giving thanks for a second successful "six months' voyage" (II, 759) of the *Cornhill* under his captaincy.

A sense of recurrence is, of course, one of the defining Thackerayan awarenesses. "Round About the Christmas Tree" (February 1861), therefore, articulates the sense of re-experiencing Christmas, as well as the attempt to say something new about the familiar. The Thackerayan speaker inevitably participates (through memory and immediate vicarious sympathy) in the experiences of happy juveniles, and also through the somewhat jaded eyes of an adult reckoning up the forthcoming bills as the quarter-year draws towards its close. Even as he foresees how today's young people will come to understand the love connundrums contained within the Christmas sweetmeats "A dozen merry Christmases more," he, as one of the "elderly folks," doesn't find "bonbons or sweeties" (III, 250); he just anticipates receiving accounts rendered.

As usual in these Roundabout Papers, he draws the reader into his process of reflecting upon experience, writing those reflections, and reading the articulate expression of that experience, as he casts up an account of "our past Christmas week" and feels aware that when "the printer has sent me back this manuscript, I know Christmas will be an old story" to his readers as well as to himself. Old and yet enduringly new. "When you read this, will Clown [of the Boxing Day pantomime] still be going on . . . and saying, 'How are you to-morrow?' Tomorrow, indeed!" (III, 251). Tomorrow—as he recalls the Horatian awareness of nature repairing its losses in the progression of the seasons (*diffugere nives*), as humankind cannot, being but dust and shadow—nevertheless brings to his mind our ability to prepare our celebrations, as the creators of pantomime do, and to prophesy the recurrence of mankind's joyful occasions as well as those of accounts payable.

Thackeray's unavoidable remembrances of schooldays occur in "On a Chalk-Mark on the Door" (April 1861), as he uses the relationship between master and pupils as a way of characterizing that between employer and servants, since in both cases subservient people, having their own lives to lead, inevitably resort to concealment in order to do so. Similarly, his speculations in "On Being Found Out" (May 1861) provide another variation on the familiar Thackerayan theme of how our private concerns keep us from being profoundly known, even to the people "close" to us. Having private concerns, concealments, even guilts, however, does not necessarily qualify each of us as a "miserable sinner" (III, 637)—the phrase from the Anglican Litany that so haunted Thackeray, as he heard it Sunday after Sunday, apparently interrogated its validity every day of the week, and repeatedly quoted it as a lasting challenge to human egoism.

Again, schoolboy experiences embody the discoveries of fundamental human knowledge, in this case as a schoolmaster unwittingly demonstrates the nature of excessive scepticism: hostile motivation, exaggerated inquiry, and uneasy awareness (in those who persecute others) of their own shortcomings. Besides being cognizant of the often inadequate motives of scepticism, however, Mr. Roundabout also knows—again using a fundamental Thackerayan as well as Perraultian metaphor—that there are Bluebeard's closets into which one should not look, however un-melodramatic their secrets. Indeed, he acknowledges that no one can know everything about another human being, and that such an inquiry would be futile as well as presumptuous. In his ensuing Roundabout Paper, "On a Hundred Years Hence" (June 1861), he once again responds to hostile scepticism and its fabrications, but in this case seeks comfort from his confidence that their distortions will be revealed by time, or appropriately ignored. Having characterized his tap as one that seeks to pour forth no more than "brisk and honest small-beer" ("On a Hundred Years Hence" [III, 756]), Thackeray entitled his next Roundabout Paper "Small-Beer Chronicle" (July 1861). Responding again to criticism, especially from the *Superfine Review*, he surveys human pretense, whether small beer proclaiming itself to be strong, or *vin ordinaire* wishing to be port. Accepting the inevitability of hypocrisy, he terms some pretentious human ambitions harmless and pardonable, concentrating instead on those that "step over that boundary line of virtue and modesty, into the district where humbug and vanity begin" (IV, 123).

Aside from magazine criticism, he amusingly reveals human bumptiousness in social behavior, the arts, the church, the House of Commons, nationalistic sentiment, and, of course, the human tendency to create heroes out of ordinary men, or to overrate men of ability, especially as epitomized by unintentionally ludicrous statues—the Duke of York "impaled on his column" in Waterloo Place, the Duke of Cumberland "on his Roman-nosed charger" in Cavendish Square, and, most comical of all, Wellington "in an airy fig-leaf costume" (IV, 125) behind Apsley House (the ridiculous "Achilles" statue, of course). By contrast, Mr. Roundabout seeks to offer "a sound genuine ordinaire," grown on his own hillside, inevitably varying in quality from year to year, as wines will do, but "offered *de bon cœur* to those who will sit down" under his arbor (IV, 123).

In writing the following month on "Ogres," he characteristically insists upon the validity of fairy tale archetypes like knights and ogres, and the reality of their continuing manifestations in everyday life: "There is no greater mistake than to suppose that fairies, champions, distressed damsels, and by consequence ogres have ceased to exist. . . . We all *know* ogres. . . . I think some of them suspect I am an ogre myself. I am not: but I know they are" (IV,

253). Implicitly recalling his own earlier days, when he was plucked and devoured by gamblers, or thinking of current illusionists promising instant fulfillment, he offers a fundamental justification for writers addressing the public: to combat humbug and other deceit. There is still a place for active knights of the pen.

Again one Roundabout Paper prompts its successor, as Thackeray's acknowledgment in "Ogres" of his chagrin at having a promising subject preempted by another writer leads to the title of his next essay, "On Two Roundabout Papers Which I Intended to Write" (September 1861). Meditating upon the frequency of thoughts that are never uttered, he argues that they "are as actual as any to which our tongues and pens have given currency." Claiming that he cannot develop the two topics he had in mind, he nevertheless speaks at considerable length of "the subjects I am going *not* to write about" (IV, 379). The first of these matters, a bizarre shooting in Northumberland Street, near the Adelphi Theatre, well-known home of sensation dramas, raises the question, "what is improbable? Surely there is no difficulty in crediting Bluebeard" (IV, 380). His comic response is to propose a sensation novel about life among the gorillas (partly inspired, of course, by Gulliver among the Houyhnhnms).

The comically appropriate desirability of a life of quietude, even mediocrity (in Horace's sense of the golden mean), is an overt theme of his next Roundabout essay, "A Mississippi Bubble" (December 1861). Recalling the splendid hospitality that he had been shown in New Orleans, with its juleps, choice French wine, and delicious bouillabaisse, he speaks of it as "the city of the world where you can eat and drink the most and suffer the least" (IV, 755), but finds that in leaving it for St. Louis, he has to expose himself to the explosive dangers of Mississippi steamers. Recalling how an Alabama river steamer blew up very soon after he had journeyed on it, and how his ship caught fire three times on the trip north to St. Louis, he understandably speaks of his Mississippi experience as a "voyage down the life stream in America" (IV, 756). Managing to keep up his courage with the help of claret and cognac amply provided by his friends for the trip, and even speaking of having claret for breakfast (shamefully diluted with water), Thackeray also finds amusement in several of his fellow passengers: "the Vermont Giant and the famous Bearded Lady of Kentucky," with her bearded three-year-old son. Naturally, in writing the essay he thinks of ogres and the eating of a sheep or two privately in the ogre den, especially since he recalls seeing these prodigies in the dining room, "all plying their victuals down their throats with their knives— . . . in such a company a man had a right to feel a little nervous" (IV, 757). Unquestionably, for a Thackerayan speaker, "To be good, to be simple, to be modest, to be loved" (IV, 760) is a condition of blessedness far exceeding the life of a prodigy, even a harmless, circus creature.

Thackeray always writes memorably about endings, doing so again in the January 1862 Roundabout Paper, "On Letts's Diary," with its illustration of an hour-glass with only a few, last, falling grains of sand. Diaries may induce hopes and expectations for the new year, but mostly of course they prompt memories. Beyond the lists of dinners given and accepted, the accounts incoming and due, are the special joys of having the sons come home for the Christmas holidays, and the liberated happiness of the boys escaping from the confinements of boarding school.

Being conscious also of painful endings arising from personal experience, however, the Thackerayan speaker evokes the death of an infant child, the departure of a beloved young relative to India, and the premature death of friends, that tell him we are going on a "down-hill journey" where "the mile-stones are grave-stones, and on each more and more names are written" (V, 125), and where "friends have dropped off, and, . . . you reach the terminus alone" (V, 126). As he had recently done in

CHAPTER SEVEN

responding to journalistic announcements, he takes his theme from *The Times*, "that great diary," but on this occasion the public statement has a thoroughly personal meaning, announcing the appointment of a cousin, William Ritchie (who was to die several months later), to an eminent post in India, and the death in India of another kinsman, Sir Richmond Shakespear.

Inevitably, Thackeray recalls, as he had just done in that month's installment of *Philip*, his own childhood separation from his family and departure from India with his cousin, William, and their subsequent consignment to a school in Southampton "which was governed by a horrible little tyrant, who made our young lives so miserable that I remember kneeling by my little bed of a night, and saying, 'Pray God, I may dream of my mother!'" (V, 127). Experiences like that may literally end, but are unforgettable and are permanently shared. Coincidentally, another connection emerges as Thackeray walks to the printer's shop to revise the last pages, sees a multitude of people in mourning for the death of Prince Albert, and writes a new ending for his essay that testifies to his joining them in sympathy.

The contemporary world also prompts Thackeray's Roundabout Paper for February 1862, "On Half a Loaf," which responds to the peaceful resolution of the *Trent* affair, when the United States released the Confederates, Mason and Slidell, who had been forcibly removed from a British mail steamer on the high seas. Thackeray also typically overresponds to journalistic criticism, especially the *New York Herald's* denunciation of English sympathy for the Confederate side. Accordingly, he impetuously sells his profitable American investments and settles for half a loaf: four percent interest in England instead of eight in America, foolishly taking nationalistic pride in his decision.

After a month's hiatus, Thackeray embarked upon a satirical extravaganza that extended over three successive issues: "The Notch on the Axe.—A Story à la Mode." A mock-sensation novel, introduced by a vignette initial depicting a boy drawing a longbow, it evokes the contemporary world of spiritualism, mesmerism, freemasonry, and even Rosicrucianism. The speaker's guide into these modish realms, inevitably, is a liar, whose name derives from that of a man notoriously mendacious, Fernão Mendes Pinto. His wild narrative carries him and his audiences back and forth between historical settings and contemporary London—as Thackeray characteristically implicates the contemporary in the historical—by having Pinto transform himself into countless figures, including even Bluebeard, mocking centuries of human folly and one contemporary sensation novel in particular: *A Strange Story*, by Bulwer-Lytton, who was an enduring source of pretentious silliness for Thackerayan satire.

A return to endings occurred in the August 1862 Roundabout Paper, "De Finibus," which followed upon the final installment of *Philip* in the same issue of the *Cornhill.* "De Finibus" is especially notable for the writer's personal presence and his openness. Longing for endings and yet resisting them, he seeks to change them into new beginnings, not only as a serial novelist, but also as he turns from the monthly conclusions of *Philip* to the beginnings of new Roundabout Papers. Freely acknowledging this compulsion, he takes comfort in the earlier examples of Swift and Johnson.

Speaking of himself sitting privately in his study after completing his novel, he exclaims: "What an odd, pleasant, humorous, melancholy feeling it is to sit in the study, alone and quiet, now all these people are gone who have been boarding and lodging with me for twenty months!" Feeling these mixed emotions, he is *not* "at ease. Far from it" (VI, 283). Accordingly, he indulges in his "I hope not dangerous mania" (VI, 282), and writes "De Finibus." Indeed, novel-writing itself is a kind of mania, for the author sees apparitions and holds conversations with invisible people (like a medium, as we saw in "The Notch on the Axe").

Thinking of the prototype of Philip Firmin, whom he knew years ago and who is now dead, he recalls his favorite lines from the "Zueignung" to *Faust*, where Goethe feels around him the shadows of departed friends, and lives in the past once again. As to the writer of "On Letts's Diary," "our books are diaries, in which our own feelings must of necessity be set down." Intimately addressing his readers, he says, "I own for my part that, in reading pages which this hand penned formerly, I often lose sight of the text under my eyes. It is not the words I see; but that past day; that bygone page of life's history."

The whole essay is a remarkable expression of personal feeling: melancholy, to be sure, amusement, as always, but also humility, as he acknowledges his "manifold short-comings, blunders, and slips of memory," and offers some embarrassing examples. In his openness, he becomes an endearing presence. Passing this particular milestone seems to have induced in him a special questioning of his ability to go on writing novels, but, thinking of an ageing friend who is still a thoroughly committed painter, he answers his questioning by saying, "In his calling, in yours, in mine, industry and humility will help and comfort us" (VI, 284).

A defense of novel-writing and novel-reading then follows, whether the work induces soothing sleep (as he willingly allows that his writings might do), or interest and excitement. Offering personal testimony of the latter, he explains how, when he is "troubled with fever and ague [as he had been for some years], that seizes me at odd intervals and prostrates me for a day . . . , for which, I am thankful to say, hot brandy-and-water is prescribed," he has found solace in novels "with the most fearful contentment of mind" (VI, 285), whether on a Mississippi steamboat (boilers intact) or in the contemplative quiet of Tunbridge Wells, reading a sensation novel: "No cares; no remorse about idleness: no visitors" (VI, 285).

In Roundabout fashion, he then moves to thoughts of his own unruly Pegasus, who, he says, is incapable of revealing a broad epic awareness, who is "restive, stubborn, slow; crops a hedge when he ought to be galloping, or gallops when he ought to be quiet" (VI, 287), but yet carries the writer into extraordinary articulations and foretellings of reality. Celebrating the imagination as a divining power, he acknowledges that his fictions emerge not simply from memory (which they certainly do), but also from what has not yet been experienced except by inexplicable anticipation. He also speaks of how his habit of addressing his readers is a "liberating [of] his soul" (VI, 286) from the confinements of secrecy, and of unshared awareness.

Thackeray's memorable catalogue of beloved novels in "De Finibus" then extends itself into his next Roundabout Paper, "On a Peal of Bells" (September 1862), which, like the very first essay, "On a Lazy Idle Boy," introduces a youngster captivated by a book of fiction—in Thackeray's case, Jane Porter's *The Scottish Chiefs*, which he had also evoked in "De Juventute." The tolling of bells, as in "A Roundabout Journey," literally as well as metaphorically *rings in* memory—not only of a little boy reading his first novel, but also of the world of a Hampshire town populated by a now-picturesque grandmother and a swarm of vanished presences. Memory, being the inspiring energy that it is, becomes his subject: "*Quo me rapis?* My Pegasus is galloping off, goodness knows where" (VI, 426).

Inevitably, he plays off against the perfumed phrases of Fanny D'Arblay's novels a series of downright, comical, contemporary Briticisms like "down in the mouth," "cut" [i.e. leave], "chaffing," "good-plucked one," and analogous comic Americanisms like "absquatulate" [i.e. leave], demonstrating his allegiance, of course, to that older language whose formality did not conceal but instead revealed emotion. As in "De Juventute," which also began with youthful reminiscence of George IV's time, he recalls being hit on the head by a schoolmaster's dictionary (source of Becky Sharp's rejection of that epitome of authoritative order?) as he was reading a favorite work of fiction. Once again, however, he testifies to his youthful enjoyment of novels as sweet tarts, and his lasting allegiance to them for the pleasures they have provided and continue to offer.

Thackeray's meditations "On a Pear-Tree" (November 1862) begin in his backyard, but take him far afield. Having had his pear-tree robbed, he finds that the intruder has also taken away—at least momentarily—his "peace of mind . . . and trust in [his] fellow-creatures" (VI, 716). As a consequence, he thinks of a host of malefactors, from Jack Sheppard, John Thurtell, and Dr. Dodd, to a criminal contemporary with him like John Sadleir. Inevitably, he also recalls first coming to London, where "I . . . fell in with some pretty acquaintances . . . , and delivered my purse to more than one gallant gentleman of the road" (VI, 719).

Retrospection is even more prominent in his Roundabout Paper for December 1862, "Dessein's," which recalls Sterne and his own youthful, surreptitious journey to Calais and Paris—an "escapade . . . of the year 1830" (VI, 771). As he had found in "De Finibus," so here too he discovers that his public confession gives him a sense of having been "liberated of this old peccadillo" (VI, 772). Once again, Thackeray immerses himself in the world of the eighteenth century, and in his earlier evocations of that world articulated in his lectures on George IV and of course on Sterne and Goldsmith, details of which reappear in this essay.

Even more, he has an imaginary conversation with Sterne, the two of them then being joined by a seedy, name-dropping Beau Brummell, whose spirit still hovers about Calais, and by Master Eustache of St. Pierre, who recounts his Calais experiences of the fourteenth century, to the bewilderment of Brummell, immersed in his own period. As this indicates, the comic spirit animating the wild gambols of "The Notch on the Axe" is very much alive here as well. Finally, the Roundbout Paper is notable as the first one that does not appear at the end of the monthly issue. Thackeray had resigned as editor in March, and was now simply a contributor.

A poor old lady of ninety living in a workhouse endowed by Queen Charlotte is Thackeray's avenue to the past in "On Some Carp at Sans Souci" (January 1863), as he takes us back through her, her mother, and her grandmother into the early nineteenth and then the eighteenth century. We exist in history, and even when our lives are as uneventful as theirs, we are fellow sharers of time. Although "Battles and victories, treasons, kings, and beheadings, literary gentlemen, and the like" (VII, 128) may have meant little to her, they are an inheritance, like Queen Charlotte's endowed snuff, or like memory itself.

She is a talisman leading him and us back into history, and if at times she seems to have no more memory than the ancient carp at Frederick's palace, she nevertheless provides a connection to what has occurred. In asking his readers whether they would "like to have a remembrance of better early days, when you were young, and happy, and loving, perhaps; or would you prefer to have no past on which your mind could rest?" he implicitly prompts us to recall that to have memory is to have an identity. Even more, it gives us a revitalizing potential. "We may grow old, but to us some stories never are old. On a sudden they rise up, not dead, but living." Offering personal testimony, he reveals how, as he was walking "in the rush of the Strand," the sight of "a pair of eyes so like two which used to brighten at my coming once" rescued him from his loneliness and made him "young again in the midst of joys and sorrows, alike sweet and sad, alike sacred, and fondly remembered" (VII, 130). Finally, then, memory also reveals to us that life—though never without Care (Sans Souci)—is a gift, a "bounty" (VII, 131), even in narrow circumstances.

Grief prompts memory in "Autour de mon Chapeau" (February 1863), the last of these essays to be termed a Roundabout Paper, though the method continues to dominate the three succeeding pieces.

friend's will. Thackeray's immediate concern was to defend his late friend against innuendo by explaining how the codicil had been written in London on Athenaeum Club stationery by his friend's lawyer and then sent to him at Chatham for his signature. Again, in larger terms, the issue is the nature of the legacy that a man leaves behind him. Though writing with a Horatian awareness of living *"sub Dio"* (VIII, 636), under the rule of implacable Death—who was to come to Thackeray himself as soon as December—he celebrated the actuality of his friend's nature and achievements: his real endowment to the future, as was to be Thackeray's own.

Unlike the man hawking old clothes in the vignette initial, we permanently retain the memory of pain—especially, for Thackeray, the parting of parents and children. Thoughts of an old clothes dealer quibbling over a few pence carry him to thoughts of club whist-players battling over small stakes, and then to the metaphor of the game of life and the question: "Shall you be ashamed of your ambition, or glory in it?" (VII, 262). In a sense, life answers this question for us, as our youthful glorying yields in the ageing process to a calmer frame of mind, and finally as we approach the ending, when "the cotton extinguisher is pulled over the old noddle, and the little flame of life is popped out" (VII, 263).

By contrast, marriage is the subject of "On Alexandrines" (April 1863), specifically the marriage of Princess Alexandra and the Prince of Wales, together with some excessive poems written for the occasion. From these extravagant verses Thackeray turns to other false behavior in "On a Medal of George the Fourth" (August 1863), beginning with the passing of a counterfeit coin upon him, and then following with a meditation on roguery and on sham conduct in general. Recalling several experiences with confidence people and other swindlers naturally leads to memory of archetypal figures, literary and historical, like Falstaff, Bardolph, Nym, Dick Turpin, Jack Sheppard, and the forging clergyman, Dr. Dodd (recently mentioned in "On a Pear-Tree"), whom he imaginatively brings to life and sets in motion. Finally, however, he moves to more broadly characterizing behavior, to "weaknesses rather than crimes" (VII, 256): false claims and hypocritical posings in the form of pretended religious devotion, bravery, high birth, poetical ability, and human warmth.

The essay appeared, like "On Alexandrines," once more at the end of the *Cornhill* issue, as did his final piece, "'Strange to Say, on Club Paper'" (November 1863), which also grows out of a specific incident: a newspaper report and subsequent club gossip regarding a codicil to a distinguished old

APPENDIX:

DENIS DUVAL

In his January 1860 Roundabout Paper, "On a Lazy Idle Boy," Thackeray had spoken of "the novels I like best myself—novels without love . . . , but containing plenty of fighting, escaping, robbery, and rescuing" (I, 126), and in his essay for August 1862, "De Finibus," he had expressed a similar view: "How do you like your novels? I like mine strong, 'hot with,' and no mistake: no love-making: no observations about society: little dialogue, except where the characters are bullying each other: plenty of fighting: and a villain in the cupboard, who is to suffer tortures just before Finis. I don't like your melancholy Finis" (VI, 285). Although these descriptions do not have much in common with Thackeray's previous novels, they are slightly more applicable to *Denis Duval*.

Denis has little love-making—especially since the outcome is given from the start—but a fair deal of love-talk, expecially as Denis expresses to us his love of Agnes, and gratefully identifies the two of them as Romeo and Juliet (without the melancholy Finis), and as a contented Darby and Joan (IX, v, 407). *Denis Duval* has only scanty social commentary but plenty of fighting, from schoolboy fisticuffs to duelling and naval engagements. It also has a good bit of dialogue, bullying and otherwise, but as for its overall direction and final punishment of a villain, one thinks of the expressive language of Henry James, who speaks of *Denis* as a "charming fragment," but one that gives us "not a glimpse of [Thackeray's] central idea; nothing, if such had been his intention, was in fact ever more triumphantly concealed."[1]

As for its method of proceeding, *Denis* has a great deal in common with the Roundabout Papers, for the utterances of the first-person speaker are often more circular than linear; Denis calls them "zigzag journeys" (IX, iv, 391). The second serial installment, where he makes that comment, can serve to illustrate the process. Beginning with preparations for the duel between M. de Saverne and M. de la Motte, the narrative mentions how the former asked that his watch "be given to the little boy who saved my—that is, her child." Then, after learning of his death in the duel, we suddenly enter the present, with the words of Denis: "The watch is ticking on the table before me as I write. It has been my companion of half a century" (IX, iv, 386).

Immediately thereafter, we hear the words of M. de la Motte, speaking to Dennis's mother, who is foster-sister of M. de Saverne's widow, and who is taking care of the distraught woman. Then Denis takes us back to a time before the duel, as he explains how he came to save the child, young Agnes. Following mention of his grandfather as a perruquier, gouging money-lender, and smuggler in Winchelsea—behavior that Denis contrasts with de la Motte's free-handed manner, especially to help maintain the poor widow—Denis glances ahead to the death of Mme. de Saverne, and to the repudiation of the orphaned Agnes by her French relatives.

He then takes us even further back in time, to mention of how a boastful letter written by de la Motte led to the duel, and how Mme. de Saverne learned of her husband's death. Following additional, subsequent discussion of his grandfather's conduct, of how de la Motte taught Denis French, and of how he provided a pension for the orphaned little Agnes, the narrator relates the consequences of his rescuing Agnes, his innocent discovery of some smuggling techniques, and details of Mme. de Sauverne's final illness and her burial. Actual reading of the narrative is a smoother experience than this detailed analysis would suggest. Nevertheless, it should be clear why one might well call *Denis Duval* an advanced example of the Roundabout method.

Denis Duval is also notable as Thackeray's only first-person autobiographical narrative since *Esmond*, and his most detailed evocation of a child's life since that novel. Perhaps the speaker's extensive immersion in his young self accounts for another distinctive quality of the novel: the relative lack of allusion, especially non-Biblical allusion, both of which gave his previous narratives such breadth and richness of human experience and awareness.

Memory of *The Arabian Nights' Entertainments* helps to define both Dr. Bernard, who gave the book to young Denis (IX, iii, 290), and Denis himself, who treasures it as his "favourite" (IX, vii, 529), but the book appears in the narrative as an illuminating fact more than as an allusion—much like Denis's copies of *Robinson Crusoe* and Pope's *Iliad* (IX, vii, 530). Similarly, memory of *"Nun ruhen alle Wälder"* refers to the literal singing of Paulus Gerhardt's *"Abendlied"* (IX, iii, 281). Even a joking reference to Claude Duval, the 17th century highwayman (IX, i, 257), calls him up primarily as a literal fact, though knowledgeable Thackerayans will also have the fun of remembering him as a mock-Newgate "hero" of the days of *Catherine*.

In the spirit of historical remembrance as well as allusion, Thackeray has Denis recall Sarah Siddons as Lady Macbeth after the murder of Duncan (IX, iv, 386-87), and Garrick at an analogous moment (IX, v, 405), and to mention Figaro, Count Almaviva, and Rosina (IX, ii, 270). Denis, like Thackeray in "The Notch on the Axe: 1" and in his personal life, treasures a print of Reynolds' image of *Lady Caroline Scott as "Winter"* (IX, v, 402-3), and he too generalizes with references to "Hop o' My Thumb" (IX, iv, 392) and "Humpty Dumpty" (IX, viii, 648).

In a narrative so implicated with historical religious struggle, Biblical awareness understandably becomes the single most frequent source of reference in the mind of Denis and of his elders.

These references can take the form of nominal terms like "prodigal" and "fattest calf" (IX, i, 258), or partly ironic references to Sarah turning out Hagar (IX, iii, 284), honoring father and mother (IX, iv, 390-91), being falsely accused like Susanna (IX, vii, 531), or correctly identified as Ananias and Sapphira (IX, vii, 533), but also can embody more resonant Biblical language, both Vulgate and English.

Thus the title of chapter iv evokes the language of Psalm 130 ("Out of the depths have I cried unto thee, O Lord" [IX, iv, 385]), while later, Denis and Dr. Barnard literally touch hands in church as they recite Psalm 138, giving "thanks to the Highest who had respect unto the lowly, and who had stretched forth His hand upon the furiousness of my enemies, and whose right hand had saved me" (IX, vii, 526). The language and awareness of the parable in Matthew and Luke regarding the mote and the beam in the eye carry over from chapter to chapter and serial number to serial number: "*Quid autem vides festucam in oculo fratris tui*" (IX, v, 405), and "*trabem in oculo tuo*" (IX, vi, 516). So too, remembrance of the parable of the Pharisee and the publican in Luke leads to mention of *The Lord's Prayer*, with its expression of gratitude for being led out of temptation (IX, v, 400).

Shakespeare, of course, also appears—not only in the forms of David Garrick and Sarah Siddons emulating Macbeth and his sinister spouse, but also in the persons of the more genially criminal Falstaff and Bardolph (IX, v, 403). The characters from Sheridan's deadlock scene in *The Critic* make their fourth appearance in Thackeray's work ("In the king's name, I charge you drop your daggers" [IX, vii, 533]), and a semblance of the nodding plumes of Hector's helmet once again comically waves over a Thackerayan infant (IX, iii, 280). Remembrance of Vergil, as usual, induces greater seriousness, as Denis recalls with renewed pain the *infandi dolores* of forty years previous (IX, vi, 517), and looks back "scared and astonished sometimes" at the past

APPENDIX 219

dangers (*discrimina*) of his life (IX, iv, 391). Unfortunately for Thackeray and his readers, the Latin word soon took on its other meaning as a dividing line. As the Virgilian quotation on the last manuscript page of what he had hoped to complete testified—*Diis aliter visum* (the gods see otherwise [IX, viii, 654]).

NOTES

CHAPTER ONE: *PENDENNIS*

[1] See Edgar F. Harden, *A Checklist of Contributions by William Makepeace Thackeray to Newspapers, Periodicals, Books, and Serial Parts Issues, 1828-1864* (Victoria, B.C.: English Literary Studies, 1996).

[2] "The History of Pendennis. His Fortunes and Misfortunes, His Friends and His Greatest Enemy." A Critical Edition, ed. Peter L. Shillingsburg (New York and London: Garland, 1991), Vol. II, ch. xxxvi, p. 347. (References identify page numbers for those readers using the Garland edition, and volume and chapter numbers for other readers.) For permission to quote extensively from my article, "Theatricality in *Pendennis*," I am indebted to the Editors of *Ariel*.

[3] A number of other actresses, circus riders, and the like, including retired performers, appear in off-stage capacities, from Miss Blenkinsop and her father (I, xxix, 281-83), Miss Rougemont, Mrs. Calverley, Mademoiselle Coralie, and Madame Brack (II, ii, 13-15), Mademoiselle Caracoline (II, viii, 84), and Fanny Bolton's teachers (II, viii, 84), to Princess Obstropski (II, xviii, 177-78), who, like Lady Mirabel, has married into society.

[4] Here, as elsewhere in *Pendennis*, when French is employed it generally serves as the language of artifice, especially when used by Blanche. Foker and his "polyglot valet, . . . who was of no particular

country, and spoke all languages indifferently ill" (II, i, 7), otherwise converse in English.

5 For a perceptive discussion of time in *Pendennis*, see Jean Sudrann, "'The Philosopher's Property': Thackeray and the Use of Time," *Victorian Studies*, 10 (1967): 359-88, especially 363-78.

6 Laura and Helen, though generally free from a tendency to behave theatrically, do succumb when agitated by wounded pride and jealousy, especially during the Fanny Bolton episode. Warrington is the character least prone to theatricalism—mainly because he is the least vulnerable to pride.

7 For more extended discussion of the narrator in *Vanity Fair*, see Edgar F. Harden, "*Vanity Fair. A Novel without a Hero.*" *A Reader's Companion* (New York: Twayne, 1995), pp. 71-94, and Harden, *Thackeray the Writer: From Journalism to "Vanity Fair"* (London: Macmillan, 1998), pp. 175-82.

CHAPTER TWO: *HUMOURISTS AND ESMOND*

1 *The English Humourists of the Eighteenth Century* (London: Smith, Elder, 1853), p. 1. For an extended discussion of the lectures, especially from a compositional point of view, see Edgar F. Harden, *Thackeray's "English Humourists" and "Four Georges"* (Newark: University of Delaware Press, 1985; London and Toronto: Associated University Presses, 1985), pp. 11-121, from which I have drawn a few phrases for this chapter.

2 "*The History of Henry Esmond, Esq. A Colonel in the Service of Her Majesty Q. Anne. Written by Himself.*" *A Critical Edition*, ed. Edgar F. Harden (New York and London: Garland, 1989), Bk. I, ch. vi, p. 49. For permission to quote extensively from my article,

"Esmond and the Search for Self," I am indebted to the Editor of *The Yearbook of English Studies.*

[3] George J. Worth briefly treats this aspect of the novel in "The Unity of *Henry Esmond*," *Nineteenth-century Fiction*, 15 (1961): 345-53.

[4] By this point in the novel, Rachel has been mother, sister, goddess, saint, and pupil to Harry, while Beatrix has been sister and pupil, and Frank brother and pupil. A number of critics have commented upon the Oedipal relationships in *Henry Esmond.*

[5] John Loofborough makes this point in *Thackeray and the Form of Fiction* (Princeton: Princeton University Press, 1964), pp. 137-38.

[6] The chief trauma occurring in his personal life during the writing of *Esmond* was, of course, the painful rupture of his friendship with the Brookfields.

CHAPTER THREE: *NEWCOMES*

[1] "*The Newcomes. Memoirs of a Most Respectable Family.*" *A Critical Edition*, ed. Peter L. Shillingsburg (Ann Arbor: University of Michigan Press, 1996), Vol. I, ch. i, p. 4.

[2] For a book-length study of allusions in *The Newcomes*, see Rowland D. McMaster, *Thackeray's Cultural Frame of Reference* (London: Macmillan, 1991), to which I am indebted, as well as to his notes to *The Newcomes* in *Annotations.*

CHAPTER FOUR: *GEORGES* AND *VIRGINIANS*

[1] *The Cornhill Magazine*, II (July-Dec. 1860), 16, 20. For a discussion of Thackeray's composition of *The Four Georges*, see Harden, *Thackeray's "English Humourists" and "Four Georges."* I am indebted to Ian Haywood's notes on *The Four Georges* in *Annotations*.

[2] I am indebted to Gerald C. Sorensen's notes on *The Virginians* in *Annotations*. Quotations come from *Works*.

[3] Henrietta Corkran records how, when Thackeray learned of her family's major financial plight, "he was most agitated, and turning to my mother he asked her what she was going to do.
"'I mean to trust to the ravens,' she answered.
"An expression of pain flitted over the great man's face, but after a few seconds of silence, he put his large hand over hers, and in a husky voice said, 'And so you may; the ravens are kind friends.'" (*Celebrities and I*, quoted in *Wisdom*, p. 349.) In this case, as in numerous others, *he* was a raven.

[4] George Saintsbury termed Thackeray's emulation of Walpole a "*tour-de-force* . . . , the superior, not merely of the sham *Spectator* in *Esmond*, but of most other things of the kind. You may go from it to the sixteen volumes of 'Horry's' correspondence, or from them to it without finding a note false or forced" (*Works*, XV, xxv). He also praised Thackeray's ability to produce uncannily persuasive imitations of Johnson's conversation.

[5] A familiar 18th century term. See a detail of the lecture on George III regarding a prison chaplain who liked to share the last meal of prisoners about to

be executed: "he is a terrible fellow for melted butter" (II, 260).

6 Here we may plausibly see the influence of Thackeray's attempt during the winter of 1854-55 to write a stage play, *The Wolves and the Lamb*, which evolved into narrative form in *Lovel the Widower*, but was finally performed as a drama during housewarming celebrations in 1862. The sixteen chapters consisting mainly of dialogue are 8-11, 14-15, 17, 25, 31-35, 50, 56, and 62, though others have extensive portions as well.

CHAPTER FIVE: *LOVEL*

1 *The Cornhill Magazine*, I (Jan.-June 1860), 44.

2 For a discussion of *Lovel's* development in manuscript and proof, see Harden, *The Emergence of Thackeray's Serial Fiction* (Athens, Ga.: University of Georgia Press, 1979), pp. 220-40.

3 One should notice the implications of his name. He may be a sugar-baker, with a name anglicized from the German "Loeffel" (i.e. "spoon" [I, i, 58]), but we should remember that "Löffel" also means "Dummkopf"—i.e. "muff"—as in the German expression, "ein dummer Löffel": a stupid spoon.

4 Here Thackeray plays with the remembrance of a waistcoat given to him in 1848 that he seems to have thought too spectacular to wear (*Letters*, II, 369-70, illustrated). In this first installment he also allows the narrator to make remarks reflecting his own sensitivity to criticism of Amelia in *Vanity Fair*, for example ("many writers' good women are, you know, so *very* insipid" [I, i, 44]), and of his portraiture in *Pendennis* of less than disinterested and intelligent journalistic criticism of literature

("You see it is 'an insult to literature' to say that there are disreputable and dishonest persons who write in newspapers" [I, i, 51]). In addition he seemingly mocks his own greenhorn efforts as editor of *The National Standard*, by way of having the narrator satirize his youthful performance as editor of *The Museum* (I, i, 56).

5 For a book-length study of Thackeray's imaginative evocation of German experience—personal, literary, and historical—see S.S. Prawer, *Breeches and Metaphysics: Thackeray's German Discourse* (Oxford: Legenda, 1997), to which I am indebted.

CHAPTER SIX: *PHILIP*

1 *The Cornhill Magazine*, Vol. III, ch. i, p. 4.

2 Juliet McMaster discusses this aspect of *Philip* in "Funeral Baked Meats: Thackeray's Last Novel," *Studies in the Novel*, 13 (1981): 133-55.

3 I am indebted to Carol MacKay's contribution to the notes on *Philip* in *Annotations*.

CHAPTER SEVEN: *ROUNDABOUT PAPERS*

1 I am indebted to John E. Wells's annotated edition of *The Roundabout Papers* (New York: Harcourt, Brace, 1925).

APPENDIX: *DENIS DUVAL*

1 "Winchelsea, Rye and *Denis Duval*," *Scribner's Magazine*, xxix (Jan. 1901), 44-53, reprinted in *English Hours* (1905). My text is taken from a more recent edition: New York, Horizon Press, 1968, pp. 288, 291.

INDEX

Addison, Joseph 30-33, 35-36, 52-53, 65-66, 98, 101
   "Evening Hymn" 33
   "The Campaign" 31, 52, 66
Adelphi Theatre 205
Aesop, *Fables* 66, 70, 87, 93, 107-9, 162-63, 168
Ainsworth, William Harrison 182
Albert, Prince 207
Alexandra, Queen [wife of Edward VII] 213
Alfred (King of England) 96
Ambrogetti, Giuseppe 198
Amelia, Princess 96
American Revolution 100, 103
Anacreon 27
Anne (Queen of England) 31, 96, 98, 138
Arabian Nights' Entertainments, The 28, 35, 65, 92, 96, 123, 163, 182, 198, 217
Ariadne 27
Arnold, Matthew, "Stanzas from the Grande Chartreuse" 139
Ashburnham, Earl of 58
Aspasia 167
Athenaeum Club, 214
Auber, Daniel, *Le Dieu et la Bayadère* 198

Beaumarchais, Pierre de, *Le Barbier de Séville* 88
   Le Mariage de Figaro 88, 217
Begnis, Ronzi de 198
Bellini, Giovanni, *Il Pirata* 156
Béranger, Pierre Jean de 27, 175
Berry, Mary 97-98
Berwick, James Fitzjames, Duke of 61
Bible, The, 26-28, 35, 57, 63-64, 71, 78, 86-87, 95, 97, 112-18, 136, 157, 160-62, 164-65, 167-70, 177-78, 197, 218

INDEX 227

Bolingbroke, Henry St. John, first Viscount 35, 59, 98
Bonaparte, Napoleon 27, 189
Book of Common Prayer, The 112-13
Boswell, James 31
Bracegirdle, Anne 48, 50
Braddock, Edward 125
Broderip, F.F., and Hood, Thomas, Jr., *Memorials of Thomas Hood* 201
Brontë, Charlotte, "Emma" 186
Brookfield, Mrs. William Henry 222
Brookfield, William Henry 222
Browning, Robert, "Love Among the Ruins" 139
   "Two in the Campagna" 139
Brummell, George Bryan ("Beau Brummell") 98, 211
Brunel, Isambard 197
Brutus, Marcus Junius 168
Buckingham, George Villiers, second Duke of, *The Rehearsal* 18
Burke, Edmund 102
Burney, Frances 99
Burns, Robert, "John Anderson my Jo" 170
Byron, George Gordon, sixth Baron, *Childe Harold's Pilgrimage* 138-39, 169
   The Corsair 27

Caradori, Maria 198
Carlyle, Thomas 102, 127
   Frederick the Great 127
   Sartor Resartus 139, 171
Caroline, Queen [wife of George III] 100-1
Catullus 108
Cervantes, Miguel de, *Don Quixote* 28, 33, 44, 48, 56, 58, 88, 175, 189, 198
Charlotte, Princess 96, 100
Charlotte (Queen of England) 212
Charon 195-96
Charterhouse School 32, 193, 196-97
Chatham, William Pitt, first Earl of 98
Chester, Miss 198
Chesterfield, Philip Dormer Stanhope, fourth Earl of 98, 109, 125
Cicero, Marcus Tullius 108

Clinton, Henry 125
Coleridge, Samuel Taylor, "Kubla Khan" 138
Comstock, Captain 182
Congreve, William 33-34, 65
   The Way of the World 95, 161
Conway, Henry Semour 98, 117
Cooper, James Fenimore, *The Last of the Mohicans* 126
   The Pilot 161
   The Red Rover 87
Corkran, Henrietta, *Celebrities and I* 223
Corneille, Pierre, *Le Cid* 88
Cornhill Magazine, The 175, 181-82, 184, 186, 188-89, 192, 194, 201-2, 208, 213, 224-25
Cumberland, William Augustus, Duke of 125, 204
Cunningham, Peter 127
Curioni, Alberico 198

Dalai Lama 43
D'Arblay, Frances Burney, Madame 210
Defoe, Daniel, *Robinson Crusoe* 159, 217
Devonshire, Georgina, Duchess of 98
Dickens, Charles 182, 196
   Bleak House 77
Dickinson, Emily 83
Dinwiddie, Robert 125
Diogenes, 26
Disraeli, Benjamin, first Earl of Beaconsfield 126
Dodd, Dr. William 211, 213
Donizetti, Gaetano, *Lucrezia Borgia* 33
Donzelli, Domenico 198
Doran, John 99
Dryden, John 27, 65
   "Alexander's Feast" 71-72, 88
Dumas *père*, Alexandre 182
Dunmore, John Murray, Earl of 125
Duval, Claude 217
Duvernay, Pauline 175, 198

Edward VII [as Prince of Wales] 213
Egan, Pierce, *Life in London* 196, 198

INDEX

Eliot, Thomas Stearns, *Four Quartets* 139-40
   "The Love Song of J. Alfred Prufrock" 122
   "The Waste Land" 139
Ernst, Duke of Celle 99-100
Eton School 3
Euripedes 109
Eustace, Master, of St. Pierre 211

Fielding, Henry 38, 102, 105, 125
   Tom Jones 32
Figg 125
Fontenoy, battle of 26
Fox, Charles James 111
Franklin, Benjamin 125
Frederick II of Prussia ("the Great") 212

Garrick, David 102, 122, 125, 217
Gay, John 33, 65, 98
   The Beggar's Opera 21, 37, 168
George I (King of England) 95, 98, 100-1
George II (King of England) 95, 98, 101, 104, 125
George III (King of England) 96, 98-100, 104
George IV (King of England) 96, 100
Gerhardt, Paulus, "Abendlied" 217
Gibbon, Edward 126, 139, 161, 183
Gladstone, William Ewart 126
Goethe, Johann Wolfgang von, *Egmont* 21, 28
   Faust 21, 28, 149, 168, 209
   "Vanitas! Vanitatum Vanitas!" 171
Goldsmith, Oliver 31, 98, 102, 183
   The Vicar of Wakefield 72, 88
Gourville, Jean Hérault de 99
Gray, Thomas 125

Hamilton, James Douglas, fourth Duke of 58-59, 64, 67
Handel, George Frederick 100, 125
   "Alexander's Feast" 71-72, 88
Harden, Edgar F., *A Checklist* 220
   ed., *Henry Esmond* 221
   Thackeray's "English Humourists" and "Four Georges" 221-22
   Thackeray the Writer 221

INDEX

The Emergence of Thackeray's Serial Fiction 224
"*Vanity Fair.*" *A Reader's Companion* 221
Haywood, Ian 222
Heenan, John 188
Henry, Patrick 125
Herrick, Robert 42
Hervey, John, Lord, *Memoirs* 96, 99, 101-2
Hitler, Adolf 188
Hoe and Company 175
Hogarth, William 31, 38, 125
    "Industry and Idleness" 73, 88, 95, 194
    "Marriage à la Mode" 88
Home, John 136
Homer 108, 112
    The Iliad 26-28, 66, 218
    The Odyssey 26, 66, 85, 96, 107-8, 112, 156
Hood, Thomas 201
Hopkins, Gerard Manley, "The Wreck of the Deutschland" 139
Horace 33, 66, 85, 107-9, 142, 147, 173, 205
    Odes 26-27, 33, 47, 50, 53, 67-68, 85, 95, 109-12, 140, 154, 156-58, 162-63, 165-69, 172, 174, 179, 202, 210, 214
    Satires 147, 168, 174
    The Art of Poetry 27, 67, 179
Howe, William, fifth Viscount 120, 125
Howell, James 182, 184

Inchbald, Elizabeth, *The British Theatre* 20
Irving, Washington 183-84

James, George Payne Rainsford 182
James, Henry 215, 225
Johnson, Esther ("Stella") 31-32
Johnson, Richard, *The Seven Champions of Christendom* 196
Johnson, Samuel 31, 98, 102, 120, 125, 208, 223
Jonson, Benjamin, *Every Man in His Humour* 175
Juno 191

INDEX

Juvenal 108
   Satires 72, 97, 168, 178

Keats, John, "Ode on a Grecian Urn" 88
   "On Seeing the Elgin Marbles for the First Time" 139
Kemble, Charles 161
Kemble, Frances Anne 161
Ken, Bishop Thomas 125
Kendal, Ehrengard Melusina, Duchess of 100
Kotzebue, August von, *Menschenhass und Reue* (tr. B. Thompson) 4-5, 20, 28
   Die Spanier in Peru (arr. R.B. Sheridan) 16

Lablache, Luigi 198
La Fontaine, Jean de, *Fables* 70
Laïs 167
Lambert, Daniel 150
Lang, Captain 182
Laurence, Samuel 154
Leroux, Pauline 198
Lever, Charles 127, 182
Loofborough, John, *Thackeray and the Form of Fiction* 222
Lord's Prayer, The 164, 178, 218
Louis XIV (King of France) 126
Louis-Philippe (King of the French) 172
Love, Miss 198
Lucretius 27, 108
   De rerum naturâ 171, 173, 182
Luther, Martin (attrib.), "Dr. Luther" 166
Lytton, Edward George Earle Lytton, first Baron, 126, 182
   A Strange Story 208
   The Lady of Lyons 19, 21, 28

Macaulay, Thomas Babington, first Baron 183-84
MacKay, Carol 225
Maclise, Daniel 154
Malibran, Maria 198
Malmsbury, James Harris, first Earl of 99
Manley, Mary, *The Belle's Strategem* 95

Manny, Sir Walter 197
March, Roger Mortimer, first Earl of 125
Marius, Gaius 27
Marlborough, John Churchill, first Duke of 51-52, 64, 66, 98, 177
Marlborough, Sarah, first Duchess of 98, 177
Mason, James 207
McMaster, Juliet 225
McMaster, Rowland, 222
    Thackeray's Cultural Frame of Reference 222
Menander 109
Meyerbeer, Giacomo, *Le Pardon de Ploërmel [Dinorah]* 198
Milton, John 65
    Comus 87
    "L'Allegro" 175
    Paradise Lost 30, 50, 87, 177
Minerva 191
Mohun, Charles, fourth Baron 36, 45
Molière, *Tartuffe* 87
Montagu, Lady Mary Wortley 99
Montaigne, Michel de 182, 184-85
Montrose, James Graham, fourth Duke of 27-28
Moore, Thomas, *Lalla Rookh* 27, 72
Morris, William 102
Mozart, Wolfgang Amadeus 108
    Cosi fan tutti 108
    Don Giovanni 26, 88, 97
    The Marriage of Figaro 88, 217
Mudie's Select Library 126

Nabokov, Vladimir, *Speak, Memory* 141
National Standard, The 224
Nelson, Horatio, Viscount 27
Newcastle, Thomas Pelham-Holles, first Duke of 98, 126
New York Herald, The 207
New York Times, The 191
Niobe 176
Noblet, Lise 175, 198
North, Frederick North, eighth Baron 98

INDEX

O'Connell, Daniel 126, 169
Ovid 66, 85, 109
   Epistulae ex Ponto 85, 166
   Heroides 67
   Metamorphoses 39, 66
   The Art of Love 28
   Tristia 67
Owen, Dale, *Footfalls on the Boundary of Another World* 200

Panizzi, Antonio 184
Pater, Walter Horatio, "Conclusion" to *The Renaissance* 139
Peakes, Richard Brinsley, *The Bottle Imp* 161
Peele, George, "His golden locks time hath to silver turned" 168
Perrault, Charles, *Histoires et contes du temps passé*, 27, 70, 93, 123, 149, 158, 162-63, 175, 203, 205
Persius 109
Phryne 167
Pinto, Fernão Mendes 208
Planché, James Robinson, *The Brigand* 15
Plato, *The Statesman* 85
Pöllnitz, Karl Ludwig, Baron 99, 125
Pope, Alexander 32-33, 35-36, 65, 98, 102
   "Epistle to Dr. Arbuthnot" 35
   The Iliad (trans.) 217
   "The Rape of the Lock" 96
Porter, Jane, *The Scottish Chiefs* 198, 210
Porto, Matteo 198
Pound, Ezra 139-40
Prawer, S.S., *Breeches and Metaphysics: Thackeray's German Discourse* 225
Price 126
Pritchard, Hannah 122
Prior, Matthew 27, 31, 65, 98
Prometheus 34
Pygmalion 26

Queensberry, Catherine, third Duchess of 33, 98, 121, 125

Queensberry, Charles Douglas, third Duke of 33
Quintilius 110

Radcliffe, Ann, *The Italian* 198
Reynolds, Sir Joshua 98, 102, 125, 217
Richardson, Samuel 125
   Clarissa 105
   Sir Charles Grandison 88
Ritchie, Anne Thackeray, ed., *The Works of William Makepeace Thackeray* 225
Ritchie, William 207
Rossetti, Dante Gabriel, *The House of Life* 139
Rossini, Gioachino, *Il Barbiere di Siviglia* 88, 217
   La Donna del Lago 161, 198
   La Gazza Ladra 156
   Otello 198
   Semiramide 161
Ruskin, John 92, 102, 139, 196, 201

Sadleir, John 211
Saintsbury, George 131, 223
Sallust 33-34, 109, 111
Sand, George 16
Saturday Review, The 189, 191, 196-97, 201, 204
Sayers, Thomas 188
Schiller, Friedrich, *Die Piccolomini* 141, 157
Scott, Sir Walter 183, 198
   Ivanhoe 159
   Kenilworth 28
   Quentin Durward 175-76
   The Bride of Lammermoor 87
Scribe, Eugène 15
Scudéry, Madelaine de, *Clélie* 95
Selwyn, George 98-99, 125
Serle, Cecilia 198
Shakespear, Sir Richmond 207
Shakespeare, William 112
   All's Well That Ends Well 65
   A Midsummer Night's Dream 26, 65, 123
   As You Like It 65
   Hamlet 5, 10, 20-1, 27, 65, 95, 121-22, 159, 170-71, 175

INDEX 235

1 Henry IV 87, 213
2 Henry IV 87, 213
Henry VIII 13
King John 65, 161
King Lear 10, 96
Macbeth 26, 122, 173, 175, 217
Othello 28, 64-65, 87, 120-21, 159, 175
Richard III 28
Romeo and Juliet 161, 215
Twelfth Night 123
Shelley, Percy Bysshe, "Ode to the West Wind" 139
Sheppard, Jack 211, 213
Sheridan, Richard Brinsley, *Pizarro* 16
   The Critic 13, 88, 173, 218
   The Rivals 9
Shillingsburg, Peter L., ed., *Pendennis* 220
   ed., *The Newcomes* 222
Shirley, James, "The glories of our birth and state" 59
Siddons, Sarah 217
Slidell, John 207
Smith, John 136
Smith, George 190, 192
Smith, William, *Dictionary* 175
Smollett, Tobias 38, 125, 198
Socrates 171
Solomon, Simeon 189
Sontag, Henriette 198
Sorensen, Gerald C. 223
Spartacus 157
Spectator, The 37, 58, 88
Spence, Joseph 99
Stanley, Arthur P. 126
Steele, Sir Richard 33, 36-39, 41, 65-66, 98, 101
Sterne, Laurence 33, 125, 211
   A Sentimental Journey 26
St. George 196
Stowe, Harriet Beecher 182
Stuart, Charles Edward 27
Stuart, James Francis Edward 55-56, 60-63, 68
Sudrann, Jean 221
Suffolk, Henrietta Howard, Countess of 99

Surtees, Robert Smith 182
Sutton, Edward 125
Swift, Jonathan 31-34, 65, 67, 98, 102, 125, 157, 208
   Gulliver's Travels 96, 136, 205
   The Drapier's Letters 35

Taglioni, Marie 17, 91, 173, 198
Tasso, Torquato, *Jerusalem Delivered* 27
Tatler, The 37
Temple, Sir William 157
Tennyson, Alfred, first Baron 140
   "In Memoriam" 139
   "Locksley Hall" 118
   "Mariana" 87
   The Princess 88
Terence 109
Thackeray, William Makepeace, "A Shabby Genteel Story" 162
   Catherine 217
   Denis Duval 215-19
   "Fitz-Boodle Papers" 22
   Lovel the Widower 143-59, 181, 191, 223-24
   Roundabout Papers 173, 181-216
   The Adventures of Philip 160-80, 207-9
   The Book of Snobs 24, 29, 82, 135
   The English Humourists of the Eighteenth Century 29-36, 38, 73, 96, 103, 211
   The Four Georges 94-104, 110, 125, 194-95, 211, 223
   The History of Henry Esmond 36-69, 103, 110, 112, 136-38, 173, 217
   The History of Pendennis 2-29, 63, 94, 105, 112, 128, 149, 152, 220-21, 224
   The Luck of Barry Lyndon 51
   The Newcomes 70-94, 96, 141, 143, 160, 162, 172
   The Virginians 102-43, 223-34
   The Wolves and the Lamb 143-44, 158-59, 223
   Vanity Fair 1, 4, 12, 17-18, 24, 29, 52, 72, 85, 88, 94-95, 110, 118, 122, 182, 210, 224
Thurtell, John 211
Timanthes 35
Times, The 207

INDEX

Trent, The 207
Trollope, Anthony 182
    Barchester Towers 182
    Framley Parsonage 182
Trollope, Frances 126, 182
Turpin, Richard 213
Tussaud, Mme. Marie 195
Twiss, Horace, *The Life of Lord Eldon* 99

Vanderdecken 161
Vanhomrigh, Esther ("Vanessa") 31-33
Vehse, Eduard 98
Vergil 66, 85, 108, 111
    Eclogues 62
    Georgics 67, 85, 95, 157, 170, 177
    The Aeneid 42, 47, 61, 66-67, 156, 166, 173, 179, 218-19
Victoria (Queen of England) 106

Wallace, William, *George the Fourth* 99
Wallack, James William 15
Waller, Edmund 27
Walpole, Horace, fourth Earl of Orford 99, 117, 125, 127, 223
Walpole, Robert, first Earl of Orford 126
Washington, George 83, 110, 125, 189
Webb, John Richmond 64
Wellington, Arthur Wellesley, first Duke of 11, 186, 189, 204
Wells, John E., ed., *Roundabout Papers* 225
Whitfield, George 125
William III (King of England) 41, 65
Wolfe, James 125
Wordsworth, William, "My heart leaps up" 97
    "Tintern Abbey" 138
Worth, George J. 221

Xerxes 177

Yarmouth, Amalie Sophie Walmoden, Countess of 95, 100, 114-15, 117, 125
Yates, Edmund 190

Yeats, William Butler 139
York, Frederick Augustus, Duke of 204

Zoffany, Johann, *Garrick and Mrs. Pritchard as Macbeth and Lady Macbeth* 175